DATE DUE

OTHERWISE
ENGAGED

OTHERWISE ENGAGED

THE PRIVATE LIVES OF SUCCESSFUL CAREER WOMEN

DR. SRULLY BLOTNICK

Facts On File Publications
New York, New York ● Oxford, England

Otherwise Engaged: The Personal Lives of Successful Career Women

Library of Congress Cataloging in Publication Data
Blotnick, Srully.
  Otherwise engaged.
  Includes index.
  1. Women—Employment—United States—Psychological aspects—Longitudinal studies. 2. Women—United States—Sexual behavior—Longitudinal studies. 3. United States—Social life and customs—Longitudinal studies. I. Title.
HD6095.B58 1985   305.4'3'00973   84-28708
ISBN 0-8160-1093-5

Printed in the United States of America
10 9 8 7 6 5 4 3 2 1

Contents

Foreword

Finding out about people's sex lives used to be difficult; finding out about their finances was relatively easy. Now the reverse is more likely to be the case. Men and women speak openly about their personal lives, especially once trouble develops, but they are reluctant to announce their bank balance. Divorce, above all, makes them feel they should "go public" with their story, particularly because they fear their ex-partners will do the same. They don't want to be characterized to strangers and business associates as ogres or maniacs.

We didn't start out to collect data on people's personal lives. Their professional and financial activities were of greater interest to us at first, more than a quarter of a century ago. Two things happened to change that, and quickly forced our focus to broaden. Women who felt there was little left to say about their business activities volunteered considerable quantities of information of a more personal sort. The fact that we already knew about their finances, and kept the information confidential, apparently made them feel that we could be trusted with "more important" information. Ironically, if we had wanted to explore their emotional lives over the long term, we couldn't have chosen a better probe than regular inquiries about their work and everyday money matters.

What we didn't realize in the beginning is that knowing a little about someone's personal life was, for us, much like trying to eat only one potato chip. Each tidbit only increased our appetite for more. Back-fence gossips in the 1950s, when we began, could probably have told us we were going to get hooked—once we heard how each saga started, we'd also want to know how it ended.

Over and over again we found ourselves asking sample members, "Whatever happened to . . . ?" We thought some would be reluctant to fill us in, but a mechanism we hadn't counted on came to the rescue. For some reason, once people tell someone the first few chapters of an event in their lives, they feel almost compelled to continue the tale. Whether it is the born storyteller in each of us, or the egomaniac ("I'm sure you want to hear what happened next, don't you?"), or just common courtesy ("Since I've piqued your curiosity, I feel obligated to satisfy it"), we don't know. Whatever it is, it allowed us to be the recipients of all the information we needed, and then some. In fact, once the stream began to flow, it was usually harder to shut it off than to get it flowing again at a later date.

For us, the addiction we had developed, together with people's powerful desire to update their autobiographies, proved invaluable. Originally, we intended to study who did well in the workplace and was satisfied there, who did poorly or was unhappy on the job, and why. A sample of 5,018 individuals—2,911 men and 2,107 women—was selected, and after monitoring the work-related activities of its members for twenty-five years, the conclusions were summarized in *The Corporate Steeplechase: Predictable Crises in a Business Career* (New York: Facts On File, 1984).

However, the rapidly expanding body of personal information we were also gathering soon began to yield results of its own. It was striking to see that some women had more satisfying personal lives than others, year after year. They had enduring intimacies that others would barely have believed possible. Interestingly, envy didn't enter the picture here. Although people are often intensely jealous of a colleague who gets even a small step ahead of them at work, they rarely think about the personal lives of their peers, some of whom have marriages that are much more stable and fulfilling than their own.

The reason they aren't envious of the difference is that they don't see or hear about it, as they would, say, of a larger office for a competitor. Bad news circulates fast, and as we've said, women whose marriages are coming apart, or already have, are more likely to be the ones doing the broadcasting. The happy couples we studied were remarkably silent, by contrast. They didn't feel that their relationships called for any comment. The upshot was that women who had unsatisfactory personal lives assumed everyone else did too. They were unaware that sustained warmth and intimacy existed, and not just in movies and novels. Perhaps if they had known, they would have tried harder to find it for themselves.

Doing so successfully requires that people gain a much better understanding than they now have of the connection between their professional and personal lives. What happens at the office (or fails to) has a definite impact on what happens at home, and that applies to women now every bit as much as to men. Some readers may say, "I don't happen to work, so this material doesn't apply to me." Women who are homemakers, and don't intend to be anything else, may feel the same way. Nevertheless, we would ask even this group of readers to seriously consider whether the conclusions reached in the upcoming chapters shed an important light on their relationships. The trends we will be discussing were so powerful, we found that they had a substantial effect on women who have never held even a part-time job.

Examining the personal lives of women through a focus that concentrates on their work lives as well will undoubtedly strike some readers as misguided. At first, in the late 1950s, we too thought it might be. At the time, work wasn't viewed as alluring by so large a portion of the adult populace as it is today. It certainly had less glamour. But much to our surprise (and delight), attitudes in the United States moved more each year throughout the 1960s, 1970s, and 1980s in a direction that made the approach we had originally taken more relevant.

The material we were gathering on people's work-related experiences allowed us to forecast with steadily increasing accuracy what would happen to them at home. The lives of working women, in particular, changed radically in ways that our study helped uniquely to illuminate. In short, *the occupational aspirations of men and, even more so, women, currently play a decisive role in their personal lives*. In fact, it usually determines whether they will have something that can validly be characterized as a personal life at all.

It is satisfying and, at the same time, discomforting to present conclusions which took more than a quarter of a century to reach. What is fascinating about them is that they allow one to see the core of a phenomenon, stripped of its everyday trappings, since it has been studied over a long period of time in a variety of different settings. The peripheral features may be colorful and diverting, but they often serve to mask rather than illuminate the essence of the events. So much for the good news.

In writing up the results of a long-term psychological study, there is always the danger that the immediacy of the feelings and behavior under discussion will be lost. In that sense, novelists and reporters have it easy. In a single episode in one person's life—say, a job change or a divorce—there is a clear sequence and palpable texture to what occurs. Someone is living the event, moment to moment, and a full description of it can be given center stage. However, where thousands of cases are being considered over a number of decades, a certain amount of distance from the events is almost forced upon both reader and author. Immediacy can still be maintained, and this is what we have tried to do throughout the book by giving a number of detailed case histories that are characteristic of the experiences of many thousands of women.

But compacting the members of our sample into one "average being" risks leaving all of them mere shadows of what they actually were. Statisticians often joke about events that exist only mathematically; an encounter between two men, one six feet tall, the other five feet in height, described as, "Two five-and-a-half footers, on average, met on a street corner." The number of women in our sample was large enough so that our "average being" is indeed representative of the majority, unlike the mythical men in the above description.

It troubles us more to be unable to have readers jump in a time machine and join us during our decades of detective work, so that each conclusion might emerge as slowly for them as it did for us. The point needs emphasis: We have finally stumbled upon more than enough interesting and useful findings to make a book many times this size both timely and worthwhile. But in the beginning we were merely stumbling around in the dark. Conclusions that we can now confidently put in italics to highlight their importance were unknown to us at the start. We had dozens of questions and no answers. It took patience and persistence, and faith that the combination would produce the answers we sought. It also required a small army of assistants and a not-so-small quantity of cash to pay them all.

The upshot, and it is somewhat unfortunate, is that in the first two chapters there are a number of conclusions that emerge almost out of the blue, seemingly without effort. The basis for the statements is apparent at the time, yet they require the rest of the book to fully support their existence. The converse holds as well, for these first two chapters shine a revealing light on the many specific events and interactions discussed in the remaining chapters. Letting the reader see early on what it took us decades to discover seems appropriate. However, it makes us realize how inadequately we have conveyed, despite our best efforts, not only the agony and joy experienced by the people we studied, but also our own, as we inched toward these findings.

To take just one instance, in a number of places we state that a particular individual was interested above all in becoming famous for his or her work. That isn't something we gleaned merely by looking at the person, or even by interviewing him or her at length. The assertion is based instead on seeing what the person fought about with others, both on and off the job. Things that were not at first apparent became increasingly obvious as we had a chance to study what people did and said in both their personal and professional relationships over a period of many years, particularly once conflict developed.

The fantasies women have about their futures, often without realizing consciously that they even have such dreams, play a major role in their work lives and, as it turns out, an even more important one in their personal lives. In this book, we have given dreams as well as realities the space they deserve.

The women we studied were special (they numbered 3,466 in all—the 2,107 referred to earlier, plus 1,359 wives or daughters of the 2,911 men in the original sample). Above average in median household income and education ($53,000 versus $20,200 for the nation as a whole, in constant 1982 dollars, and with 72% college graduates versus 25% for their peers as a whole), they lived primarily in urban and suburban settings. Their median age when the study began was eighteen. We deliberately selected such women because we felt that trends which affected personal spending and occupational aspirations would make themselves felt first in the major metropolitan areas of the United States. (Remember, the financial and professional activities of these women, and their male peers, were our original focus in the late 1950s. The selection process and study procedure are described in the Appendix.)

Our view of American cities as the birthplace of new social trends was repeatedly confirmed during our study, though for reasons we had only partly anticipated. First, the demand for specialists was, and is, consistently higher in cities, and as Chapters 1 and 2 will discuss, that made urban areas the forerunners of attitudes that would soon prevail in the entire country. Rural settings, by contrast, were significantly more inclined toward generalists. Physicians provide a good example of this; there are few general practitioners in large cities, while in more rural settings, even highly trained specialists often find themselves forced to play the role of GP. Attorneys in the two settings report similar pressures. During the period of our study, 1958–1985, specialization was increasingly demanded throughout the nation in every line of work.

The second reason that cities turned out to be so fertile a soil in which new social trends could grow had less to do with the residents already there than with the steady flow of people constantly arriving. Demographers who state that the population of many major American cities has been declining for the past quarter of a century are right but are omitting an important dimension. The majority of adventuresome young men and women we studied would not have been happy anywhere else. That doesn't mean they thought of the particular city in which they took up residence, once school was through, as a Garden of Eden. However, they did recognize that they were now in a place that afforded them the maximum number of opportunities and, equally if not more appealing, the chance to become tops in their chosen field.

There were ambitious young men and women who had come to the same cities decades earlier with similar dreams. For most, the dreams never came true, though the attempts provided rewards of their own. Having had enough of the negative aspects of urban living, many left for more pastoral or small-town settings. Fresh blood arrived daily to take the place of those who grew weary of what they called "the rat race," or who had retired and were heading for warmer climes. These transfusions not only lessened the damage caused by the hemorrhaging, they also gave new life to the patient, in some cases even more than it had had before.

As we'll see, the inconspicuous but massive comings and goings had a powerful effect on the personal lives of the women in our sample. More to the point, by monitoring *all* the relationships the women had—everything from one-night stands and brief affairs to long-term friendships and live-in lovers—we were able to obtain a much richer and more dynamic picture than any previously available. This persistently microscopic approach allowed us to gather the data needed to cut through the sweeping generalizations (based on superficial evidence) that plague writings on this subject and offer instead a fresh view, one that we think working women who truly want to improve their personal lives will find useful and effective.

ACKNOWLEDGMENTS

While gathering material for our study required prolonged effort, analyzing and condensing it was even more demanding. With more than three tons of files, plus 26 gigabytes on disk memory, the task seemed Herculean. It took the assistance of dozens of people to help shape this mountain into a manuscript. One who stands out is Facts On File's gifted Editor in Chief, John F. Thornton. Without his contribution the present work would have been twice as long yet contained only half the material.

Of the more than 600 individuals who assisted during the course of the study in data collection and processing, or who provided valuable suggestions and guidance, the following deserve special thanks: Robert Anderson, Carol Chen, Anna Garcia, Mary Giordano, Marie Lambert, Judith Luscher, Rick Miller, Janet O'Connor, Michael Perry, Fred Shoenberg, Lynn Stern, Barbara Stevens, Nancy Thompkins, and Steve Weinstein.

OTHERWISE
ENGAGED

PART
ONE

1 / Reaching for the Brass Ring

Few people can work hard day after day without being thanked. Social beings that humans are, they want their labors to be recognized and rewarded by others. High pay is one way, applause is another, and important positions in a firm or organization are a third, yet when all is said and done, what matters most is that recognition in some form is finally theirs.

How much sweeter the reward is when it comes from one's country. Even people who have no great fondness for the president in office at the time, and who don't give a hoot about politics, still sense that a prize awarded by the nation as a whole represents something special. Bypassing the president is better still. The ultimate acknowledgment of the worth of one's labors has to be recognition that flows directly from the American people en masse, without first being funneled through the White House.

Movies, television, and newspapers now make that possible. Instant recognition is available to anyone who achieves something noteworthy. However, in most instances, the renown comes to people slowly at first, and for labors that have been long and difficult. Every nation has its heroes, and long before one tries to carefully analyze a topic as specific as the personal lives of successful women, one needs an understanding of the background forces that help shape those lives. Heroes are a good place to start, since they provide a revealing reflection of the nation's top priorities. These pressures are particularly important to the young, who in response to them are molding behavior and attitudes that will later be difficult to change. Individual differences, of course, affect such things as the stability of marriages and the degree of one's sexual satisfaction, but in a subtle and powerful manner, so do the nation's aspirations.

What are America's top priorities? The answer changes as the years pass. During World War II, the brave soldier was clearly the nation's idol, as was Rosy the Riveter, who made good fighter planes for the boys overseas. The end of the war brought about a shift during the next thirteen years that seemed primarily to involve men but actually had major consequences for women to this present day.

The 1950s have been characterized repeatedly as a time of conformity. Endless rows of houses that seemed the same were springing up in suburbs that also seemed interchangeable. Interest in politics among both adults and adolescents was minimal. The country's priorities were evidenced in the most popular choices of college major: for women, teaching, and for both men and women, the liberal arts. In fact, it was precisely those most interested in the humanities who spearheaded the attack on the conformity they thought they saw in offices as well as homes.

The attacks were completely ignored, as the public happily went about its business. Books such as *The Organization Man*, by William Whyte, stridently insisted that people should be more individualistic. They often became bestsellers because people found the message a comforting cliché. What was overlooked in the flood of articles, books and speeches about the "man in the gray flannel suit" was *why* he had become so in the first place. Instead of being Madison Avenue types all their lives, these men had been national heroes during World War II. That sounds like a glorious position for young men to have been in, but when we began our research in the 1950s, they quietly pointed out to us that it had been hell on earth, not glorious in the least.

Watching hundreds of their fellow soldiers die or be maimed stripped war of all its romance in their minds. They had gone off to battle scared and excited, but those who came home were glad that it was over and wanted nothing more than to live in peace and to forget what they'd seen. That wasn't easy for some, and when we asked them to tell us as accurately as they could what it had been like, the chilling reports made it clear why they no longer wanted to be in the national limelight. They had been there, and it hurt.

They therefore reacted to the prevailing "tough guy" image popularized by screen idols such as Humphrey Bogart, John Wayne, or Jimmy Cagney by unwittingly producing the reverse. Men who had been in a real war found the film and fiction version of the Tough Guy hollow, if familiar. The G.I. Bill allowed hundreds of thousands of returning veterans to get college educations and graduate degrees. The life that permitted them to lead didn't require muscles and guns for success.

Here, for the first time, we realized how powerful an impact national priorities have on the love lives of men and women. "Don't women *want* you to keep playing the tough guy?" we asked them. "Some do," one replied, voicing the view of the majority, "but that doesn't matter. They'll find it elsewhere, from other men, if that's what they want. I, personally, don't feel it's necessary anymore. World War II is over, and so is Korea." They were almost consciously reshaping their self-images and attitudes in a responsible civilian direction. The many photographs of Eisenhower on the golf course, rather than striking them as ludicrous, were a reassuring symbol of a distinguished military leader on permanent R & R. People who stayed home during World War II and worried that when it ended, millions of men who were now in effect trained killers would be returning to our shores turned out to have nothing to fear. The vast majority of veterans avoided VFW clubs and went relentlessly private.

That is, until Sputnik was launched in October 1957. A new breed of national hero was suddenly needed to meet the challenge. The ex-soldiers knew that they weren't it, though their children might be. This time, it was scientists and engineers, laboring on behalf of their country in an international technology competition whose stakes were every bit as high as those in previous military conflicts. The atmosphere became electric as soon as the news of the successful launch was announced, and it remained that way for the next dozen years. Yet most of the young men and women we began to monitor at this time were convinced that it would have little relevance to their professional aspirations and none whatsoever to their personal lives.

The first hint of how distressingly wrong that forecast had been appeared soon after Jack Kennedy took office in 1960. The appeal of the man was so great, and young adults felt so much closer to him than they had to Ike, they barely noticed that the temper of the times had shifted dramatically in just a few years. Previously, liberal arts majors, and their generalist's approach to the problems of the workplace and of everyday life, were riding high. Thanks to the attitudes that predominated in the 1950s, they felt superior, while the tech types, majoring in everything from biology or chemistry to engineering or statistics, felt somewhat like second-class citizens. Now, the tables abruptly turned. Elite status was accorded, with proud presidential approval, primarily to people who were technically trained.

People can adapt to almost any change if it occurs slowly enough. This was nothing of the kind. Kennedy, responding to the threat the Russians posed, magnified its importance and accelerated its pace. Since it placed a premium on youth, the young were pleased. Yet the fact remains that for every person suddenly elevated to elite status, many more lost status, since they weren't in science-related fields. The loss clearly wasn't apparent to most at the time.

Even if it had been, they certainly wouldn't have blamed Kennedy in any way. True, they had been seriously demoted, evicted from the good life they had been led to expect in the near future, but they simply couldn't see him as the enemy because he was *theirs*. They identified so closely with him, wanted so much to be like Jack and Jackie, that hating him was nearly impossible.

American political scientists and historians have written some incisive analyses of what happened in other countries when large numbers of educated young adults were suddenly disenfranchised. However, the most important part of what was happening in their own backyard escaped their notice. The education and professional preparation of millions of intelligent and energetic young Americans had been rendered archaic and irrelevant almost overnight. It is hardly surprising that these young people too came to feel that way. They may not have been able to hate Kennedy, may not have thought of him as associated in any way with their growing plight as the "haves" pulled ever further ahead of the "have-nots." But once he died, it was inevitable that the nation would explode in a paroxysm of hatred.

Lyndon Johnson, and everything he did, could easily be despised. Did those recently demoted hate the war in Vietnam? Of course. Did they want to avoid being drafted, while their technically trained peers were exempted on the grounds of national need? Definitely. Yet something larger, more enduring and almost as threatening was also at issue, and it would be there long after the Vietnam war had ended: their ability to earn, love and think well of themselves.

EXTRAMARITAL RELATIONS

What in the world, the reader may be asking, does any of this have to do with the personal lives of successful women? The answer is: everything. Ever since 1960, the top two priorities in the United States, for both young men and young women, have been, first, to become specialists, and second, to become outstanding in the chosen area of specialization. Merely settling upon a speciality isn't enough; attaining renown in the field is as important as finding it in the first place.

The request or, more accurately, the demand, seems reasonable at first glance, yet it has a major and unexpected impact on the love lives of people who try to act in accordance with its dictates. Having pigeonholed themselves at work, they want to take flight once the workday is done. We aren't talking about the mere alternation of work and play, which, like being awake part of each 24-hour day and asleep the rest, is normal. What is being discussed instead is the process when it is pushed to its extremes—and the emotional and erotic hungers it generates.

Human adaptability has been a precious possession for millennia. The flexibility and resourcefulness people display in a hundred forms, large and small, allowed them to move from warm climes to cooler ones, using clothes to adjust for the differences; and to engage in a wide range of productive labors, everything from hunting, fishing and farming to construction and manufacturing, to keep themselves alive and healthy. Now the modern world began to insist that each person who would be a citizen in good standing throw away all fields but one; within that field, find a subspecialty that he or she can lay claim to; and last but by no means least, become well-known in that area.

Wanting the acclaim, and convinced that the subspecialty they eventually chose would be satisfying in itself and rewarding as well, most people after Sputnik's launching in 1957 attempted to follow the dictates. The hidden guideline affected their actions even more deeply once Kennedy became president in 1960. What we then noticed, in monitoring the progress of those in the limelight, was that the majority had increasing difficulty keeping their marriages intact, more so than people in less glamorous fields. They focused intently on the same topics day after day, and they badly wanted some variety in their lives when evenings and weekends rolled around. Make that "when weekends rolled around," for their evenings too were often devoted to their work. In many cases, they worried more than they worked, but the toll on their emotions was the same. Keep in mind that the people we are discussing weren't mere job holders, content to work nine to five and leave their professional activities in the office until the next morning. These people wanted not only to be highly competent, but also to be publicly acknowledged as outstanding—and they openly said so. They had few illusions about how difficult a task that would be to achieve.

We couldn't find even one who said, "My area of specialization is *so* narrow that when I'm finished working, I want to break free and run around as though I weren't married." Yet they behaved in a manner that made their feelings about the matter quite clear. Men were hit by the pressures first, since the nation, in its technological race against the USSR, was praising primarily physical scientists and engineers, professions chosen even today largely by men. As is typical in the United States, the carrot was used instead of the stick; monetary rewards and public applause were offered; no one pointed a gun at anyone's head or threatened anyone's parents with imprisonment or disgrace. Yet the inducement was powerful enough to constitute coercion, even though those who accepted the challenge did so voluntarily.

When we interviewed our subjects, it was apparent that they had no explanation for the rapid increase in their inner restlessness. They felt thrilled to be laboring away knowing that the national limelight was shining on them as a group. That was indeed thrilling because it automatically solved the problem of how they were to meet the second and equally important of the nation's top two priorities—namely, to become famous in their fields. As things now stood, all they had to do was earn from their peers the right to stand up and take a bow. The national audience was already assembled.

Instead of bringing them peace, and encouraging them to concentrate single-mindedly on the first national priority of becoming highly skilled at their specialties, it seemed only to make them more nervous. At first we thought that these prized professionals were under added duress precisely because they were inescapably in the spotlight, and that made the stakes they were playing for higher. However, that turned out not to be the pivotal issue. Examining a wide range of comparable cases allowed us to see that the most critical contributor to their sexual restlessness was their closeness to their professional goals. Being closer made them try harder—which fed their appetite for variety once their work was through for the moment.

The public's perception of people in the computer, electronics, engineering, physics, mathematics, statistics and aerospace fields is distorted by the handful of careful and disciplined workers they have encountered, if any. Many are indeed retiring types, who cherish their reclusive involvement in the day's activities and would probably continue them as a hobby even if they couldn't earn a living doing them. What needs to be said is that even quite inhibited men, and as we'll later see, women as well, wound up filing for divorce. That surprised us and, even more so, their friends.

What we found is that, extroverts or introverts, these limelighters were on average nearly twice as likely during the 1960s to have (or just as significant, to want to have) extramarital relations as people who were not on the national stage. The hypothesis that they were "peacocks," seeking to exploit the extra plumage the country had awarded them merely for selecting the right professions, provided only part of the explanation for the elevated level of desire. For *within* each field in the spotlight, it was precisely those men who were most intent upon attaining renown, as measured by their own statements to this effect, who most readily wandered sexually, or wanted to.

Interestingly, the least motivated men in these fields were doing the same. They were casting an interested eye in a wide variety of directions outside work to make up for what they sensed they were unlikely to achieve within it. If the dedicated needed diversion far more than they realized, the indifferent needed a more ordinary style of ego boost. Sex with an appropriate stranger was supposed to provide it. If anything can accurately be described as peacock behavior, this was it, for these men felt they deserved extra attention solely on the basis of their being in a highly regarded field.

THE EVICTION OF HOMEMAKERS

The people in these professions constituted only 3% of the work force. Thus, it is important to see how the majority of young workers and students in non-technical fields, who had been abruptly demoted by the nation's sudden infatuation with science and engineering, felt about their own activities. Many had no trouble articulating their feelings when we asked them to discuss their own career prospects, given the nation's emphasis at the time. Two words capture the essence of their remarks: anger and defensiveness. The country apparently no longer needed their skills, or if it did, was unwilling to applaud them for having the skills. That made it impossible for them to become citizens in good standing. Even if they became enormously knowledgeable in their chosen subspecialties, national acclaim was unlikely to become theirs and they knew it. There was no audience waiting. No one cared.

One area of activity took a beating under the new guidelines that far exceeded that sustained by any other: namely, that of being a homemaker. Here was one line of work that was anything but specialized, as is apparent by listing the various professionals who have to be called on to fill the shoes previously occupied in each case by one woman. Not only was this activity a failure as measured by the first of the nation's new top two priorities, it was even more so when judged according to the second. Being private instead of conducted in the public arena, it stood no chance whatever of bringing any practitioner widespread acclaim, no matter how exceptional she might be at her work. The very idea of the Housewife of the Year, popular in the 1950s, now struck both the young men and women in our sample as quaint and a little ludicrous.

There were many women for whom housework was drudgery and looking after their children not much more satisfying. For them, the pressures sweeping everyone into the work world were a blessing. They weren't sure they'd ever become renowned at their jobs, but now at least they had a chance. However, there was a comparable number of women who wanted to work only part-time. "If we can manage it financially," one told us at age twenty-seven, in 1960, "I'd like to stay home with my three children."

The point, and it is an important one, is that these women, who previously felt appreciated for what they were doing, now felt inferior. And judged by the nation's new guidelines, they were. The jobs they felt pressured to take often involved at least as much drudgery as they had been shouldering at home. They put up with it because they realized subconsciously that they were more modern this way, living in accordance with the nation's unwritten new dictates. However, this group of women rarely developed a real fondness for the office work they were doing.

Above all they sensed that much of what they were doing was not voluntary. Like men who were sent to Vietnam during the period, they couldn't erase some nagging doubts about the forces moving young men and women to and fro.

A growing proportion of the young women we studied were taking their educations and their initial positions in the work world seriously, and they had no interest in devoting themselves solely or even primarily to being homemakers. However, they had more in common than they thought with those who continued to prefer this role. The similarity between the two groups lay in the inability of either group to find enduring relationships with men. It didn't matter whether the women wanted to marry and work, or marry and spend full time raising a family. Partners seemed to be vanishing before their eyes.

They didn't notice that fact in the early 1960s because Kennedy's magic made everything still seem possible. Nixon and Johnson served the purpose of keeping boys and girls together even better, thanks to their being widely despised presidents. A common enemy made young men and women, who were actually drifting apart, still feel somewhat close.

If psychological pressures caused high-tech limelighters to become philanderers, as much in mind as in fact, plenty of men should have remained available: namely, those whose professions alone excluded them from the spotlight. But they weren't. For the bitterness and disappointment that many of these men chronically felt soon spilled over and poisoned their personal relationships. They had been permanently rendered second-class citizens merely because of their choice of a profession. Women who hadn't selected the physical sciences or engineering for their life's work were equally unable to feel they were citizens in good standing. Like their male peers, the frustration they were experiencing in trying to find a secure and proud place for themselves in the world made them defensive and angry. Couples formed, of course; there was never any doubt that they would. But the big question in our minds was whether they had enough glue left under the circumstances to be able to stay together. The seething hostility they were aiming first at one president, then at another, as the 1960s progressed, spilled over and made them bark at one another with alarming frequency. It prevented them from finding within themselves the peace without which even good relationships become endangered. It is hardly surprising that from the launching of Sputnik in the late 1950s, and continuing through the next decade, the divorce rate steadily climbed.

In short, the decade of the 1960s was characterized by two radical changes. First, it demoted most young men and women in the eyes of their country. Second, it evicted women from their homes, since their work there was no longer viewed in a positive light according to the nation's new criteria for judging the worth of any profession. An elite of scientists and engineers had been given a monopoly on the spotlight, since they were now the front-line soldiers in a tense technological rivalry with Russia.

It was as though these men had quietly been conscripted into an army, just as those twenty years before had actually been. Women whose husbands had been sent overseas during wartime had it easy by comparison to what was now taking place. During this go-round, the men with whom they were—or wanted to be—involved were still there, tantalizingly close, yet in actuality unavailable. They had become a mirage.

FLEETING ENCOUNTERS

It is always easy to blame someone else for our troubles. There are many readers who will feel that the previous pages indicate that Kennedy and Johnson were responsible for the serious problems that beset young men and women in the 1960s. History gives us many pictures of egomaniacal leaders who sacrificed large portions of their countries' populace to grandiose and demented schemes. However, that isn't what was happening in the United States at this time, and if we are truly to understand what is happening to women today, we should look briefly at an alternative explanation.

When a country becomes as affluent as the United States, internal pressures develop and accompany the visible signs of plenty that are seen everywhere. Since it now takes less than 3% of the labor force to feed the entire nation, and less than 20% to manufacture everything the country consumes, the key question that arises is: How are the other eighty million workers to keep themselves gainfully occupied? Economics 101 provides the entertaining and instructive answer: "Let them take in one another's laundry." The 1970s and even more so the 1980s would unwittingly take this simplistic answer to heart by keeping almost 20% of the labor force busy taking in one another's money instead. Mushrooming activity connected with pensions, IRAs, Keoghs, charge cards, checking and savings accounts, financial services of all kinds, provided employment for millions.

Responsible leaders didn't really care *what* the activity was that kept citizens off the streets and productively occupied. What they feared most was the reverse: complacency. A country that grows fat becomes vulnerable. Arnold Toynbee expanded this realization into a monumental work[1]

1. A. Toynbee, *A Study of History* (Oxford: Oxford University Press, 1954).

that repeatedly says, in essence, that countries that were challenged, and met the challenge, survived and grew; those that weren't challenged by an external threat languished and then withered. What this great Toynbean perspective overlooked, and few psychologists would fail to notice, is that nations that aren't faced with a real external threat can readily manufacture one internally. That applies especially to the United States. After all, a country that has synthesized everything from rubber to diamonds should have little trouble turning some molehill into a mountain and scaring itself into remaining vigilant and active.

How much better it is, then, when the threat posed by another country—in this case, Soviet Russia—seems very real indeed, thanks to its undeniably belligerent and expansionist actions. These weren't responded to immediately, so Eastern Europe was lost. As we mentioned, Americans first needed to recover emotionally from the effects of World War II through a prolonged period of normalcy. The McCarthy era in the early 1950s showed that the knee-jerk tendency to whip up a little hysteria and stay alert was still functioning well. But it wasn't until the end of the 1950s that *Time* magazine, assessing the nation's mood in the summer of 1959, could say that the United States was a land "in which fear and fretting were made ridiculous by the facts of national life." That was enough complacency to trigger the survival instincts in almost any healthy human, particularly since Americans had been enjoying a prolonged period of R & R along with their President Ike.

The nation leaped to its feet under Kennedy and labored enthusiastically to match and then surpass Russia's lead in space. But the point that needs to be made here is that, far from being manipulated by its president, the nation manipulated the president into giving it what it sorely needed psychologically at that moment: a challenge. It did so by responding excitedly to certain things he said and not to others—man on the moon, *si*; Bay of Pigs, *no*. Phrases such as, "Ask not what your country can do for you; ask what you can do for your country," gave the public precisely what it wanted. Meeting this primitive psychological need— one connected with survival—eventually caused millions of marriages to collapse. However, that was normal during wartime, hot or cold. Love mattered, but not nearly as much as preventing the populace at large from becoming fat and lazy.

By the late 1960s, it was clear that human costs of meeting the challenge were too great to continue using this route. Making people once again heed the warning to stay lean and mean had finally made them, after a decade of screaming the warning, just a little too lean and far too mean. In accidentally stripping them of the possibility of establishing satisfying and enduring intimacies, it turned them into the equivalent of atoms in a gas at high temperature, crashing into one another in what turned out to be fleeting and painful encounters. The country had gone too far. It had stimulated for too long the survival apparatus located in the base of the brain of each of its citizens. A respite was called for; an era needed to end.

It did, as spending on the Vietnam war, Great Society programs and the space race wound down rapidly. When it did, engineers and scientists, instead of being brought home from the front and given a hero's reception with a parade up Fifth Avenue, were fired by the thousands. For them, the recession of 1969–1970, which was caused by the huge spending decreases, was more nearly a Depression, as well as the occasion for a major loss of prestige.

The public at large, working men and women in their prime earning years, had tolerated and were even pleased about the elite status of scientists and engineers throughout the 1960s because each hoped to profit personally from the activity of this group. The usual way in which celebrities share their status with the public is to sign autographs and send signed photos of themselves. Tech types in the 1960s, the real celebrities of the period, were able to carry the process a two giant step further. They formed thousands of small high-tech companies all across the land and sold stock in them to the public. Better than any measly autograph, these shares stood a chance of making their new owners fabulously rich. Not surprisingly, workers who knew nothing whatever about microelectronics and computers eagerly snapped up the shares, buying them through stockbrokers who often had to beat back rabid customers who seemingly wanted them at any price. In fact, a good way to think of this period is in terms of frenzied players of high-tech stocks, while overtly hostile youngsters were rallying everywhere. That is, as millions of young men and women roamed the streets, their non-tech professions making them feel inadequate and angry, their parents were excitedly hoping to cash in on the huge profits generated by the firms that had recently been founded by high-tech professionals.

Once the nation abruptly demoted its scientists and engineers, just as it had done a decade before to its liberal-arts generalists, the stocks of high-tech companies plummeted. The government was no longer watering this garden, feeding it lavishly, and that caused the plants to wither fast. The number of stockbrokers was cut almost in half, and the public took a thumping loss. Its decade-long infatuation with the wonders of modern technology was over for the moment, leaving most with a bitter taste in their mouths.

That should have been good news for women—those who wanted to work, those who wanted to be homemakers, and those who wanted to be any combination of the two. It should also have been good news for the majority of young men, who weren't in the science and engineering fields. It should be clear by now that these groups had much more in common than has previously been thought. Both suffered during the 1960s, and for the same reasons. Now at last, women and non-tech men could hope to be looked upon favorably by their country.

RENOWN FOR FEMALE MBAs

How were they supposed to make that happen? We've been talking all along about the power of prevailing attitudes, not politics, on the professional and personal lives of young men and women. The attitudes may have seemed political because they were being funneled through the office of the president. This time, and throughout the decade of the 1970s, the White House was unavailable to create the next national hero. Nixon's psychological problems and then criminal activities, Ford's physical clumsiness and inability to locate Poland, and Carter's greater involvement with God than with his country made this trio irrelevant in the minds of the vast majority of people in our sample. None of the three was popular or believable enough to fulfill the traditional presidential role of Perceiver of Threats. At first glance, that made young people now seem to be solely on their own.

Yet each country has a way of making its priorities known to young adults who are embarking on a career. Job openings and the size of starting salaries communicate the message clearly. The dethronement of scientists and engineers was a liberating event of great importance for the majority of workers. Women seized the term, and the phrase "women's liberation movement" suddenly became popular. But it is critical to note that until tech types lost their monopoly on the national limelight, there could not have been—and there wasn't—a women's liberation movement. Before the end of the 1960s, when the event took place, millions of women worked, as did non-tech men. However, neither group mattered. Now they could be important, but only if they went into business.

We'll see in a moment why this area of professional activity was accorded top priority in the United States in the 1970s. First, let us look at the comment that the women's liberation movement broke up families. Of all the criticisms of the movement, this is the one that is voiced most often and most bitterly. It is also the most inaccurate. The evidence flatly contradicts this criticism. In each year of the 1960s, there were women who told us that they yearned to be homemakers, and nothing but homemakers, yet the activity was *already* considered déclassé and dated. These women knew the truth about prevailing attitudes in an immediate and painful way that would take others years to grasp. "What are you now when you're a housewife?" one member of our sample asked us rhetorically at age twenty-four, in 1962, and proceeded to answer, "A nothing, that's what." The point is that even if she had had the strength to ignore the prevailing attitude, it is unlikely that she would have found a partner to settle down with happily and permanently. Too many pressures were working against that outcome throughout the 1960s.

Couldn't she have found such a mate in the 1970s? The answer, unfortunately, is no. Things had gotten even worse for women who wanted to be happily married. In the 1960s parents were betting (in the stock market) on the success of the very professionals who had displaced their children in the job market. The children eventually felt they had no choice but to riot and revolt, and there was an abundance of hatred in the air by 1968–1969. The recession of 1969–1970 apparently gave adults all the time they needed to lick their wounds after the bursting of the technology bubble, for even before it was over, they had erected a new national idol to take the place of the old. Scientists and engineers were out, MBAs were in.

Women and non-tech men knew they had no chance of transforming themselves into physicists and electronics engineers. The distance was too great; these disciplines and their own differed in too many ways. But the distance between themselves and MBAs seemed blessedly smaller and quite bridgeable. This they could become, even if they had majored in English as undergraduates. Hatred in the 1960s was therefore replaced by frenzy in the 1970s. Tens of millions of recent and not-so-recent college graduates, male and female, were suddenly liberated in 1970 to find their place in the sun, but only if they devoted themselves to business.

Why, then, were women who were seeking partners even worse off now than they'd been before? Because they no longer had any excuse for not trying to live their lives in accordance with the nation's top two priorities: become highly competent in a specialized sphere of occupational activity, and renowned for it as well. Previously each could claim that she had indeed become highly skilled at her chosen profession, but since scientists and engineers were hogging the spotlight, there was no room for her, no chance to meet the second criterion. Now there was. There was no doubt after 1960 that she had been evicted from the world of homemaking, so one hand was already pushing her into the business world. After 1970, two were. She had no arguments left for not adopting the kamikaze approach. Her chances of establishing a satisfying marriage had been drastically reduced, and for a very simple reason: *Now anyone could hope to work too hard—in business—and secretly hope to become famous, as well as rich, by doing so.*

The race was on, and the sheer number of people chasing the same goal guaranteed that most would end up badly frustrated. What is fascinating psychologically is that, after an inital burst of optimism and enthusiasm, the amount of hostility many began carrying in the 1970s was no less than it had been in the 1960s. The situation had deteriorated; at least during the 1960s, they were able to aim it in an outward direction, at convenient targets such as Johnson and Nixon. Hating Ford and Carter, the "Bumbler" and "Little Goody Two-Shoes," as the majority of our sample characterized them, was much more difficult. As one put it at age thirty-one, "It's kind of hard—you know, far-fetched—for me to blame them for my troubles."

But the troubles were serious, and they persisted. Even though the dethronement of scientists and engineers had set the stage for a vast democratization of ambition, the rewards that were being realized in the quest were plainly minimal. Someone had to be at fault. If the White House was sitting this decade out, caught up in its own misdeeds and fecklessness, the finger would have to be pointed somewhere else. Those who had partners could find only two people to blame: themselves and their partners. Both parties wound up with a faceful. The 1970s turned out to be a decade of masochistic self-criticism for Americans—and still higher rates of divorce.

Resenting one's partner became a national pastime, particularly for women. Many had waited in limbo an entire decade for their chance at success to arrive, and now that it had, they could see that the payoff would be pitifully small. Someone had to be responsible for that; it couldn't be themselves. "I've done *everything* I can—believe me, everything," a twice-divorced mother of a young daughter told us at age thirty-four, in 1976, "and I'm going nowhere fast." Who did she feel was at fault? "Men," she answered, without hesitation. "They're holding women—holding *me*—back."

What made the reply, and the enormous number like it during the decade, so odd was that the men in our sample were stunned by the changes that were taking place in the relationships between the sexes. Previously, at least, young men and women had been able to huddle together and listen to the soothing music of anti-war activists and rock stars. Sex took place, and so did marriages, though not many lasted. Those that did were admittedly rocky. Now, even that possibility began to seem remote. As a twenty-nine-year-old attorney, looking very much to get married, put it in 1971, "How did *she* wind up with an exclusive on being the angry one?" It shocked men to realize that the old togetherness had disappeared in less than two years' time. They couldn't continue to espouse their old militancy, side by side with their female contemporaries, because *they* had suddenly become the target of a new militancy, one that their gender precluded them from espousing. The rift between the sexes widened quickly in the early 1970s. Women alone claimed the right to be militant, while men went on the defensive.

For women to then complain that such men were having trouble "making a commitment," and were "afraid to open up," was truly bizarre. The men committed themselves instead to business with a single-mindedness that made loving husbands in the 1950s look lazy by comparison. Without realizing it, women who were openly expressing their hostility toward men were creating two beds of nails to lie on, one at work and another when it was done.

Deciding that men were the cause of their personal and professional troubles may have been the easiest—and perhaps the only—choice that seemed available to women, if they were not to blame themselves. However, what it tragically overlooked was that men and women were in the same boat to an extent that few could have dreamed; in fact, neither sex was at fault, and they could have helped each other enormously to handle their common plight, rather than repeatedly turn on one another.

POLITICIANS AND CELEBRITIES

For that to have happened, or more to the point, for that to happen in the future, they would need a better understanding of the powerful pressures in the atmosphere that move our feelings first in one direction and then in another. We are embedded in our times to a much greater degree than we realize; whether we like it or not, we are affected by them in a host of large and small ways. Women, and men too, who hope to have satisfying personal lives must not only examine where they are now, but also the damage done to them by painful events in prior years—damage that they are still carrying. This is an especially opportune time for them to do so. The pressures that have relentlessly been tearing couples in half since the late 1950s are finally easing. That will allow people more flexibility in their choices and more love in their lives—but only if they rid themselves of the self-destructive habits they unwittingly put in place during trying times in the past.

Some readers, trying to avoid yet another round of disappointment, may be wondering whether the grounds for optimism are justified. In their view, the situation between men and women is every bit as bad now as it was in the 1970s. They think that such encouraging signs as a steady decrease in the divorce rate since the late 1970s are merely a result of the recurring recessions we've had since then. Economic concerns, the cynics insist, not love, are holding these pairings together.

A brief review of developments during the last fifteen years on the fronts we've been discussing should make it clear that important changes for the better have taken place just recently. Thus far, we've been examining the effects of two fundamental forces on the personal lives of women. The first is a psychological one, connected with maintaining vigilance, that we all seem to trigger from time to time; we generally look to our political leaders to tell us when. We leave it to them to perceive the most important dangers for us—that is, when we're in the mood to be reminded of a danger. Otherwise, we think rather little of this bunch.

The second force is more social than psychological; it is associated with the two criteria that the United States has been using since 1960 to judge the merits of anyone: how good is the person in a *specialized* field of endeavor, and how much *public recognition* has he or she attained in that field. One without the other of these two is no longer considered sufficient. It is almost the same as lacking both.

That either of this pair of fundamental forces should be allowed to play so pivotal a role in our lives is perhaps unfortunate, but we certainly seem to be stuck with them. Vigilance maintenance was undoubtedly an invaluable survival tool at one time, but the ease with which we scare ourselves nowadays about trivial or even nonexistent threats has produced a paradox: sometimes our readily induced state of hypervigilance is more of a menace than the alleged menace itself. Not only is the state of tension usually unproductive, given the nature of modern work, but it is also hard to shut off once we've triggered it.

In fact, we are so oriented toward maintaining chronically high levels of anxiety, we use a hidden rule for testing the validity of any statement we hear. The rule is, "Optimism sounds superficial; only pessimism strikes us as profound." And we cling to that belief even though, in the economic arena, for instance, it is the optimists who have almost always been right in this century, while the pessimists were profoundly wrong. Pointing to the Depression, though, pessimists can proudly retort, "But look how terrible it can be if I'm on target even once." Given the nature of our nervous systems, we buy the logic of the argument too easily, and alarm ourselves far too often for our own good, as we'll soon see.

The second force seems to have a sounder justification for the central role in modern life. Namely, it helps to move goods, especially consumer goods and services, which account for two-thirds of all economic activity in the United States. It does so in a very simple manner. Since there are so many offerings on supermarket and department store shelves, the public needs some way of winnowing down the number in each category and settling upon one or two. Advertisements help drive a few names home, and so do celebrities. However, celebrities aren't born, they are made, and the system that creates them centers around the two criteria we've been discussing: these are people who have become outstanding at something, such as tennis, acting, or football. And they have become famous at it as well. If they use a particular underarm deodorant or motor oil, then we too should, of course.

In short, a good, compact way of thinking about the two fundamental forces is in terms of politicians and threats, and celebrities and products. That is, a key part of what politicians do is make certain threats believable, when we're in the market for some; and a key part of what celebrities do is make certain products believable, when we're in the market for some.

Americans were certainly *not* in the market for threats to disrupt their complacency in 1970. There wasn't very much complacency—not yet, at least. What there was at the time was a massive swing in public sentiment away from small companies and toward large ones instead. Why? Because small companies depended on scientist-entrepreneurs and had just cost investors a fortune. Large companies, on the other hand, didn't depend on any one person, and thanks to their size, they had literally attained lives of their own. Management, not innovation, was their secret of success. In a shift that had major consequences for women, MBAs replaced tech types with surprising rapidity in the ensuing swing in sentiment in the early 1970s. The result was the sudden emergence of the "nifty fifty," as they were widely labeled at the time—fifty of the nation's largest companies whose shares now began to sell for the kind of absurd prices that high-tech stocks had commanded only three or four years before. The pendulum had swung way over to the other side; complacency about the prospects for very small companies had been superseded by complacency about the prospects for very large ones. An excess of anxiety is clearly destructive, but so is an excess of self-assurance. For it is likely, when punctured, to be transformed into panic.

The Arab oil embargo in 1973 thus hit the United States like a nationwide tornado. No politician had to fulfill his or her duty and make this one convincing; a gathering recession, plunging stock market, and long lines at the gas pumps made it all too real. What happened next was very revealing. Once we adjusted to the new power of OPEC and began paying the higher prices it sought, a growing number of business people came to believe that the biggest threat to the United States wasn't coming from the other side of the Atlantic. It was coming from the other side of the Pacific.

Anyone interested in how the process of knee-jerk vigilance works in individuals and in nations would have been enthralled by the unfolding of subsequent events. Americans generally felt a bit foolish at having been so vulnerable to what most saw as a bunch of camel riders in bed sheets, who just happened to have oil under their sand dunes. After people have been shocked, they don't relax so quickly. "Once burned, twice shy," would be psychologically more accurate if it read, "Once burned, hyperalert for a while after." Americans were looking for a threat on the horizon and found one in the direction of the setting sun.

They had something to build on. The Japanese attack on Pearl Harbor on December 7, 1941—"A day that will live in infamy," Roosevelt called it—had by no means been forgotten by business leaders in the United States. Now executives, many of these men had been teenagers when the attack came, and they enlisted or were drafted soon afterward. Few needed to be reminded of how ruthless and driven the Japanese could be. Since the White House was sitting this decade out, able to do little more than shoot itself repeatedly in the foot, the business community took charge. If the president of the country couldn't handle the nation's psychological need for vigilance, business people would do it themselves.

Books and articles about the subject poured off the presses and immediately became bestsellers and the topic of heated conversations. Americans weren't interested in the culture and personality of the Japanese, though nearly every TV set in America was tuned in to "Shogun" when it was aired at the end of the decade. What they focused on instead was Japanese management practices. It was a sign of the times in the United States.

Every believable threat to a nation creates the need for a savior. In the 1940s, our soldiers were saviors; in the early 1950s, Senator Joe McCarthy was thought to be, until it was realized that he himself was manufacturing the threat; in the 1960s, scientists and engineers were our saviors from the Russians; in the 1970s, MBAs were, from the threat of Japanese economic invasion. That it was too late seemed not to matter. Japan had already "Pearl Harbored" Detroit, and its technical prowess was being amply displayed on our shores in the fields of consumer electronics, cameras, motorcycles, steel, shipbuilding, semiconductors, apparel and textiles.

American soldiers weren't likely to be tapped as saviors this time, since many were watching a Sony and driving a Datsun or Toyota, and they saw little reason to get upset about it. Scientists and engineers weren't likely to be tapped either, since it was too soon. The public still hadn't gotten over those thumping losses it had taken in the stock market. The position of MBAs was therefore strengthened further as the nation went through another round of "hypervigilance in response to a threat." Even though Japan was graduating more scientists and engineers than we were at the time, the secret of Japanese success was seen to be their production abilities. "Their genius lies in manufacturing," we were told, "not innovation." Since they had paid the United States nearly $10 billion to license our technology in the prior thirty years, the argument seemed sound. Management was in its heyday and graduate schools of business were jammed.

As we've said, the relevance of all this to women, and to non-tech men, was that *anyone* could try too hard to succeed in business and become famous for saving his or her country. Hope lifted the spirits of many. The nation had issued an urgent call—remember, it wasn't being funneled through the White House this time—and women who devoted themselves diligently to business seemed certain they'd finally be able to meet both of the nation's criteria for mattering. Next to that, having a personal life simply couldn't be deemed important. In fact, on a subconscious plane, a large proportion of the women in our sample viewed it as a distracting self-indulgence. They were in the army now, having enlisted without realizing it, and love was something to find only on the run. Fleeting sexual encounters were bemoaned as unsatisfying yet actually accepted as the best one could do under the circumstances. This was no time to play. Grim was in.

Well, it may have looked like war, if judged by the behavior of these women, but it was merely the nation going through yet another round of "let's all scare ourselves in response to a threat." This round wasn't as gripping as the one a decade before, and so even though far more people were eligible for the role of savior ("wealth *and* fame can be yours"), management never attained the elevated position that tech types held in the 1960s. Nothing quite as stirring as Kennedy's speech, stating that "the shortage of PhD's [in science and engineering] constitutes our most critical national problem," was heard. And since these bouts of self-induced anxiety usually don't last very long (a decade at most), "Japan and management" were soon in need of replacement as a threat and its solution. Reagan, reacting to the nation's need for a new prod, chose one that was tried and true. "Russia and high technology" was the program we helped manipulate him into giving us.

The Soviet Union, not Japan, was therefore declared the big threat of the 1980s. To meet it, scientists and engineers would once again have to be dusted off and drafted, via a huge increase in the defense budget. It was hardly surprising that the *The New York Times*, and many other publications, soon began running articles on "Raising the Status of Engineers."[2] Similarly, the National Research Council established panels in 1984 to "explore ways to improve media access to the engineering community." Physical scientists were having an even easier time of it, thanks to the expansion and historic success of the space shuttle program. Technology once again was king. This time, the public was participating more broadly than it had before, buying high-tech stocks and products. Sales

2. "Raising the Status of Engineers," *The New York Times*, 9 February 1984, D2.

of microcomputers boomed. Magazines in the computer field, devoted to hardware, software, or both, found their readerships soaring. Books about Russia replaced those about Japanese management on the best-seller lists.

The majority of working women we studied only knew that, with the coming of the 1980s, they had become neither rich nor famous. And without knowing precisely why, they sensed that the chances of becoming either had suddenly decreased. They could see the evidence plainly in their everyday work lives. Although the nation's focus during the 1970s on management, multinationals and big business obscured the fact, small companies were flourishing. In fact, they were sprouting up and doing well as never before, in the stock market and in sales and earnings, thereby providing employment for tens of millions of people.

Instead of being good news, this arrangement struck both the younger and older working women we interviewed regularly in the first half of the 1980s as something less than Nirvana. Small companies were supposed to be pockets of innovation, but the women saw them as hotbeds of insanity. Entrepreneurs were being widely heralded as our secret weapon against both the Japanese and the Russians. Those whose firms produced new high-tech products were held in particularly high regard. Yet the women working there found such places chaotic and emotionally draining, and felt their annual turnover rates were nearly unbelievable. "What in God's name," they kept asking, "am I supposed to build with *this* as a foundation?"

DELUSIONS ABOUT SELF-ESTEEM

Many of the women in our sample who viewed themselves as moving ahead far too slowly tried to escape the grip of the second fundamental force, the one connected with superlatives and celebrities. They were happy to continue striving to be competent (the first criterion) but wanted to dismiss the importance of becoming renowned in their field (the second criterion). That in itself was no easy task. Men and women have been trying for more than two decades to ease the pressure induced by the second criterion. And an enormous pressure it is, since it says, in essence, "Only the famous in America are individuals. Everyone else is, at best, deservedly part of the anonymous crowd." Home remedies sprang up to ease the pain. "It doesn't matter what anyone else thinks of you, as long as you like yourself," was a common bit of self-stroking found in pop books and an endless number of articles in women's magazines. "You should be your own best friend." It didn't work, because it couldn't.

As much as we'd all like to believe that thinking well of ourselves is sufficient to make us happy, it is not. As it turns out, unless others also think well of us, eventually we don't either—and that is especially so if we want them to think well of us for our work. However satisfying the activity, if it consumes a major portion of each day, it is also supposed to earn us a certain amount of acclaim. People who insist that "You have to start to *really* like yourself," and that "self-esteem is the key," are kidding themselves. There is no reason for us to be similarly deluded. This seemingly private, almost masturbatory concept is in fact a very social one. High self-esteem begins with and is maintained by the approving reactions of others. We recognize instantly that there is something amusingly wrong with the statement, "He is a legend in his own mind." The substitution of the word "mind" for "time" shifts the focus from a vast audience of his contemporaries to an audience of one, himself. That strikes us as pathetic, and given the people to whom this witticism is usually applied, appropriately so. Regardless of how hard people pitch the concept at us, we know that self-love just won't do.

So much for the good news. The bad news sounds bad indeed. If the world at large has to give us a standing ovation to make us feel good about ourselves, aren't the overwhelming majority of people doomed to lifelong disappointment? After all, not more than a minuscule proportion of the professionals in any field are likely to—or can—become renowned. This depressing reality seems, at first glance, to be statistically unavoidable. However, like Malthus's famous doctrine that population expands faster than food supply, and therefore the starvation of millions is a mathematical inevitability, the conclusion turns out to be false. Food is food, but applause can come from two entirely different directions, each of them capable of providing the required nourishment.

To state our finding in its simplest form: acclaim can come either from one person who truly matters or many people who don't. Both are able to make the same impact on one's need for feedback and approval.

"That's all well and good," someone may protest, "but there is a business dimension here that mustn't be overlooked. If you get millions of people interested in your work, you may just wind up rich. The other way, with an audience of only one person besides yourself, the best you can do is wind up loved and appreciated."

That isn't even close to being accurate. The reason it isn't true is so important, it forms the basis for this entire book. What we found is that people with close partners who really mattered to them and to whom they really mattered were significantly more likely to succeed in business. It may sound paradoxical, but men—and even more so, women—with a satisfying personal life increased substantially the odds that they would eventually become admired by many people they didn't know. A steady stream of applause from an intimate later led to applause from the crowd.

In short, the real recipe for success is an enduring intimacy plus ambition. Ambition alone won't do. We will be exploring the details of why that is so in every chapter that follows, but let us state briefly here the key reason. The best way to grasp the underlying dynamics is to use the old saw, "A watched pot never boils." The women we're about to meet wanted so badly to succeed in business they could almost taste it. They had either graduated from college in the 1960s and had been held in the starting gate so long they were now champing at the bit, or they graduated in the 1970s and considered work right from the start to be their top, and often their only, priority.

Talented, educated and energetic, if anyone seemed destined to go places, they did. But they haven't, and with each passing year it becomes increasingly clear that they aren't likely to. *Precisely because they never take their eyes off the goal, the goal never seems to get any closer.* They hadn't counted upon how slowly they'd be progressing in what had become by then a very crowded business world. The result is that they have concluded time and time again that they are making no progress at all. Their feelings of being repeatedly foiled and defeated ate them up inside, while their moody, hostile and uncooperative behavior at the office did the rest.

When all is said and done, as some of the brightest women in our sample realized all along, women were liberated in 1970 to do one—and only one—thing: work. Nothing else was to be allowed to matter. It is our hope that by the time this book is through, it will be painfully obvious why this totally unbalanced approach produces only frustration and failure, both at home and on the job.

2

An Identity of One's Own

It is all well and good to talk about a nation dangling a carrot in front of its young and inviting them to pursue it, but unless they receive encouragement at home they might not make the effort. During the decades of our study, it was common for youngsters to point to the war poster that proclaimed, "Uncle Sam Wants You," and react with, "Who cares what Uncle Sam wants?" *They* did, without realizing it, but they weren't inclined to respond positively during this period to posters or speeches trying to persuade them to enlist.

Other pressures were making themselves felt more strongly during these decades, pressures that would ultimately result in these youngsters being labeled "narcissistic" and "self-centered" even after they became adults. To begin with, there were changes on the home front. With the exception of the post-World War II baby boom, the birthrate in the United States had been declining in a relatively steady manner for the past two centuries, reaching an all-time low in the late 1970s. At the same time that the number of children in contemporary households was declining, the number of elderly living there also decreased. In fact, between 1950 and 1970, the percentage of the elderly living with their children plummeted by more than two-thirds, to under 10%. By 1985, less than 3% of the households of the elderly were receiving income from their children, a striking shift, and these amounts constituted less than 1% of the income of the elderly. Social Security, and a variety of other programs covering food and medical care, picked up the slack. Few workers complained about the increasing bite being taken out of their paychecks by Social Security taxes, for they vaguely understood that much of the money was making its way to people they would otherwise have had to support directly, if they could.

Households were shrinking steadily in size, and that made the people in them focus ever more on the larger world "out there." At any given time during the past quarter of a century, approximately 30% of the women we studied were living alone. The age of marriage reached a post-war low in 1956, but during the 1960s and 1970s it rose significantly; people married later, had fewer children, and had them later in their marriages than they did in the 1950s. Young adults found that their household setting was being reduced in importance while the technology for making contact with the world was expanding dramatically. The phrase "overnight success" had always been something of an exaggeration. Now it became an electronically based reality that these young adults wanted for themselves.

MARRIAGE AS A CONSOLATION PRIZE

What one generation sees as the chance to make all its dreams come true, another may find merely silly. Mining precious metals, for instance, seemed a once-in-a-lifetime possibility to people, many of whom were well-respected members of the middle class, who made the long, life-threatening overland trek to California as part of the Gold Rush of 1849.[1] In the early years after World War II, young adults thought of a modest but pleasant material setting and a strong family life as goals worth pursuing. Ike and Mamie, as President and First Lady, underscored the message, expressing their approval by living it themselves. After 1960, neither goal was accorded top priority by the people we studied. The change had been abrupt, so people continued to state that they were still interested, but their actions indicated otherwise.

It was revealing to hear many in their twenties and early thirties now saying that their material desires were interfering with their desire to have a happy marriage. In their view, they hadn't yet made enough money to live in the style to which they hoped to become accustomed, with or without someone else by their side. And until their no-longer-modest material aspirations could be met, they felt that it was appropriate to put these aspirations first.

A number of demographers have stated that the level of material comfort we experience at home as adolescents determines the level we strive to maintain or surpass as adults, as well as how we measure success or failure in judging our own material attainments.[2] No doubt there is a

1. J. S. Holliday, *The World Rushed In: The California Gold Rush Experience* (New York: Simon and Schuster, 1981).
2. R. A. Easterlin, *Birth and Fortune: The Impact of Numbers on Personal Welfare* (New York: Basic Books, 1980).

certain amount of truth to this hypothesis, though there is less than was originally thought.[3] Of greater importance in certain periods, we believe, is how the president lives. At the dawn of the era we are discussing, President Kennedy's affluence, a legacy of his wealthy, self-made father, gave many young adults in our sample a standard that they sorely wished to emulate, if not precisely match. The picture of Jack and Jackie out on the town inspired these young adults to put financial and social aspirations above all else.

Others in our sample—in fact, the majority—eventually put their careers first. They said that money mattered to them, yet they wanted eminence in their profession even more. Until it was in their grasp, they acknowledged that personal relationships might well get nudged accidentally onto the back burner.

As the years passed, we began to realize that neither of these "either/ or explanations" was valid. A seesaw with money at one end and marriage at the other, or career at one end and family life at the other, seemed the appropriate picture of the choices confronting young adults during the 1960s, 1970s and 1980s. However, a far more powerful force was making them feel they had to choose one or the other, and that they couldn't possibly attain both without major difficulty.

As we saw in Chapter 1, once Kennedy became president, charisma was on the minds of young adults every bit as much as Camelot, and the youngsters felt that they too possessed it. If there was a spotlight somewhere—anywhere—in the nation, they also wanted to be in it. They knew that the profession they were in would be important in determining the maximum amount of public acclaim they could receive, especially if it were going to be funneled first through the White House. Nevertheless, that didn't stop them from wanting as much applause as anyone else was currently getting, an inner demand they considered perfectly reasonable in a democracy, where all are supposed ultimately to have access to anything an elite manages to acquire for itself, even temporarily.

The impact of all this on the personal lives of young men and women was profound. The spotlight might move on, favoring one profession, then another, but the appetite of Americans for this type of widespread special attention was growing steadily. Once they knew it was "in the air," they could no longer ignore it. *The desire for renown became the single most important goal of young men and women after 1960. Increasingly, fame became the top priority, supplanting money and marriage.* In fact, the latter two often

3. M. MacDonald and R. Rindfuss, "Earnings, Relative Income and Family Formation, Part I: Marriage" (unpublished manuscript, Center for Demography, University of Wisconsin, Madison, 1980). Also, R. Rindfuss and M. MacDonald, "Earnings, Relative Income and Family Formation, Part II: Fertility" (unpublished manuscript, University of North Carolina, Chapel Hill, 1980).

came to be viewed as poor substitutes—consolation aims—for those who failed to attain the former.

SHARING THE REWARDS

Why did fame and marriage have such difficulty fitting together? Are they really all that different as a pair of goals from money and marriage? They are indeed, and a good way to see why is to think about a $10,000 couch. Not many people would make such a purchase even if they were wealthy, but let's assume for the moment that they did so anyway. Sharing such an object with one's partner could hardly be easier. There is room for more than one person to sit on it, so it doesn't much matter who owns it. If we went through a comprehensive list of the most expensive items that people would like to own, and would actually buy if they were rich enough, it would quickly be apparent that the majority of items on the list have this same characteristic. Clothes and jewelry are exceptions, though less so than they might seem at first glance, given the expanding social aspirations of most couples who rapidly became rich. But a $100,000 car has seats for more than just the driver, and a $2,000,000 mansion is designed with others in mind, perhaps many of them, rather than being inherently a home for a hermit. In fact, most people are struck by the incongruity of only one person inhabiting a residence that large.

To avoid even a hint of conflict over the issue of "mine versus yours," most of the happy couples we studied had a clever way of sidestepping any potential trouble. "I bought it for *us*," they warmly insist, even if the object serves the purposes mainly of the purchaser. The people who voice such a comment seem to mean it, so the worst they can be accused of is temporary stupidity, not selfishness.

Fame, unlike a material possession, cannot easily be divided. Pairing up with a famous partner or even becoming good friends with such a person often leads people to say that one is "basking in the glow" of this public figure. Nevertheless, no one has any illusions about whom the renown belongs to. As with the couch, more people than just the owner may make themselves comfortable about the celebrity status, which is every bit as real in their minds as the couch, yet there is never any doubt about who its owner really is.

Although the 1950s have long been thought of as a decade in which Dad worked and Mom stayed at home with the kids, anyone who was regularly interviewing both parents at the time knew that wasn't so. Mothers frequently had to be reached at the office, more so each year. The "labor force participation rate," as it is called, for women living with their husbands and with children of their own under the age of six, jumped from under 10% in the late 1940s to more than 20% in the early 1960s. Those living with their husbands and with children of their own between the ages of six and eighteen increased their rate of participation from approximately 25% in the late 1940s to more than 40% in the early 1960s.[4]

The stereotype was far from the reality. Feminism, out on the horizon, clearly had nothing to do with any of this, though, amusingly, feminists have been trying to take credit for it ever since they arrived on the scene more than fifteen years later. As one noted economist recently put it, feminist writings won't "be viewed by future historians as a basic cause of social change but primarily as a rationale and rhetoric for changes that were already occurring for other reasons."[5]

The "other reasons" for working full- or part-time weren't hard to find then, and the women we studied spoke about them freely. The extra money was nice, they said; the work provided social pleasures as well as interesting contact with a wider world, and it gave men and women more in common rather than less. Educated women, in particular, liked the idea of picking up where they had left off. Their college major was supposed to be preparation, if indirect, for some kind of rewarding work in their adult years. Now, having had a family, they felt they could attempt to fulfill that inner expectation.

As we saw in Chapter 1, the work world was changing rapidly at the time. Blue-collar positions in everything from mining to manufacturing were surrendering their primacy to white-collar office work. That much is clear from the data.[6] Two shifts that are of critical importance and don't show up as readily in the data are, first, that white-collar office work centered around the idea of a career, not merely a job; and second, people expected to be publicly praised, not just paid, for this kind of work.

Let's take the second topic first. Then, in the next few chapters, we'll see what is involved in having not only to show up at the office day after day for decades, but also to keep oneself highly motivated while there, day after day for decades.

BECOMING PROFESSIONAL

We have focused thus far on young adults, the experiences of men and women in America primarily between the ages of fifteen and thirty. Par-

4. *Employment and Training Report of the President* (Congressional Printing Office: Washington, D.C., 1980 and 1981).

5. V. Fuchs, *How We Live* (Cambridge: Harvard University Press, 1983).

6. R. K. Shelp, *Beyond Industrialization: Ascendancy of the Global Service Economy* (New York: Praeger, 1981), and V. Fuchs, *The Service Economy* (New York: National Bureau of Economic Research/Columbia University Press, 1968).

ticular attention has been paid to the external pressures and the opportunities they faced while coming of age between 1958 and 1985. However, there were important internal factors as well that affected youngsters in every region of the United States and in every decade of the century. One of the most pivotal was theatrical behavior in children. The power and persistence of the desire to put on a performance for one's parents undoubtedly had a survival value at one time, though a parent who becomes annoyed by the demand for attention can also be a threat. Nonetheless, young children act as if the guiding rule is, "The show must go on, even if it has to be postponed a little while Mommy or Daddy calms down." Patience is hard to come by at the single-digit ages we're discussing, so the curtain may go up a bit too soon anyway and the show may seem to viewers as though it has been (and will be) running forever. As far as kids are concerned, it is better to risk irritating an adult than to be ignored and suffer, perhaps fatally, from neglect.

It was fascinating to see the teenagers in our sample wrestle with these powerful exhibitionistic impulses. Unfortunately, many never realized how normal and natural they are, not only during one's teen years, but (to a somewhat lesser extent) in one's twenties and thirties as well. In wishing them gone, these youngsters might as well have expected their arms and legs to vanish just by blinking. We knew from parental reports that ten years earlier these same youngsters had done a variety of things, some truly hilarious, to call attention to themselves. The innocence with which they were done at the time was genuine, as was the overwhelming desire to be noticed.

High school and college may be looked at in many different lights, but for now, let us view them in terms of the relentless attempt by the vast majority of teenagers to elicit applause. It is a tempestuous time for them, especially once the glandular storm of puberty hits with full force and gives them sexual impulses to learn how to manage as well. We can better understand the path most middle- and upper-middle class youngsters end up taking by noting the major milestones they pass along the way.

As teenagers, they haven't yet settled upon the field that will form the basis of their livelihood as adults. They may know that their skills lie in the social, literary, scientific, verbal, musical, or manual area, but that predilection is still far from being developed to the point where it affords them stable membership in a profession, with an appropriate manner to match. For the moment, they want above all to be loved for themselves; for the charm they possess, the good manners they display, the athletic feats they perform, the good grades they get, the appealing personality they can radiate when they want to—and usually, for all of the above. With each passing year of high school and, especially, college, they become more willing to allow themselves to be judged by their abilities in their chosen field. That encourages them to think of themselves in increasingly realistic terms as potential employees. They are developing skills that, one way or another, they hope to be able to market.

We saw in Chapter 1 that, particularly after Kennedy became president, the market demanded more specialized skills than it ever had before. There was nothing new in this trend; division of labor is as old as recorded history, and affects insects too. But with urbanization and the industrial revolution, the transformation picked up speed.[7] It moved into a still higher gear with the advent of the space race in the 1960s. Even in fields that didn't qualify for the spotlight at the time because they couldn't help the nation in its military and technological race with the Russians, the process we are discussing continued unabated. Whether a college major was "hot" or not during this era made little difference in this regard. The psychological aspects of the process of *professionalization* were taking place among students in every academic department we studied.

What are the most important steps involved in this process? First and foremost is the heightened valuation of the opinion of people in one's field and an accompanying devaluation of the views of people in any other field. It isn't too surprising that social science majors become estranged from those in the natural sciences, and that both become estranged from those in the humanities, and vice versa. Many of the personal characteristics which help produce these choices in college are already present in high school and make themselves felt there. But it is revealing to follow these young adults year in and year out and see that the vast majority who enter a field soon become estranged from those in every other subdivision except their own. English majors look askance at sociologists, and go on to find political science majors just as remote. Chemists eye physicists and mathematicians as somewhat alien beings. The word we really need here is "foreigner." People who select a major and then go on to become a member of the profession might as well be choosing a new nation to inhabit. It becomes the only place in which they feel intellectually at home, and it inclines them to see the members of every other field as foreigners.

We will see in Chapter 7, on women's magazines, why people don't wince in pain at this progressive narrowing, and why, paradoxically, they are usually exhilarated by it instead. For the moment, we are interested in seeing what effect the process of professionalization (in an era that values highly specialized skills most) has on the attempt by young adults

---

7. F. Braudel, *The Wheels of Commerce: Civilization and Capitalism, 15th–18th Century*, Volume II (New York: Harper and Row, 1983).

to gain control of their exhibitionistic tendencies. Does the narrowing increase or decrease their desire for applause? We found that it does neither. It merely changes the nature of the audience from whom they want it. Professionals insist that it is only their peers who can really judge them, and therefore it is the public approval of this group alone that counts.

In brief, the teenagers we studied started out with a hunger for *fame* and ended up, a decade later, claiming that what they wanted most was *recognition*. The difference between the two words seems vast, at first glance. Fame means that the public at large, the informed and the ignorant, know one's name. And one may or may not have done something meritorious to achieve the renown. Recognition, on the other hand, implies that a much more limited and sophisticated group, the members of one's field, have bestowed their blessing on one's efforts, and, indirectly, on oneself.

SWITCHING FIELDS

Why discuss all this in a book about the personal lives of successful women? Because the vast majority of women we studied who became professionalized in one field wound up in another. The switch had a huge, and in many cases permanent, impact on their personal relationships. Millions of American college students who were certain that their major in sociology, education, English, economics, chemistry, psychology, art, or history would bring them the eminence they sought ended up instead in the business world.

Their switch from the academic or artistic to the commercial sphere was an abrupt one. Less than 2% had a chance to make a serious attempt at attaining the recognition they sorely wanted in their field *before* having to take a job at almost any company that would have them. To listen to these recent graduates talk about their transition from school to work (and forget, as they had, the things they said while still in school), pay was a key criterion in deciding which firm to join. If they previously were "academic dreamers," as some started labeling themselves in retrospect, they had become "hard-headed realists." As one twenty-three-year-old put it proudly, "I've become bottom-line oriented," referring to her interest in the firm's net profits, as well as her own annual earnings.

People in their twenties spoke convincingly throughout the 1960s and even more so in the 1970s and early 1980s about their desire for pay increases and promotions. The typical twenty-six-year-old who was in the work world between 1960 and 1985 had become extremely articulate about his or her financial goals and managerial aspirations. No doubt these were things that were really wanted. Few people in any field scoff at a high income and a top position at the firm for which they have chosen to work.

However, our study slowly led us to the conclusion that a third appetite was also in operation here, one that was stronger than the other two combined. These young men and women wanted renown. Wanting it is one thing; getting it, another. Not only couldn't they ask for acclaim, they couldn't even discuss it candidly, since their peers all wanted the same thing. Keep in mind that one of the main achievements of these young adults during the prior ten to fifteen years of their lives had been to rein in their exhibitionistic impulses. They had learned to ask others polite questions, and to appear to be interested in the answers, rather than just rattling on endlessly about "I, me, my." They seemed to have made substantial progress in overcoming the egomania of adolescence, a degree of self-involvement that surpasses even that of childhood because so much of it is conscious. There is an expanding ego present, and it can easily become all-consuming.

The most effective tool that these young adults could find to shoehorn their demands for applause into a very small container had been to choose and take seriously their college major. As we've said, that made them write off the approval of almost everyone else except colleagues in their own specialty. Then, suddenly, they no longer had a specialty. They had a job. Without them being aware of it, the box containing their hunger for applause had burst.

They may never have gotten the recognition they wanted, and now that they were working, they no longer cared if they ever did become recognized in connection with their former college major. But they weren't about to be denied acclaim a second time, especially since they had automatically reverted to their pre-professionalized stand, when all votes counted. Anyone could applaud their efforts now and be noticed.

Summing up, between 1960 and 1985, American youngsters made the transition while in school from yearning for fame to settling for recognition as a goal. Entering the business world and leaving their college major behind made them once again want fame, this time without realizing it. For they continued to use the vocabulary they had learned, and with good reason. It was far more acceptable, even respectable, to say that one was seeking recognition than fame. The effect on their personal lives was immense and enduring.

DOMESTIC QUARRELS

Couples paired up in the 1950s, and as we've seen, after having children, 40% of the women with children over the age of six were working by the end of decade. These couples made it clear to us that their primary goal was to earn enough money as two-paycheck families to live the way they wanted. It was a time of modest living standards, and couples were thrilled in the late 1940s and throughout the 1950s merely to be able to move to the suburbs and buy what they considered a nice house. What Thorstein Veblen called "invidious distinctions," an attitude of "my home [or car] is slightly better than yours," still prevailed. It always does. But to someone in the 1980s, the differences are barely noticeable. Basically, these young men and women found what they were looking for as residents of pleasant suburbs that centered on the family and community.

Couples pairing up in the 1960s tried to use their parents' approach and increasingly found that they couldn't. Something fundamental changed in 1960, and has been doing so more each year from then till now. A young man and woman could still pair up and have a family that was important to them. Yet unlike couples of a comparable age only a decade earlier, family was no longer enough. A number of astute observers have said that a key to understanding countries around the globe in the period since the end of World War II is that a "revolution of rising expectations" has occurred. The observation is fine as far as it goes, but it doesn't go nearly far enough. After people have a certain amount of money, they usually don't continue to view accumulating more as their top priority. In the United States, we found that another goal came to occupy that slot: becoming a star. Youngsters took their parents' material achievements for granted and went on from there to a different hierarchy altogether.

That doesn't mean money ceased to be important to them. It couldn't. After they finished school and started working, they were among the first to comment on the fact that they weren't living in the lap of luxury. They recognized that a moderate bread-and-butter income was needed just to cover the basics. Still, it wasn't as electric a subject in their minds as becoming renowned. Money was an annoying necessity they had to have and could talk about openly; public acclaim was an exciting extra they sorely wanted and had to talk about using euphemisms and circumlocutions, if they were willing to risk talking about it at all.

Conversations between young adults and their parents during the 1960s and 1970s made it plain how far the two sides had drifted apart on this front. Trying to offer encouragement, parents told their children who were still in school or who had recently graduated to look for jobs that paid well. That struck them as the most realistic approach. Many students did this anyway, of their own free will, since they wanted the high incomes that doctors, lawyers and MBAs were making at the time. However, the majority couldn't bring themselves to choose these fields because they were after more than just sizable earnings. The clashes between parents and their children during these decades were a result of words that now had different meanings to the two groups. *To parents, "doing well" meant "earning well"; to their achievement-oriented children, it meant becoming well-known. Small wonder the two sides so often fought. One was discussing money; the other, fame.*

Once these young men and women went to work, whether they were in business or the professions mentioned above, they spent the whole of their twenties and thirties seeking "recognition," as they called it. Remember, to them, recognition was the appropriate word, for it implied that the acclaim was being received for *work* they had done and, equally important, it was being given by an allegedly *knowledgeable audience.* However, the hunger for acclaim was so strong that anything they did could conveniently be classified as "work," even dressing well, and anyone who complimented them could instantly be accorded "knowledgable" status.

Who they themselves were and how well they functioned as part of a team—problems that plagued their twenties and thirties—were left unanswered in all the jockeying for compliments. Yet it was precisely this unending search for praise and the inability to be part of a team, seen in case after case, that finally made us understand why marriages began falling apart at a record rate during these decades. To summarize our findings in this area briefly: *People who evidenced repeated reluctance to be part of a team at work were more likely than their peers to end up divorced.* And the more hostile they were to the idea of teamwork on the job, the greater the likelihood of divorce.

To look at the situation from their point of view for the moment, they insisted that they had good reason for preventing themselves from becoming anonymous cogs in a well-oiled machine. The comment we heard most often was, "I won't get any pay raises or promotions if I don't make certain I'm noticed." Their argument seemed to be merely financial and managerial. Yet their behavior made it apparent that they had a much larger goal in mind, one that went well beyond the confines of the firm. They expected their work somehow to bring them applause, first from their coworkers and eventually from the world at large. As it turns out, even in *their* minds recognition was nothing more than first-stage fame, a mere prelude to the wider glory they were really seeking.

They acted the same way at home, without realizing it, and did so for precisely the same reason. *There are couples who break up because one partner becomes enormously better known than the other. But for every such couple there are thousands of others who break up because neither partner has become famous and both want desperately to be.* So they fight about every crumb of what looks like public acclaim. Even an innocent compliment from an outsider may set off a furious domestic quarrel. For when all is said and done, what *is* a compliment? It is applause from an audience of just one person. It may not sound like much to a passerby who overhears it, but to people who are starving for public approval, it is a morsel as big as a meal. That makes it well worth fighting for. The pair fight even harder to prevent themselves from being ruled out as eventual candidates for thunderous applause. What would cause them to be excluded from consideration? Being wrong. The battles that develop about who is right, who is smarter, are intense because they appear to the participants to be a matter of life and death. Each party feels that he or she is the only one deserving of acclaim, and each wants to be ready and waiting gracefully for it whenever it finally arrives.

REVEALING SECRETS, ON THE JOB AND OFF

One of the most interesting definitions of a psychologist is an expert who tells you that your secrets are the same as everyone else's secrets. The things we worry about most turn out to be remarkably similar to those our peers are fretting about. Some of the anxieties are timeless; people in every century are concerned about threats to their health, the possibility that they may be stricken by a fatal or, even worse in some ways, a permanently disabling disease. However, other anxieties are very much a product of their times. Their socioeconomic origin makes them harder to trace, since a host of pressures exerted by the people we know, the work we do and the goals we seek to attain may all be involved. These factors give rise to anxiety every bit as much as does a pain in the stomach or chest that we fear may be the beginnings of cancer or a heart attack.

Finding out what people are striving for and worrying about is frequently much harder than anticipated. They may talk openly about certain topics and not want to discuss others, even on questionnaires that they are asked to fill out anonymously. A large part of the problem is that people may be uncomfortable about the fact that they are pursuing aggressively something they aren't supposed to be pursuing at all. It should be clear by now that our study indicates that renown is what men and women in their twenties and thirties were intently pursuing between 1960 and 1985. Why would they be so uncomfortable with this pursuit that they couldn't discuss it, even in confidence?

The answer is that they knew that acclaim, if it were really deserved, would come their way without any public relations effort from them. Their work, their merit, would speak for itself, resulting automatically in a growing pool of admirers. Over and over again they told us, "A compliment from someone doesn't mean anything if you have to twist the person's arm to make him or her give it to you." The same thing applied to affection: "How much credence can I give an 'I love you' that I practically had to beg for?" Love or praise therefore had to be spontaneous if it was to be viewed by the recipients as worthwhile. It is appropriate that this guideline was carried from the old arena to the new and used by people to judge how well they were doing. None wanted to be in the position of being vulnerable to the charge, "Of course you have a circle of friends— you bought them."

The upshot was that they pretended both to themselves and to everyone they knew that they weren't interested in renown. This show of indifference was intended to convince any skeptical listener they met that since they didn't care about public approval, they weren't doing anything to get it. Just going about their business. If acclaim arrived in spite of their indifference, it would have to be considered genuine precisely *because* of their indifference. Millions of ambitious young men and women thus wound up painting themselves into a corner. They couldn't acknowledge even to themselves the magnitude of their most important desire. Paradoxically, the more open they were about wanting applause, the less its arrival would mean. Only by turning their backs on it, and denying altogether that they wanted it, could they allow themselves to pursue it on the sly.

A variety of social commentators[8] came to the conclusion during these decades that one reason—and maybe the main reason—for the collapse of intimacy and the soaring divorce rate was that people no longer had any real secrets to tell one another. The style of the time seemed to be "Let it all hang out." Americans discussed their sexual activities so openly that their hidden erotic desires could no longer bond each pair into a unit. Having become cocktail party chatter ("Just the other day I was telling my shrink that I climax best when . . . "), the information was now useless for helping to ensure the longevity of the relationship.

Our study indicates that this conclusion could hardly have been further from the truth. The first clue we had that it was wide of the mark appeared when business executives in increasing numbers began telling us in the early 1960s that they would no longer readily disclose company secrets to prized subordinates. Their reason was simplicity itself: "Why should I teach the people who work for me the tricks of the trade, so that they can go elsewhere and use them against me?" Job changes had rolled onto the scene as a major factor disrupting the flow of knowledge from the top to the middle layers of the firm. Thanks to the blithe manner in which employees now quit to go to another company, or start one of their own, top corporate officers became wary of what they said to subordinates. These executives did indeed have valuable company secrets and

---

8. Cf., for example, N. Postman, *The Disappearance of Childhood* (New York: Delacorte, 1982).

business wisdom to pass on, but job-hopping by the most valued members of the junior staff made senior staff members clam up.

The increasing rate at which marriages began to dissolve after 1960 and, especially, 1965, made us suspect that similar influences were in operation in the personal as well as the professional sphere—this time on a horizontal instead of a vertical plane. For instance, the men and women we studied often ran rather than walked to their nearest book or magazine store to read the secrets that suddenly became public when a divorce occurred in which at least one of the partners was well known. If both were, so much the better. The public fully expected one of the partners to "spill the beans." Revenge was the first motive they named as the reason for the spilling, while the second was financial: "It sells. People want to read about it." No one we interviewed had any doubts about the huge public appetite for gossip.

The possibility that they themselves could be involved in a similar exposé, in a less public way, didn't escape them. As the divorce rate continued to climb, the possibility turned into a probability. By the end of the 1960s (for those under thirty) and early 1970s (for the entire sample), virtually everyone we surveyed reported that they had close friends who had gotten a divorce, or that they themselves had. People now had sound justification for playing their cards close to the vest not only out in the world, but at home as well. Letting their guard down anywhere could prove very costly later. In short, both on the job and with one's spouse, there was growing reason for people who had important information to disclose not to disclose it.

Anyone interested in studying how a self-fulfilling prophecy actually works on a broad scale couldn't have done better than to watch what happened once the prevailing attitude became, "I can't trust my subordinate [or my spouse] because he [or she] is probably going to leave anyway." Social scientists and commentators weren't wrong to assume that secrets help glue people together in pairs, but they were very wrong in their assumption that there were no longer secrets left to serve as glue. Quite the contrary, the number of personal secrets being carried by the people we studied soon reached backbreaking levels. Their reluctance to take anyone completely into their confidence, especially the person to whom they were married, made them feel isolated. Since they couldn't explain to themselves why the feeling was there, in spite of their having a partner, it was natural for them to conclude that they had the wrong partner. That caused them to become even more suspicious of what might happen to them if the relationship disintegrated—which only made the relationship disintegrate more quickly. The process fed on itself. Secrecy merely created more of the same and eventually made strangers of the pair.

Neither partner was willing to level with the other about the most important secret of all: namely, how much the idea of achieving renown really meant to them. Why didn't they own up to this burning desire? Because most didn't even know they had it. Their actions made it quite clear that they wanted renown more than anything else, but the words they uttered made it sound as though they were seeking a tiny little thing, not all that important, called recognition. And it was to be for their work, of course, not for themselves. Quite a number told us, with a straight face, "Nothing personal about any of this, you understand."

The psychologists and psychiatrists to whom many in this group turned had little aid to offer. Both professions suffered a serious decline in public esteem. Therapy sessions concentrated on timeless problems, which are always worth discussing anyway, but therapists ignored the real-life setting in which their patients were trying to love and achieve. More than 45% of the nearly 2,600 male and female therapy patients we interviewed during these decades complained that the sessions were "irrelevant." The majority labeled them "not worth the bother." As one put it, voicing the view of most, "We might as well be having our conversation on the moon." Too little of what these people faced in the present and, much more important, dreamed about as their future was entering the interchange. When psychotherapists know a secret, they can help someone harboring it to bring it to the surface. It didn't work in this case. They knew the secrets that people had kept to themselves in the past, not the ones that were disturbing their present.

Sociologists, demographers and economists, with their readily available abundance of data (most of it gathered for them by government agencies), moved to the fore as interpreters and came up with some interesting explanations. However worthwhile the contributions, and some were undeniably so, they were far from the whole story, even when taken en masse. Reading them did nothing for the people we studied who were troubled by their own behavior, not to mention that of others, and who were trying to understand its source. The data presented on page after page of sociological, demographic and econometric studies provided none of the insights they needed to change their lives and exert some control over their destinies. Unfortunately, fantasies are harder to quantify than divorce rates and illegitimate births, and are especially difficult to study statistically if people think they aren't supposed to be having them in the first place.

AUDIENCE ADULATION

Were all the dreams of fame merely neurotic? Had millions of able and ambitious Americans in their twenties and thirties suddenly developed a serious psychological malady? Hardly. What had happened instead was that the United States, without issuing any formal notice, had changed its way of *identifying* its citizens. For centuries, it had been important to own land, and this was the prime way of deciding who was a member in good standing of the community, and therefore of the nation, and who was not. In fact, in many colonial towns, people who weren't landholders couldn't even vote. The rise of the merchant class—shopowners, manufacturers, and import-exporters—helped bring about a new mode of identification, in which being in business was every bit as acceptable as owning land.[9] Still, from that day to this, many merchants who did well hastened to buy some property, to give their membership in the community a more traditional and tangible basis.

By 1960, with a tidal wave of baby-boom children on the way, and with land running short and serving no productive purpose for most owners, the nation decided subconsciously that an even greater intangible had finally become not only acceptable, but necessary. Fame moved to center stage and ceased to be merely part of the yearnings of adolescents. From then on, even adults would be judged in both the old ways and the new. How much land or money they had, how many businesses they owned directly or indirectly, through publicly traded shares, mattered. But so too would how well-known they became. It is hardly surprising that many observers after 1960 viewed the United States as having entered a state of permanent adolescence.

As we'll see, in some ways it had done just that, yet the real purpose of doing so was simple: people needed something to keep them striving. Renown was it. Our factories and farms were so productive at this point, and our material needs were being met so easily, that there was the uncomfortable possibility that the nation might fall into a state of torpor. Monarchs in prior centuries encouraged their nation's most venturesome citizens to find land and gold and kill for it, if need be. The reward was a share of the spoils. Captains of industry received the same pat on the back in nineteenth-century America for building, at any cost, the infrastructure of roads, ports, railroads and factories we've been using ever since. That became old hat after 1960, when a more humane way of keeping the citizenry motivated—and, as it also demanded, its hands clean—was finally inaugurated.

There was nothing new about the idea of devoting one's life to a

---

9. J. T. Maine, *The Social Structure of Revolutionary America* (Princeton: Princeton University Press, 1965); B. Bailyn, *The New England Merchants in the Seventeenth Century* (Cambridge: Harvard University Press, 1955); M. J. Rohrbaugh, *The Land Office Business* (Oxford: Oxford University Press, 1968).

search for fame, in much the same way Ponce de León had sought the Fountain of Youth. A small proportion of each nation's citizens had long thought themselves worthy of a wider reputation.[10] To take one of hundreds of examples from past centuries, listen to Johann Bernoulli, an outstanding European mathematician. In 1697 he announced to his colleagues, in writing: "I, Johann Bernoulli, greet the most clever mathematicians in the world. Nothing is more attractive to intelligent people than an honest, challenging problem whose possible solution will bestow fame and remain as a lasting monument. Following the example set by Pascal, I hope to earn the gratitude of the entire scientific community by placing before the finest mathematicians of our time a problem that will test their methods and the strength of their intellect. If someone communicates to me the solution of the proposed problem, I shall then publicly declare him worthy of praise."

Of the more than 12,000 people to whom we showed this quote in the period between 1960 and 1985,[11] only 4% thought that a present-day person who was normal would have written it. Approximately 62% felt that it smacked of megalomania. Typical remarks: "Sounds to me like a pompous ass," "I can't tell if he's 16 or a demented 60," and, "The guy is a little full of himself, wouldn't you say?"

The most revealing part of their reactions was how prim and proper people now were when confronted with someone who was openly comfortable with the idea of attaining renown. Precisely because they too wanted it, in many cases desperately, they found his approach too naked. We might as well have been showing a prudish group a passage from past centuries that was sexually explicit. In that case, the respondents would at least have realized that they hadn't invented sex. In this case, some were shocked and amused to realize that they hadn't invented the idea of striving for worldwide and lasting renown. And that is the key point here: after 1960, instead of a favored few clamoring for the spotlight, the vast majority of young adults in America accepted this goal as their chief aim in life. Money, marriage, and enjoyable work mattered too, but what good was any of it, they quietly asked themselves, if it didn't produce fame? People called it the Age of Aquarius, but it was nothing of the sort. *It was the age of celebrities; audience adulation was in the process of replacing love as a top priority, and marriage in America was well on its way to becoming Hollywoodized.*

10. To find the real basis for many of these attitudes, one must look at least as far back as the twelfth century; see C. Morris, *The Discovery of the Individual: 1050–1200* (New York: Harper & Row, 1973).

11. The 12,000 consisted of 5,000 from our original sample plus 7,400 selected at random from the readership of a national business publication.

THE JOYS OF BEING A SUPERSTAR

A broad-scale social change can only be understood, and the validity of the concept tested, by seeing how it affects the lives of individuals. Do they even know about it? More important, in what specific way do they make contact with it and incorporate it into their own attitudes and actions?

From 1960 on, young men and women became involved with the idea of finding their own *identities*. They still are. After 1970, and continuing to the present, women became even more caught up in this search than men. If we are fully to grasp how the trends we have been discussing made themselves felt in the personal lives of American men and, especially, women who were in their twenties and thirties during the past twenty-five years, we must look more closely at this word.

Every man and woman in our sample with whom we discussed the term insisted that it represented a personal, inner search. It was a voyage of discovery that they were conducting deep within themselves, hoping to find out who and what they really were. One's identity, they wanted us to believe, is a wholly private matter.

Nothing could be further from the truth. On a desert island, one has no need of an identity. Even if a few others are present—say three others are there too—the idea of an identity would soon be vestigial. Each would come to know the others cold, if they didn't already, in which case having an identity would become meaningless. However, in a crowded world, particularly one in which people change locations, partners and positions frequently and easily, the concept becomes important. Corporations talk about their "image" in such a world, where distance and anonymity are facts of life that make almost any image they wish to concoct believable to some. A convincing TV commercial, an appealing slogan or memorable jingle, makes all things possible, or so the company hopes.

When all is said and done, *what people who are searching for an identity really want is an audience*. "My own identity" means "my own audience." And not just any audience, but an uncritical one that, as corporations also hope to find, will accept at face value the specific picture of themselves that they are presenting at the time. People can't say that that is what they are looking for. Companies can. Corporations conduct this type of advertising and public relations campaign daily, without a second thought, since they view it as a "business necessity." Most Americans are squeamish about doing anything of the kind on their own behalf in public, in large part because they know it would be received badly. Instead, many walk around in T-shirts proclaiming that a particular beer, soft drink, team of professional athletes, or automobile is "Number One." They don't have the courage to put their own names on the shirt, announcing to the world that, at least in their own opinion, they themselves are the best. So they do the next best thing and become walking bill-boards for companies boldly doing what they themselves are too sheepish to do.

Forgetting their discomfort for a moment, let us ask a crucial question: What makes people think they have to have a following in the first place? Why do they feel it is so urgent for them to broadcast their distinctiveness, even though the very thought of doing so, much less the act itself, makes most squirm? Here above all we want to know what it is they see and respond to in their everyday lives that tells them that this is the appropriate—indeed, the most important—thing for them to be trying to do, day in and day out. Regular reminders must be coming from somewhere, since a single message to do this, even if it were received early in their lives, would not give the quest so central and persistent a part in their lives.

The answer is: incessant public and therefore media attention to well-known figures from the worlds of sports, politics, and entertainment. Look at it from the point of view of the ambitious men and women in their twenties and thirties whom we have been discussing. How did—how *does*—the world really look to them? As far as they are concerned, America is a land of ghosts and superstars. As ghosts, they are reminded in a countless number of ways each day that that's all they are. It's not their names they see in the daily papers; it's not their faces they see in magazines; it isn't events from their lives that constitute "the news"; the biographies they read don't include their own, since theirs haven't been and probably won't be written; they aren't the ones singing the song millions are buying, or playing the lead part in the film hordes of moviegoers are lining up around the block to see, or giving the speech throngs want to hear. They didn't write the bestselling novel everyone is reading; they haven't broken any long-standing world records lately, and they didn't cause a traffic jam at the last hotel at which they stayed, because no one noticed them. They're not important.

Greek gods may have been tucked safely away in the starry skies and on mountain tops, but superstars aren't a heavenly constellation. They're right here, everywhere; not just in advertisements, billboards, posters, movies, theaters, magazines, books, ratings, reviews and programs, but also in executive suites, high-priced restaurants, banks, capitol buildings, fancy suburbs, the best vacation spots, grand openings and premieres, limousines, expensive co-ops and mansions, limited edition sports cars, tennis courts and ski resorts, enclosed estates and interesting gossip.

Superstars inhabit everything that is sold in the United States. Their endorsement, sometimes direct, often indirect, makes a product not only acceptable, but necessary. They are the only ones capable of legitimating a mode of dress, way of life, or place to live. They determine hair lengths and styles, animate customs, approve gestures, validate accents, popularize expressions of speech, populate conversations and initiate migrations. In a revealing twist, in past centuries people became renowned because they led others to a new land—Moses, Columbus, Brigham Young. Now it takes a celebrity to get the migration going in the first place.

Often, today, the mass movement involves money, not people. If a celebrity is known to have invested in a particular tax shelter or venture capital deal, thousands of normally hard-headed investors also jump in. Throwing caution to the wind, blinded by the glow radiating from the celebrity, they grinningly assume that nothing can go wrong. Similarly, a restaurant that is known to have been patronized by a celebrity is more than four times as likely to be patronized by the people we studied as one of equal quality that hasn't served a star.

Unfortunately for those who view themselves as ghosts, there doesn't appear to be any in between, no comfortable state of mediocrity. Everyone in the middle is classified with the ghosts. Superlatives abound in America, and they hide the fact that anything not describable in such terms is no longer worth describing. Things that aren't excessive barely exist. The good must be exceptional, and the bad, abominable. Negatives are subject to the same pressures that positives are: something must be hideous or revolting to even merit a comment. If it is only moderately bad, it doesn't deserve much notice and hence is ignored by people always on the run. To be of interest, it must be truly awful.

The fact that most products now have an endorsement ends up making the buyer feel like a fraud. The typical purchaser of sporting goods provides one of hundreds of examples we could choose. The golf clubs, skis, baseball cap or glove, basketball, or helmet, tennis racket, sneakers, or ice skates are all endorsed—in the higher price ranges, some even "signed"—by the celebrity. The implication is clear: "This equipment made the celebrity a celebrity and will do the same for you." There is an additional fantasy here that is every bit as important to customers: "Using the equipment makes you and the endorser indistinguishable—identical—the very same person." Somehow, the celebrity is magically "in" the equipment which bears his or her name, and the user will be dramatically elevated, both during the event and afterward, just by using it.

It usually doesn't take more than a few days' use of the equipment for users to realize that the magic isn't working. If they remain willing at that point to continue believing that the celebrity is still "in" the equipment, they are forced reluctantly to conclude that they simply aren't as good as the item they have purchased. A few more less-then-perfect moments with it and, frequently, depression hits. The whole experience backfires. They were solidly convinced for a while that they were superstars, and now they are equally convinced that they are merely ghosts, always were and always will be. They may further chastise themselves at this point for being suckers. What they mean is that they recognize that they were faking it. They're not superstars, they *know* that and keep coming back to that realization, but they had briefly made themselves believe otherwise. For the time being, the pretense is over. Hiding the pair of skis or tennis racket, to avoid having it reprimand them mutely, suddenly seems appropriate.

However, the event was nearly inevitable, and before taking themselves too strongly to task, they should be aware of the likelihood that it will be repeated many times in the future, in ways large and small. For we found that people who view themselves as ghosts get joyfully preoccupied rather infrequently. In fact, they become expansive primarily when they feel themselves to *be* superstars. Conversely, if they become ecstatic, whatever the reason, they suddenly feel themselves to be superstars. Nothing comes close to equaling the ability of their (fleeting) superstar self-image to get them excited, or, on the other hand, to express any excitement they happen to feel. They don't like being "nothing" and yet, no matter how much of an ego boost they receive from what they do, own, or are, or from the people they know, they still don't feel they have escaped from the realm of "nothingness." The superstars are everywhere, but one seems never to have joined them. The ghosts thus keep on trying.

No matter how hard they try, very few succeed, in spite of more than a quarter of a century (in many cases) of endless effort aimed at achieving this goal. Superstars are everywhere in the world of the ghosts—everywhere, that is, except in these people's everyday lives. All the people ghosts actually encounter daily are also ghosts, so ghosts can only conclude that superstars hang around strictly with superstars. Ghosts and superstars appear not to mix, unless there is a business dimension to their brief get-together. If nothing else, the ghosts we studied have an abundance of determination and are willing to keep trying. As they keep telling themselves, they may be successful one day in bridging the huge abyss that separates the ghosts and superstars and find themselves famous overnight. Indeed, the gap is so great, they imagine that it will *have* to be bridged in a blink, if it is ever to be bridged at all. They know that it has happened before. "It could easily happen to me," many say, strictly in confidence. In any event, as far as the possibility of fame goes, no self-respecting ghost sees himself or herself as being truly beyond hope.

People are unique, more so than they'll ever know. However, in the view of the people we studied, uniqueness is no longer enough. It must be public as well. The majority complained at one time or another that modern society has already reduced everyone to the point of being unindividualized, impersonalized beings, each little differentiated from the next and all characterized increasingly by numbers in a government data bank somewhere. What we found instead is that the audience for their individuality is so crucial to these people's sense of uniqueness that without the audience they don't feel unique. In fact, a closer look at their behavior indicates that they want the audience far more than the individuality. So, paradoxically, they gladly copy someone famous, hoping to quietly steal for themselves, even momentarily, a portion of the celebrity's following, in spite of their having to erase themselves totally to do it successfully.

The lack of an audience shouldn't make that much difference to their personal and professional lives, but it does, because superstardom demands nothing less. There is one, and only one, launching mechanism capable of thrusting someone from ghosthood to superstar status: an enormous public. It is no longer sufficient to have only a small audience, a local following. The public one gathers must be huge and nationwide as well. Many people would indeed be happy to be, as they put it, "the big frog in a small pond," but there don't appear to be any small ponds left; they have all become linked (electronically) and flow into one another, merging to form one very large sea in which all must sink or swim. It simply won't do to be a "local bigshot" or a "regional bigwig." On the contrary, it is so inadequate and provincial now, it is merely a parody of the celebrity status people desperately seek. "The best on my block" is sufficient as a goal today only for tots and pre-teens. After puberty, nothing less than the entire country will do.

THE NEW PRUDERY

Summing up, even couples who were very much in love in the 1960s, 1970s and 1980s found themselves increasingly unable to be honest with one another. A new prudery about fame gripped the United States, and it proved far more destructive than the old prudery about sex. At least sex was an undeniable fact of life, an act in which couples had to engage merely to make their marriage legal, not to mention produce the next generation. Couples who never once discussed the subject still found it possible to embrace one another warmly, even erotically, and enjoy this aspect of their relationship.

Where the search for renown was concerned, they were prevented from doing the same for a number of key reasons. Fame, unlike sex, cannot be shared. It belongs unalterably to its original owner, and, to a lesser extent, to others who helped produce it in the first place. Interestingly, it often worsens the public position of people who sidle up next to a celebrity, just as stars in the sky vanish when the sun is out. Couples in the 1950s could pool their earnings and reap a standard of living higher than either partner on his or her own might achieve. After 1960, couples could and did pool their earnings, but a powerful tug-of-war had developed about something that both partners wanted more than money and which couldn't be pooled.

Since acclaim was supposed to come to each spontaneously, in order to be labeled genuine, neither was in a position to ask openly for it. Nor could they level with their partners and say that renown is what they wanted more than anything else in life. Tragically, that forced them to deny its importance to the very people who loved them most. Then they became furious when they didn't get the applause they had just denied wanting. Their extraordinary ambivalence about the subject made them torture themselves first and their partners shortly thereafter.

The subject was so important in their lives, it couldn't remain absent from their everyday comments. So, circumlocutions had to be found, paralleling those that people used in previous decades and centuries about pregnancy ("indisposed") and death ("no longer with us"). The two great euphemisms of the period from 1960 to 1985 were, "I am seeking *recognition*," and, "I want my own *identity*." Men used the sentences more than women did in the initial part of the period, after 1960; women used them more than men after 1970. However, both used them so often, the difference was insignificant. They wound up attacking each other without even knowing why, rather than helping one another—the only way either one could have wound up with what both were seeking and *still* have had a satisfying personal life in the process.

How, specifically, were they supposed to be helpmates instead of enemies and attain what was out of their grasp as singles? What did successful women do then and now, usually without realizing it, to guarantee themselves greater happiness and effectiveness both at work and at home? We will later examine the answer in detail, but the material will make more sense if we first look closely at the emotional fuel ambitious women have been using in recent years.

Remember, the business world was moving relentlessly during this period in a direction that compelled people to think of their work in terms of a career, not just a job. They could enlist in the army for a few years, and then be free, but if they enlisted in the work world, they were expected to enlist for life. Specialized white-collar professions need people who stay with them, year in and year out, for four decades. Young workers who were highly motivated tried to internalize this value and make it their own.

As we'll see in the next five chapters, there is a right way and a wrong way to do this. One leads to success on the job *and* enduring personal relationships. The other, chosen by the majority, we now know produces failure in both arenas.

PART TWO

3

Better to Have
Loved and Lost...

It may seem like an odd suggestion, but the next four chapters will be more worthwhile if the reader forgets temporarily the background material discussed in the last two. Seeing the events in people's lives merely as examples of a general trend drains them of their importance. The flesh-and-blood men and women involved become two-dimensional and mechanical in some ways. The social sciences can be uplifting, for they allow us to discover and understand large forces that often exert a major influence on people's thoughts and actions. Yet these same sciences are also distasteful to many people, for their approach to human behavior tends to leave out humans. Experiences become interesting only insofar as they confirm or deny a social scientific hypothesis.

The women we are about to meet are important in their own right, and they deserve to have their experiences looked at in a light that isn't colored only by the trend under discussion. Seeing them as specimens mounted on a corkboard for a lecture class deprives their lives of the richness and depth that were present in the events under discussion, and which no book can adequately convey.

We still seek themes common to the majority, if any patterns at all are to be found, since there is always something to be learned from knowing what most others are doing, thinking and feeling. But it is essential for us to drop down to the plane on which the information (from which our generalizations were constructed) was gathered to begin with.

For those who lived through them, the decades of the Fifties, Sixties, Seventies, and Eighties are as different from one another as, say, major U.S. cities. Yet, on the plane of individual experience, there are some important similarities present after 1960. There is a common refrain in the answers given us over the years by women in response to questions about what life was like for them in the prior ten years, answers that differ from those we got in the 1950s.

Some time in their late teen years, they told us at age thirty, they met someone with whom they fell deeply in love. In most cases, the young woman later married the man. In many others, she merely lived with him. Either way, what these women remember most is that the relationship ended unhappily. There were good times, of course, many of them. But in retrospect, these were overshadowed by all the negatives that subsequently surfaced. The collapse wasn't sudden, and it seemed to take place in spite of everything both parties were willing and trying to do to close the gap. Nothing worked. Invisible forces drew the two together in the first place, and forces that were equally invisible and even more powerful drove them slowly apart.

"It is better to have loved and lost than never to have loved at all" is a centuries-old belief, and it was one these women didn't have to be told. That is indeed what they had done: loved, and then lost. What puzzled them was *why*. To this day, few understand the trying events that occurred. In fact, rather than being active participants in the process, exerting their wills at every step, they felt themselves caught in the grip of something that was truly bigger than themselves and their partners combined. In their view, something wrenching and unforgettable happened to them.

Three case histories are sufficiently representative to tell the story of countless others. The women whose experiences are presented here are drawn from the more "driven" end of the spectrum. These ambitious individuals were selected for two reasons. Women who had little interest in their work turned out to be among the least successful members of the sample. Yet we want to focus above all in this book on what it takes to achieve success and still have a satisfying personal life.

The second and more important reason for taking a closer look at the lives of highly motivated women is that they thought of themselves as "the cutting edge," "trend setters" and "opinion makers." They were right. A large number of women who didn't possess their degree of motivation nevertheless eagerly adopted their attitudes. Since it had become fashionable to seem very ambitious, women who weren't soon learned how to look and sound convincingly as though they were. In some instances, it even earned them a promotion, much to the chagrin of women who really wanted and had worked hard enough to earn the position.

Projective tests are one of the psychologist's favorite tools. They are easy to administer and at times reveal things that the test taker may have brushed aside and would prefer to keep hidden, if he or she knows about them at all. The trouble is that most people are well aware that they may disclose things about themselves that they'd rather not, so they are reluctant to take the tests in the first place. Also, the tests have numerous inadequacies. Finally, we were interested in knowing what people actually did, not just their attitudes toward their own and others' behavior.

One of the main projective tests we therefore settled upon involved the partners they chose and how they behaved with each. There were pluses and minuses with the approach. Women who avoided serious relationships altogether prevented us from seeing what they were like in the midst of such an involvement. There is an ancient insight, dating back more than 2,500 years, to the effect that "a man doesn't know himself until he lives with a woman." The same applies to women, but approximately 11% of the heterosexual women we studied neither lived with nor married a man. Not only do they not know themselves well, according to this saying, we don't either. Much of what they are remains buried, and we had to depend on the comments of their coworkers, lovers and friends, as well as the evidence offered by their own words and actions, to try to understand what they were after (or afraid of) in each case, and why.

The upshot is that the women we'll be looking at are more sexually active than is average for our sample. Each has had as many as forty partners, whereas the median number for the sample is approximately twenty-six. Prurience isn't our primary reason for giving these women so prominent a place. What interests us more is that they were, unwittingly, making their wants and needs evident, if not with some partners, then with others. There were women in our sample who were very active sexually, yet revealed little of themselves either to their lovers or to us. Their promiscuity was part of a very effective smokescreen. However, the large majority of women who were sufficiently interested in men to at least have sex with some allowed us to see the *kinds* of men they chose. That, together with the texture of each relationship, proved more revealing than we had hoped even in our most optimistic moments.

PEOPLE WHO CAN BE BOUGHT

Many of the characteristics that distinguished Ellen Porter at fourteen were still there decades later. Above average in height and intelligence, she wanted to do well in school, at that point more for her parents than for herself. Her grades were high enough for her to get into a good college, and like so many others from the upper-middle class suburb to which the family had moved when she was three, she went happily. There never really seemed any doubt that she wouldn't.

By the time Ellen began her junior year in high school, she had reached the 5'8" height she still is today. Physically, she described herself as "thin but shapely," with wavy, long brown hair and wide-set eyes; psychologically, she rarely appeared mopey or depressed. Ellen was outstanding in English and liberal arts subjects but found her science and math classes difficult and uninteresting. Teachers were impressed with her ability to write and to speak her mind, especially once she became even mildly annoyed. This was no tongue-tied teenager.

The friends in her social circle were as bright as she, but as later events were to prove, they were less motivated. The bulk of the time that she and they spent together outside of school was devoted to talking about boys. Ellen's preferences at this stage were clear: she liked good-looking, athletic, clean-cut types who were very popular. By her actions even more than her words, she made it plain that she had no interest in boys who seemed destined to spend their lives in the business world. For example, a classmate and neighbor of hers, Steven, used to help his parents in the family toy store—and liked it. He looked forward to running and expanding the store one day, perhaps into a chain. Money and business were natural topics to him, and they entered his conversation regularly. Ellen couldn't have been less interested in him if he'd been a bookworm—something he certainly wasn't. She labeled him dull and the things he discussed even duller. Physically, she found Steven "pasty" and unappealing. The phrase Ellen used to describe him to us, when both were sixteen, was deadly: "He's middle-aged, if you know what I mean." When his parents and hers asked them to go to a party together (neither happened to have a date for it), she balked. "He's not someone I want to be *seen* with," she told her mother, and wound up not going to the party at all.

Once Ellen had been in college for a while, her tastes in men changed. It was no longer so important that her partner be an athlete, much less an outstanding one. Nor did he have to be widely known and admired. "The BMOCs [big men on campus] are pretty callow youths," she told us during her sophomore year. "They're mindless jocks and rich kids, for the most part." That represented quite a shift in attitude. In high school, Ellen was attracted primarily to popular boys, and the more popular they were, the more likely she was to fantasize herself petting (in private) and being seen with them (in public). On occasion the fantasy turned into reality; one of them became the first partner with whom she had intercourse, while she was babysitting on a Friday night just before the fall term of her senior year. The relationship lasted through the first five weeks of the new term, until both parties seemed to lose interest and became just friends. "He's nice but not too swift," she commented.

In college, Ellen demonstrated a decided preference for bright young men who appeared headed for eminence in their fields. Not just any field, however. She was still put off by business majors and even more so by those who were interested in business itself, as an activity rather than as an academic discipline. Ellen had little trouble articulating her reasons for feeling negatively toward people in the business world and those who would soon be. Since her stand regarding them was central to later events in her life, we have filled in between the lines and spelled out her views on the subject in greater detail than she did at the time.

First, she considered this group too money-oriented, whereas she saw herself as people-oriented. She faulted the engineers in her class for the same reason: "All these guys are too interested in *things*." That made her see the young men in business and engineering programs, the two majors most commonly chosen by American males then and now, as "insensitive." By that she meant "insensitive to people and their feelings."

Second, students with an interest in business didn't seem sufficiently serious to her. During their college years, Ellen and her friends were convinced that they had a mission in life. It was their destiny, they believed, to reshape the nation and perhaps even the face of the globe. That give their every thought, action and utterance a deeper meaning and higher purpose. Some had joined the Peace Corps. Although Ellen never used the word, she felt inspired—and considered business majors uninspired, lacking in idealism of any sort.

"Business people are nothing more than wheeler-dealers," she said, sounding like a prosecutor stating a criminal charge at the opening of a trial. As she saw it, that meant they were willing to deprive anything of its meaning and reduce it merely to an object to be manipulated. Their goals and plans were too loose, with everything geared simply to making money. They clearly weren't motivated by high ideals and in fact couldn't even be thought to have a sense of direction. "They go wherever the money is," she said with a sneer, contemptuous of the idea that they could be bought so easily.

People with a real profession, on the other hand, seemed to her to have a built-in sense of direction that saved them from such constantly shifting mercenary considerations. It rooted them almost of necessity in a world of ethics and prevented their becoming "scavengers," as she repeatedly labeled budding businessmen. At this time in her life, Ellen was questioning everything and dreamed of changing the world. Business types, by contrast, seemed to accept the world as it was and obviously weren't dreamers with a mission, imbued with lofty visions. In short, they were modern-day outlaws, immoral and unethical, not playing the game of life by the same set of rules as the professionals with whom she intensely identified. Worse still, they were selfish. She and her friends were givers, trying to make a contribution, whereas business people merely wanted to grab whatever they could.

"I don't want anything to do with them," she said flatly. Her attitude

wasn't expressed verbally as part of a conscious philosophy. Instead, Ellen's actions revealed her real opinions even more clearly than her statements did. For example, Ellen had met and come to like two young men
in her class, Peter and Richard. In her initial descriptions of both, they
seemed rather similar in appearance and manner. Yet she was vividly
aware of one important respect in which they differed. Peter was much
more involved than Richard with the liberal arts major all three had chosen: political science.

Peter struck her as the more sexually appealing of the two men ("I
like his intensity"). He also seemed twice as interesting. His involvement
with his field exceeded but more closely resembled hers, and that gave
them much to talk about. "We look at things the same way," she remarked
offhandedly, glad to have finally found someone with whom she could
talk for hours on end. Richard's indifference, on the other hand, his attitude of "I'm only doing this to get a degree," made her think of him as
not only less appealing, but also as someone less likely to succeed. By
the middle of her junior year, Ellen and Peter were married.

RELIEF FROM LONELINESS

We expected these two bright and resourceful people to graduate and find
a place for themselves in the business world far more easily than most.
They didn't, and the main reason for that failure was precisely that the
man Ellen had chosen was so dedicated to his field. Dedication, in and
of itself, needn't be a problem. Had his major been accounting or engineering, for instance, the evidence indicates that Peter—and his marriage—would have been subject to much less inner strain while he and
Ellen made the transition from school to work. The gap between what he
had studied in class and the attitudes and actions expected of him by an
employer would have been significantly smaller.

As it was, Peter's high degree of involvement with his liberal arts
major compounded the problems that others in his field normally encounter once their years of schooling are through. He simply couldn't walk
away from his profession, dismissing it right after graduation with "That's
enough of political science; now it's time for me to make some big
money." Richard could say that, and did. In retrospect, it was clear that
the choice of partners that seemed best to Ellen while she was in college,
given the views she held while there, interfered with her ability to become comfortable in the business world she entered after graduation.

Fights broke out and became a regular feature of the evenings and
weekends they spent together. Since the topics of dispute were so varied,
it was hard for them to see the source of the friction. Peter told us that

he felt cornered and unhappy no matter which way he turned ("I don't want to go to graduate school, not yet anyway, and I really don't want to be a businessman"). Ellen began to wonder if she even knew who he was. They simply could have gotten a divorce, and many in their situation did just that. However, Ellen didn't want to move too hastily. It seemed the wrong thing to do as long as there was some hope left. Two more troubled years passed. It had been three years since the pair had graduated. "We meant so much to each other once," she commented during that third year. The words were said with disbelief and sadness, almost as though she was discussing another couple she had once known, who had died.

Within four months of voicing that comment she began an affair with a man she had met and come to know in the financial services firm for which they both worked. The usual explanation for such sexual encounters is that the woman in Ellen's position is having little or no sex with her husband (that was true in this instance), and the minimal amount that is taking place is doing very little for her. Revenge and loneliness are also commonly listed as motives—even by the people directly involved—for the woman who allows herself to engage in an extramarital fling during a period of marital turmoil.

These forces all made themselves felt here, but we found a fourth factor that was equally if not more important than the other three combined. When Ellen was in high school, she told us repeatedly that boys who were interested mainly in making money left her cold because they seemed "out of it." In college, she echoed the refrain, this time in a more sophisticated fashion, and stated that such men struck her as "too mercenary and narrow-minded." At various points in her undergraduate years, she described them as "frumpy," "unexciting," "gray," and "crass." During high school and college it was impossible for her even to envision herself happily paired up with such a man. That wasn't the kind of partner with whom she wanted to be seen in public.

Now, circumstances and her own ambitions were making it essential for her to find a place in the arena such men had made. Ellen and her intellectual "in crowd" were no longer able to characterize the business world as being populated with alien beings. Her burning desire to become outstanding in a line of work of her choosing, coupled with the need to make a living, made her view businessmen in a light that was slowly becoming more positive.

The sex she had one afternoon with Ed, the man from her office (they were supposed to be on the other side of town at a meeting, which was postponed at the last minute), met the three physical and emotional needs discussed above. But it did more. For the first time in her life she saw a money-oriented business administration major—one who made no secret of his beliefs and goals—as having real sex appeal. "I get aroused just thinking about him," she told a friend a few days after the first sexual encounter had taken place. What made the comment striking was that she had always shunned men like Ed.

Some readers may say, "Ellen was simply aroused, looking for some-one—anyone—to sleep with, and this guy was handy." That, at first, is what we too believed. It was only after we had examined a large number of similar instances (more than 160) that we realized that *in every case* there were plenty of other non-business types available of the kind she had previously prized. Some of those around Ellen even possessed the features she had most admired about her husband. She didn't select them as bedmates, and neither do the vast majority of other women in her position.

Far from seeking revenge, a mere sexual fling, or relief from her loneliness, Ellen was using the sexual encounter to ease her post-school transition. She was helping herself to embrace the new business mentality, the one that formed the basis for her present daily reality, by erotically embracing someone who embodied that mentality.

However, she wasn't yet ready to marry such a man. First of all, she was still married, if unhappily, and second, some of the old reservations remained. Her affair therefore represented a toe in the water, a preface to throwing herself wholeheartedly into the pond a few years later. Ellen wasn't consciously aware of any of the transition purposes that were being served by the liaison. When she thought about the subject—something she frequently did ("It's never far from my mind")—she dwelled on the character of her two partners and the many contrasts between them. A typical comment she voiced at the time was, "Ed is so upbeat, and Peter is always grumpy."

GROW OR DIE

Thus far, it may seem as though the developments we've been describing were seen only in the lives of women who were married to someone seriously interested in a liberal arts field. However, the same pattern was seen in single women who had chosen a liberal arts subject. Anne Wallace was an English major, one who took her work seriously, as both her good grades and extracurricular readings made clear. Although she dated a number of young men while in college, and slept with more than twenty, she married none of them. Like Ellen, she selected men who seemed to her sensitive and humane, as judged by their choice of a major. Without being aware of it, she too shunned bedmates who were in business, engineering and finance. "Babbitts," she referred to them once, during her junior year. "People with a mole-eye's view of everyday life."

Anne's shoulder-length hair contained blonde highlights and swung freely as she moved. At 5′6″, most of her weight distributed itself around her hips and thighs, much to her dismay, yet her long arms and legs made for a limber appearance. When reading, she propped wire-rimmed glasses on her nose and a thumbnail between her teeth, totally absorbed and lost to all. She had a serene and somewhat frosty manner that many men wanted to melt because they suspected a certain mischievousness beneath.

Once she graduated from college, Anne was certain she would be able to keep intact the world view she had absorbed at school. The field of publishing attracted her, as it did many of her classmates who shared her interests and attitudes. She landed a job at a national magazine as an editorial assistant and was thrilled, though not for long. Without making her thoughts on the subject explicit, Anne felt sure that her choice of an industry (publishing) and position within it (editorial) would ease the transition from school to the business world by reducing the gap between the two.

In the beginning, at least, it seemed to do just that. Nevertheless, within six months of being at the magazine, the business pressures to which it was continually exposed as a going concern had filtered down and made their presence felt. "We need stories that appeal more to both our readers and our advertisers," she was told. At first Anne tried to argue with the message ("I thought the magazine was doing pretty well"), but when her argument was met with the response, "Like everybody else, we have to grow or die," she realized it represented the voice of reality. It was a sentence she herself had used in the past. Anne switched to another magazine after three years with the first, and found the atmosphere there every bit as "bottom-line oriented," that is, concerned with making a profit and expanding its readership. The move had originally been made to help preserve her old academic outlook, yet encountering the same conditions elsewhere resulted in a lowering of her resistance to change.

Anne's choice of sexual partners during this period reflected these ongoing changes. Her self-concept and view of the world around her were evolving, and that slowly made her begin to see potential lovers and husbands in an altogether different light. Men who were interested in business, who were previously the recipients of nothing but her scorn, stopped seeming like ogres and predators to her. The first clear sign that Anne's perceptions of this group of men were shifting significantly was when she reported that a stockbroker she had met at a party and a building materials salesman she was introduced to by a coworker each had a good sense of humor. "They're very funny," she said, remembering a joke the broker had recently told her. "I feel relaxed around them."

In the past, she'd have found neither one amusing in the least and would have been even more uptight in their presence than she usually felt. The hostility she bore this breed hadn't vanished by any means, but it was decreasing substantially during this, her fourth year in the business world. Both men became her lovers. The first relationship, with the broker, lasted approximately seven months. The second began as the first one was waning and continued for four months until the salesman was transferred by his firm to another part of the country.

Again, the reader may protest that it is hardly surprising that in the business world the bulk of Anne's lovers turned out to be businessmen. However, the objection ignores the fact that the industry she had chosen was full of men who more closely resembled the partners she strongly preferred while in school—men more interested in culture than profits, and in idealism over income. Not only were there many more of them, but she also spent a much larger portion of her work and leisure hours in their company. By any measure, they were more readily available and willing than men who were caught up in the nuts and bolts of business.

Nor is the explanation that business majors are more aggressive than those who study English literature valid here. Anne noticed that difference herself while still in college, and she considered the heightened aggressiveness repulsive, not arousing. Only a revised view of herself and her profession made these men more acceptable as partners. Even then, she avoided the loud, back-slapping salesmen and promoters, choosing to become intimate instead with businessmen who, as she put it, "were well-mannered, and respect and understand quality." The mixture she was seeking in them matched the one she was trying to construct internally at the time: maintaining her own integrity while recognizing the realities needed to keep the firm for which she worked in existence.

That proved a more difficult inner struggle than she imagined, and we will see later how it contributed to her remaining single for the next fifteen years.

"HE WAS MY FIRST"

Of all the students we followed, those who were majoring in business or business-related subjects seemed to us destined to make the leap from campus to corporate life with the greatest ease. Differences between the mentalities of the two spheres appeared likely to be minimized for this group of women, whether they were single or married during the transition period.

Barbara Herndon was a socially active teenager, a cheerleader whose friends usually described her as "cute," "bouncy," and "pert." She was 5'4", had a round face, perfect teeth, straight, sandy blonde hair and a slightly square build ("chunky," she called herself, though she was the only one who did). Barbara also had energy to burn and an IQ of 140. While in high school she considered every college major that would allow her to be active rather than sedentary. Even physical education was held up as a possibility, an idea that appalled her teachers, but it was finally dropped. "I want to do something with my mind," she said intently during the summer between high school and college, "and not be out of a job if I break my leg."

She entered a large state university that fall, not knowing what she would settle upon as a major. During the first two years Barbara took courses in a variety of different departments. In the fall of her sophomore year she was still undecided about her ultimate choice, yet she was putting together a growing mental list of majors she knew she would not select. "I'm winnowing it down," she said at the time, apparently intending to find the most appropriate one by a process of elimination. The business courses she took didn't excite her, but they at least had a utility, a practical dimension, that she was seeking and didn't find in her other classes. "They're too theoretical and abstract," she said, dismissing the rest.

Barbara's choice of boyfriends in high school was limited, as she put it, to "friendly superstars." Along with most of the other bright and sociable girls in her class, she favored boys who were gifted both academically and athletically—and who were very popular. Let's call the period when this type of partner is most preferred "stage one." Larry, the captain of the baseball team and an outstanding tennis player, was her favorite. He was good-looking, had good grades and, Barbara reminded us, "a horde of horny girls always chasing after him." That, as we were later to learn, was an exaggeration, but she obviously viewed him as quite a catch and chased him without, she was convinced, ever tipping her hand.

They moved in the same circles, ran into one another regularly, and paired up early in her senior year in high school. Larry became her first lover during November of that year, and once she started having sex, she found herself wanting it all the time. Without her mother knowing it, she had started taking the Pill, thanks to a prescription written for her by a relative who was a gynecologist. "Whenever we get a chance, we do it," she said with a girlish giggle. "If his parents are away—or mine—or in the back of parked cars—we don't need hours and hours to make it fun." The words conveyed her sense of pleasure and play, and seemed neither coarse nor overly romantic.

She and Larry went to different colleges the following fall, though the two schools were located less than an hour's drive from one another. The distance was sufficient, however, to allow Barbara to try a number of new partners and still get together regularly with Larry. It was revealing to see that, during the next four years, her choice of lovers consisted almost solely of the kinds of partners she had favored in high school. Now, though, most were majoring in business.

What did she dislike about men who were dedicated liberal arts majors, the usual stage two of women who went on to become college graduates? We didn't ask her this question, nor would an inquiry posed in such general terms have been appropriate. Instead, whenever she discussed a classmate who fit the general description of a stage-two male, some of whom lusted after her with real persistence, we asked her what she found unappealing about the particular young man. Her answers throughout the four years made use of one phrase more than all the others combined to characterize the more than a dozen that she rejected: they were "too reclusively intellectual" for her. On one occasion during her junior year she talked about one who had asked her out five times; "As soon as he's finished making love, he'll either fall asleep or go back to his books. I can tell." Barbara liked things open and aboveboard, not guarded and subterranean. Business majors, rather than scientists, historians or sociologists, struck her as sexy and accessible.

Larry continued to interest her, in spite of the approximately twenty-five lovers she had during the four years. "He was my first," she said in an untypically sentimental mood, "and maybe that counts for something." Larry had decided to major in economics and found the program at his school absorbing and easy. That helped him resist the idea of trying to make a living as a professional athlete. He told her more than once, "I think this can be a lucrative field for me if I play it right." Sports continued to appeal to him and he vented his energies through tennis; he and Barbara often played doubles with friends. At the end of the fall semester of their senior year, they decided to get married the following spring. "I'd like to be a June bride," Barbara told him, "and besides, we'll be finished with school by then."

After graduation, they got married, as planned. Barbara landed a job at a large consumer goods company and Larry found a position in the economics department of a bank, talking to corporate customers about the outlook for the economy. Within a year, Barbara was pregnant and very pleased about it, giving birth eventually to a baby boy. Things were a good deal less rosy than they seemed, however. The marriage was beginning to seem empty to her. "I just don't like him as much as I used to," she commented, almost as if she were surprised to hear herself saying the words.

Among the many negative developments that emerged at this time, and which grew steadily worse over the next few years, was the extent to which Barbara and Larry interrupted one another's sentences. Both were inclined to talk at a pretty rapid clip, and since they knew one another so well, each was often able to finish the other's thoughts—and did. Now they started doing so in an aggressive and even hostile manner on a regular basis. In essence, each was trying to silence the other.

Later, we'll see where Barbara wound up, and why, but before moving on, let us note one key point about this decade of her life, from her mid-teens to her mid-twenties. As mentioned previously, the vast majority of women we studied who went on to become college graduates drew their boyfriends and bedmates from three different pools of men.

In stage one, while the women were in high school, the boys they chose tended to be good-looking, athletic and popular. During stage two, when the women were in college, they tended to choose articulate, lean, and intense men who were intellectually involved in a liberal arts major. In stage three, after the women had entered the work world full-time, the men they selected were likely to be involved primarily in business affairs and money. They were also more playful and entertaining than the men chosen during stage two.

What is striking about Barbara's case, and that of many women like her, is that she bypassed stage two. Her interest in attractive and intelligent athletes was superseded by an interest in potentially successful businessmen. There wasn't any middle step in between.

THE CHANGING IMAGE OF THE IDEAL PARTNER

The three women we've been discussing had been very different as teenagers—Ellen, the political science major who married someone in her field; Anne, the English major who remained single throughout college and her early years in the work world; and Barbara, the most business-oriented of the three, who majored in the subject and married someone with similar interests. Yet in spite of their initial differences, all three ended up a decade later with the same point of view toward the men in their lives.

That was odd. Anyone who monitors a large group of Americans over the long term can't help but notice the enormous amount of conformity seen during adolescence. Even those who are rebelling during this period are usually conforming, since they are taking the mainstream picture that is supposed to be their guide and trying to live by its opposite. With so many others their age behaving in a similarly rebellious way, it is easy for them to tell whether they are acting in the appropriately inappropriate manner.

However, as the years pass, one expects more truly independent thought and behavior to emerge, if for no other reason than that peer pressures become less intense. Once school is through, the group that may have been together since childhood disperses, giving each more elbow room to be whatever he or she really is.

That isn't what happens in the lives of young women who become seriously interested in attaining success in the business world. Each may develop her own unique plan for attaining that success, but her attitudes and actions toward her sexual partners display a remarkable similarity to those of other women who share her professional aspirations. By the time Ellen, Anne and Barbara were in their mid-twenties, they all had pretty much the same view of the men with whom they were close.

The three were unaware of the convergence. There certainly wasn't anything regional about it. In fact, the three hadn't even met, since they went to high school and college in very different parts of the country— Ellen in California, Anne in the Chicago area, and Barbara in New York and then Boston. Nevertheless, with each passing year, they became more alike in the way they perceived the men with whom they were intimate.

What happened to them was happening to the majority of women their age in our sample: their lives were undergoing a three-stage evolution toward an adult reality. The choice of partners that they made while in school had trouble surviving once the women entered the business world. A parting of the ways was nearly inevitable in many cases. The very basis of the romantic and sexual attraction was rapidly evaporating.

Generally speaking, the transition from high school to college is quick and smooth, at least in this area. Being popular is high school's central value, so popular men are considered the most desirable partners. This is stage one. In college, potential partners who show promise of being outstanding professionals in their academic field come to be prized most. That is stage two. Reality asserts itself to some extent here, making most young women give consideration, though not always consciously, to their partner's prospects. They want partners who will do well.

What the typical ambitious woman we studied overlooked at this point was that her image of the ideal partner was going to change. The bright liberal arts major she frequently picked while in college would no longer appeal to her later. The men she once found sexually arousing, even across the room, would leave her increasingly cold as she became an integral part of the work world. Far from being a quick and smooth transition, this one generally takes years, sometimes decades. Two things prevent it from being as easy as the one between high school and college, from the first stage to the second.

To begin with, it takes her a number of years to free herself from the standards and goals she adopted during her undergraduate days. If she goes on to graduate study in her chosen field, the attitudes are reinforced. The more seriously she dedicates herself to living by the academic standards that surround her at this stage, the more difficulty she is likely to have leaving them behind once she enters the business world and tries to make herself at home.

The second and equally important factor that affects the rate at which she adapts to the business world is her partner, if she has one. Two people can create a universe for themselves, especially when they are in love. The men selected at this stage help bring substance to the picture. Two people taking the same approach to life make it seem far more real than one person, on her own, usually can. Thanks to the right choice of partner, it becomes effortless for her to see herself in the present and, even more so, in the future as living in full accordance with her academic beliefs and hopes.

A change in her aspirations requires a corresponding change in those of her partner. In many cases, that does indeed happen. The two separately and together make the transition from school to work, leaving behind the old attitudes they adopted on campus, while quietly adopting the new. In fact, we expected the majority of young couples we studied to be able to do this without difficulty. Each, we thought, would help the other over any rough spots, large or small, that surfaced during the transition period.

We were wrong. The evidence indicates that most couples handle the strain poorly, particularly during an era that pits men and women against one another in a race for renown. What would otherwise have been a manageable problem that they could have helped one another to solve becomes instead a threat, and it contributes significantly to the likelihood that they will end up divorced. What puzzled us initially was that even couples in the same field, such as Ellen and Peter, had trouble making the transition together. Peter's interest in the subject somewhat exceeded Ellen's, although hers was considerable. Yet even when we studied couples who were classmates and whose level of involvement with their college major was very nearly the same, it was common to see them get "out of step" with one another after graduation.

It took us a number of years to find out why. Put briefly, the reason is this: there is no significant difference in the rate at which couples majoring in business, business-related subjects or the natural sciences make the transition to the work world. However, there *is* a significant difference in the rate at which men and women who major in the liberal arts or social sciences do. Women in the liberal arts make the transition 34% faster, on average, than their male peers, and those in the social sciences make the transition 26% faster, on average.[1]

Whether one chooses to view the man's greater attachment to his college major once school is through as admirable persistence or as the behavior of a dreamer is a matter of interpretation. Sometimes the attachment leads to great results years later; in a much larger number of instances, it produces decades of alienation from the work world. In either case, it produces problems for the pair.

What complicates the matter severely is that college couples rarely have the same major, with both possessing the same degree of interest in that major. Instead, they are normally in different departments and often in different years. The problem here is that even if we look at a pair of identical twins majoring in different fields, they leave behind them *at different rates* the mentality they adopt in school. For instance, if an accounting major pairs up with a classmate in a field whose members generally make the transition more slowly (for example, an English major), the partners are likely to end up feeling out of sync with one another after they graduate.

It is no illusion, though the excuses they give for the gap usually are. When such couples are monitored regularly during their early post-school years, they claim that the arguments they are having are due mainly to income differences. They are having fights about money. That is true to some extent, for professions with a low transition time tend to earn more than those whose transition times are high. It is almost unfair—insult added to injury. Nevertheless, that difference does make life uncomfortable for the couple to whom it applies, for it means that not only has one partner entered the business arena more quickly than the other, but that person is earning more money than the other as well, and will probably continue to do so.

The underlying source of friction in their relationship is therefore two-fold: there is a financial factor, of which the partners are well aware, and there is also a psychosocial one, which the partners usually don't notice. With one still living the mentality of the academic world (even if the person is no longer in school), and the other now fully a part of the business world, they might as will be living in different countries.

It is hardly surprising that they start to misinterpret one another's sentences and quarrel, since certain key words no longer mean the same thing to both. When one says, "I had a really great idea today and it could change my future," two entirely different pictures are likely to appear in the minds of the pair. To the first, the idea may be exciting because it

---

1. How such transition times are computed for men and women, and hence how these percentages are derived, is explained in *The Corporate Steeplechase* (op. cit.).

sounds as though it could lead to professional eminence; to the other, it may be exciting because it sounds like money in the bank.

THE POINT OF NO RETURN

People who have been arguing can make up, especially if the differences about which they have been fighting begin to decrease. However, if the animosity between them becomes intense, and each one, believing he or she is fighting for life, makes remarks that are hurtful, patching things up afterward may be difficult or even impossible. The smoke may clear, yet each side remembers very well the blows received, not the ones successfully delivered.

Even with both parties dishing out exactly the same amount of abuse and the fight presumably a draw, it can still escalate rapidly. Each side moves to a higher and higher level of hostility, to make up for the subjective impression of having gotten the worst of it in the previous interchanges.

Somehow the happily married couples we studied intuitively understood how the process worked and deliberately prevented it from getting out of hand. They sensed that any disputes they had, no matter how minor in origin, could quickly spiral out of control and lead them to say things they shouldn't, insults that couldn't later be unsaid. Keeping the relationship intact thus meant keeping their comments civil, even when they felt moderately murderous in their hearts. Ellen, Anne, and Barbara never consciously scoffed at the approach. But their words and actions during quarrels that arose with their partners over the years made it apparent that, once a fight broke out, they felt there was less and less reason to prevent it from hurtling past the point of no return.

The fact that Peter and Ellen, for instance, started at pretty much the same point and were becoming part of the business world at different rates was a common development and needn't have proved fatal to the relationship. Nevertheless, the sheer weight of numbers, the high proportion of pairings that were failing to endure, made us suspect that the marital difficulties they were having once school was through were based on more than just a difference in transition rates. In fact, it slowly became clear that no sooner had they finished handling this problem when they were faced with another one, considerably thornier. If the first blow rocked the relationship during the couple's early years in the work world, making them feel that they were living alone together, the second had a much longer duration, often lasting decades.

Moreover, it affected single women every bit as forcefully as it did those who were married. An important finding emerged. We are used to thinking of a fight as taking place, in its simplest form, between two people. Verbal, emotional and perhaps even physical weapons are used, but the enemy is visible and has a name. However, as we'll see in the next chapter, the most intense combat in which the women we studied engaged between the ages of twenty-five and forty took place internally, where they wrestled with an enemy whose name kept changing and whom no one else but they could see. In the end, the inner battle left them too exhausted and confused even to have a personal life.

4 Going It Alone

The period of life between the ages of twenty-five and forty is unique, for it is the only one in which most people are convinced that time has nearly come to a standstill. They can see from the calendar, and the dates they write on checks and letters, that the years are indeed passing by. There are important milestones along the way, such as having children and buying a house or co-op. However, their bodies, the real clock they use to tell them what year of their lives it is, seem to them almost in a state of suspended animation. Most are convinced that anything they could do at twenty-five they can do at least as well and perhaps better at thirty, thirty-five, and forty. That sets this period apart radically from the ones before and after it.

The ages between fifteen and twenty-five present people with an ever-changing panorama, one that frequently leaves them gasping for air as they race to catch up with the person they are becoming. Some of the sentences they blurt out during these years strike them as pure gold and leave them even more surprised than their audience, as they wonder whether to take credit publicly for the sparkling remarks they have just made or to search themselves for strings, to see if a brilliant ventriloquist moved their lips for them at just the right moment.

The years after forty present them with the same vivid awareness of change in themselves, this time poignantly so, for they now can sense the beginnings of a slow but steady loss of youthful vibrancy. For many, this represents the loss of what they have long viewed as their strongest suit. It allowed them to "fly blind" into any number of situations and emerge on the other side unscathed, having used the mental agility and natural exuberance of youth to see them through.

The sense of being on automatic pilot made most of the women we studied less introspective between the ages of twenty-five and forty than they had been before these years and would be again after them. That was a blessing in many ways, since it allowed them to better concentrate on the world around them instead of being immobilized by self-consciousness, which had previously been a painful problem. In fact, some deliberately overreacted during these years, forcing themselves to stay relentlessly focused on the problems they confronted daily on the job and off, so as not to turn back into the "pillar of salt" that their constant self-scrutiny had rendered them, in their own minds at least, in the past.

However valuable the approach was, and in many cases it was undeniably so, it made them overlook a critical change in their own psychological makeup. Their action orientation prevented them from listening to something valuable that their emotions were telling them. More attuned to signals from the outside world, they ignored a key inner indicator that would have allowed each to assess how satisfying her personal life really was and what its future course was likely to be.

To see what this powerful test is, and why it works so well, it is well worth our while to see what Ellen, Anne, and Barbara were doing during these years.

HIS VERSUS HERS

The fights that Peter and Ellen had during the first few years after graduation were largely attributable to the different rates at which they were adapting to the business world. Eventually, they both made the transition fully, as did the vast majority of other college graduates. The different rates at which they did so should thus have been only a temporary problem. If the two had seriously wounded one another's egos during their school-to-work transition fights, that would have been sufficient to prolong the hostility, perhaps indefinitely. But they hadn't. Their arguments remained restrained, more full of tension than of attacks on one another's jugular vein.

Instead of the second through fourth year of their post-school lives together resulting in a lessening of tension as the transition gap between them closed, a new, more lethal variety of conflict began to emerge. The combination of their incomes gave them enough money to consider making a succession of purchases for their apartment. Individual differences in taste can always turn such shopping expeditions into public skirmishes that continue at home. However, two people who care for one another and view the relationship as worth preserving usually find such trips satisfying. They are part of the nest-building process that induces each to take into account the likes and dislikes of the other and arrive at a common choice both are happy to live with.

Peter and Ellen seemed to be getting worse rather than better at locating such mutually acceptable choices. By their third year in the business world, with both now twenty-five, they were able to get into heated arguments not only about the items they were thinking of buying, but also over the ones they had already bought. On a sunny Saturday morning in the middle of October, Peter and Ellen went to a large department store that was having a sale on furniture. Full-page advertisements in the local newspaper caught their eye and made them think they might find, at reasonable prices, a sofa and an armchair or two for which they were looking. Both had decided that the few remaining hand-me-down pieces in their living room, given them by Ellen's parents to get them started after graduation, were beginning to look a bit threadbare.

Ellen liked things modern, while Peter liked them comfortable, regardless of their appearance. The difference was hardly insurmountable, since many manufacturers were claiming at the time that their lines of furniture met both requirements. Nevertheless, Peter and Ellen were growling at one another after only twenty minutes in the store and barking at each other within an hour. They left without buying anything and spent most of the weekend arguing about all sorts of things.

"She doesn't think of anyone else, but only about what she wants," Peter later commented acidly. "All she worries about is how it looks—for company—which we don't have a lot of anyway." Ellen's version of this latest in an accelerating series of conflicts was, "There's no reason why the living room has to look like his old college dorm. It really is time to grow up." Their taste in people also differed. He preferred old skiing buddies from school days, whereas she was seeking new friendships, mostly from work situations. As Ellen put it frequently, "All his friends are unsophisticated. They have no idea what's really going on in the world." Rather than wanting to spend time alone as a pair, as most good couples did, Peter or Ellen always made plans to be with other people. The fact that the practice created additional reasons for fights did nothing to deter them.

When they did go out alone, they fought over the choice of restaurant. Ellen liked to dress up, while Peter was happy to take off his tie after work and not put it on again until Monday morning. "It is important to be seen at the right places," she said, trying to sound casual. "All the people at work brag about the latest place in which they've eaten. If I left it to Peter, we'd never get out at all. The neighborhood coffee shop is his speed."

Virtually all the couples we studied came to such minor impasses repeatedly, and many managed one way or another to resolve their differences. Sometimes it took time, days or weeks, for each to modify his or her own position enough to make a decision both could live with. Rather than feeling put out by such internal modifications, happy couples found them to be a secret source of pride. Both partners felt pleased about the many things they were doing, large and small, to help shore up the relationship at no real sacrifice to either. "We weren't disagreeing about anything very earthshaking," an attorney who had also been shopping for furniture told us. "My wife likes nubby fabrics on a couch and I like them smooth. It's no big deal." It was to Peter and Ellen, and became more so from their second through their fifth year in the business world. Their marriage was deteriorating, and while they hadn't unleashed any lethal blows during the initial round of transition-period fights, they certainly were doing so now. The restraint that characterized their earlier disputes was evaporating.

KEEPING THINGS LIGHT

Anne Wallace was single during both her school-to-work transition years and afterwards, when she finally came to view herself as an integral part of the business world. Since she was no longer on the outside looking in, the disagreements she had with the businessmen she dated stopped being cultural clashes. By the time she was in her mid-twenties, she had enough in common with the men who became her lovers to argue with them about other, more personal matters.

Ken, the stockbroker Anne met during her fourth year at work, was twenty-eight at the time, two years older than Anne. Although still young, with more than $100,000 in the bank he had already made enough to start looking beyond next week's paycheck and think instead about enriching his life in ways that weren't financial. His courses in college and interests until recently had been mainly mercenary, and he made no apologies for that. "Without money, you're nothing," he told Anne at dinner, during a discussion of his outlook on life. Similar sentences had incensed her in college and in her first few years in the work world. Yet when she heard it from Ken, she didn't protest. Nor did she even feel the urge to. It had come to have a certain logic, one she now considered more desirable to fall in line with than resist forever.

However, she wasn't the only one trying to bridge the distance between his approach and hers. Ken wanted more culture in his life, and Anne had little difficulty providing it. For her, going to plays and museums was as natural as it was for Ken to watch football and hockey. Not once did she have to twist his arm about seeing an opera or a show on the weekends they began spending together. Also, while Anne worked for a magazine, and liked it, she preferred to read books. That was something

Ken rarely did ("I'm too impatient"). However, once he and Anne became a pair, he was surprised and pleased to find himself on many a Saturday or Sunday afternoon doing just that, with Anne nearby doing the same.

There were many other pieces that seemed to be falling into place; their sex life was satisfying, and they could talk quietly for hours on end about topics that would not have interested anyone else. The majority of couples we studied who got as far as these two did soon found themselves being pulled further along, without thinking about it, toward marriage or living together. The process by then had attained enough momentum to carry the pair almost automatically in the appropriate direction.

Not in this case. Soon after the idea of settling down and having a family entered the conversation seriously for the first time, Anne started finding fault with Ken. She let him know it too, in a variety of ways. Suddenly he seemed "not good enough" to her. Flaws that she hadn't noticed before, or found easy to overlook, now stuck out like a sore thumb. One aspect of his behavior struck her as particularly offensive. "He's so full of himself," Anne said. The tone of the remark made it sound as though she was just becoming aware of it as she spoke, but the ease with which she voiced the words made it clear that she had recently rehearsed them, internally, many times. "Ken is flamboyant, likes to show off for whoever is watching—waiters, friends, it doesn't matter who. He plays to the crowd."

Similar assessments from Anne appeared in the next few weeks, and like this one, they were accompanied by an almost palpable sense of relief rather than depression. Other women we studied who were in Anne's situation, and who were doing the same thing she was to rid herself of a partner who had gotten too close, gave a more convincing portrayal of sadness. Anne either didn't know how to do that or else didn't realize that she was supposed to. The evidence indicates that it was the former. Even during her early twenties, a theatrical period for the overwhelming majority of workers, Anne never had to worry about being compromised by any dramatic tendencies she possessed. They were too well leashed to ever get her in trouble, on the job or off. Within six weeks of her initial barrage, she and Ken drifted apart. He later married a woman with whom he worked.

As the relationship with Ken was waning, Anne was introduced by a coworker to a building materials salesman named Victor. At first she showed no interest in him, but when he asked her out a second time, she said yes. "How come?" we inquired, after the two had gotten to know one another better. The answer was an unusual one for Anne: "His sense of humor is priceless. I like that he can make me laugh."

Others had had the ability before Victor, especially classmates and coworkers, but none had found quite so receptive an audience in Anne. She and Vic spent less time together in the subsequent months than she and Ken had in the prior ones; there were no long weekends devoted just to sitting around her apartment, reading, talking, and making love. The relationship was characterized by other kinds of activity instead. "We go places and do things—constantly on the move," Anne said, trying to project a picture of happiness, this time convincingly. "There's so much to see and do."

Apparently, the idea was every bit as much Vic's as Anne's, since he tried to maintain their previous pace even when she wasn't feeling well for a few weeks and wanted to slow down. "We should drive out to the country for the day," he told her, "and get some fresh air." Their lovemaking sessions were briefer than the ones she had had with Ken, a change she welcomed. In fact, she used the occasion of mentioning it to us to get in one last dig at Ken: "I think he took so much time before climaxing because he was trying to show me how long he could keep it up."

After four months of seeing pretty much only Vic, Anne heard that he was being transferred by his firm to a different part of the country. That allowed us to see how loose a bond had actually existed between the two, since neither made much of an effort to contact the other after the move a few weeks later, much less attempt to keep the relationship alive. Revealingly, the partners Anne had in the next six years were more like Vic than Ken. As Anne herself put it two years later, "I don't want any hassles."

"WHY ARE YOU SO IRRITABLE LATELY?"

Barbara liked being pregnant, and after her son, David, was born, it was obvious that she was happy to have him. "No toy, no possession, is as much of a gift," she said, after she had returned to work six weeks later. "I think about David waiting for me at the end of the day and it makes me glow." She seemed more tired and anxious than usual during the next twenty-four months. Being awakened repeatedly in the middle of the night disturbed her sleep, and like most of the first-time mothers in our sample, she fretted excessively. "I guess I overreact to a lot that he does," she said, knowing that she would keep on doing so. "Whenever he gets sick, I worry. I look in on him in the middle of the night to be sure he's still breathing."

Her relationship with her husband Larry, on the other hand, was filled with a different kind of tension. At first we thought that the fatigue generated by a newborn baby in the house might be causing husband and wife to be short-tempered with one another. That happened frequently, even to couples that have loved one another from then till now.

What was happening here was different. As Barbara said in a number of ways, her feelings for Larry were changing, and not for the better. She found herself less inclined during the evening to listen to his descriptions of events that had taken place during the day. The arrival of a child didn't start the process, but it did serve to hasten it. If nothing else, it provided the excuses Barbara needed to voice a steady stream of disapproving remarks. "He isn't as good with the baby," she said, comparing her handling of David and his. Ten minutes later she complained that he wasn't helping her out with the baby nearly as much as she wanted him to. "I change a lot more diapers than he does," she said sarcastically. In her rush to criticize, Barbara overlooked the glaring contradiction between the two comments. She did the same on a number of subsequent occasions.

Larry was slow to recognize the change in Barbara's attitude, attributing the remarks instead to her moods. By the time David was two, however, Larry was running out of rationalizations. Then he started asking Barbara openly what was wrong when she was acting out-of-sorts. He expected his question "Why are you so irritable lately?" to help clear the air. "I'm not irritable," Barbara snapped back. "There aren't enough hours in the day to get my work done. And you analyzing my every mood doesn't help." Not having a ready answer to so vague an accusation, Larry slowly retreated into the reports and papers he brought home from the office each day.

Getting out of Barbara's way was no help. She took to constantly rearranging his favorite objects, never happy with where he left them. Larry put up with not knowing where his favorite chair or book or magazine would turn up but lost his temper when she threw out his list of clients. "Good thing for you it was still in the incinerator room," he yelled furiously. "How could you do such a thing? My livelihood depends on that folder." Barbara merely shrugged and said, "In that case, you ought to keep it locked away instead of in a sloppy file."

Between her baby and her job, Barbara seemed to need nothing else. Moving the furniture around, straightening up continually—this was her way of moving Larry out of their home physically in the same way that she was moving him out of her life emotionally. One nightmare that Larry had never even imagined, especially with the birth of a child he too loved, had finally come true: he had been rendered irrelevant in his own home.

READY, AIM, ACHIEVE

There was little difference in the behavior of Anne, Ellen, and Barbara in a business setting. The fact that Anne was single and the other two had husbands wasn't evident during office hours, as she experienced the same daily ups and downs and mood swings as her married contemporaries. She considered being single an advantage by comparison. "I don't have to answer to anybody when I come home," she said proudly at twenty-six. "No one is sitting there, if I come home at 7:30, with a 'How come you're late? I'm hungry.' I can do as I please."

There were two other respects in which the three women seemed the same. First, their career aspirations were growing. Their desire to become successful was increasing by the day. Second, the three were being pulled in a similar direction, feeling ever more alone. Given the different starting points of the three, that was a conspicuous development. Ellen had chosen political science as a major; in college, at least, her aspirations were vague and largely academic. "I can imagine myself teaching the subject," she said tentatively in the spring term of her junior year, "contributing to the political awareness of students." Anne's college major was English, and while she had a less clear picture of her professional future than either Ellen or Barbara, in the spring of her junior year she could still describe an "ideal work day" ten years hence. "I would write essays and critiques, and maybe book reviews for some prestigious literary quarterly. That would be interesting and fun."

Barbara had the least difficulty envisioning herself five to ten years later as part of the work world. Right after her junior year ended, she said, "I don't really want to *have* to work, but be doing it because I like it. That way, it would always be mine. I would spend most of the day working with people. That's what I do best." If there was ambition here, and there was indeed, it lay primarily in the direction of being admired by the coworkers with whom Barbara imagined herself active.

Ellen's, Anne's, and Barbara's initial images of themselves as future professionals differed considerably while the three were in college. But with each passing year the images became increasingly alike, a process that accelerated once they had entered the business world. The point is that not only did the images finally come to resemble one another to a large extent, but the degree of ambition they contained steadily rose as well.

For example, people who came to know Ellen, Anne, or Barbara when each woman was in her early thirties quickly concluded that she had always been that ambitious. But that was false. Two of the three had hoped to avoid the business arena altogether. The third, Barbara, knew that was where she was headed but hardly considered it something to cheer about. It merely seemed the most appealing choice given the low income prospects and "unreality" of the alternatives.

Now all three had become quite eager to succeed in the business world. Surely in part, but only in part, that was because they were re-routing any ambitions they had long had, funneling them in a new, more commercial direction. That had become much easier for them to do in recent years. It is normal for adolescents to mask their desire to advance themselves. During their teen years, belonging to an approving circle of friends is every bit as important to them as making great strides in the area of professional or self-development. Any aspirations to excel that they possess are often muted.

Only later when the social group disperses does this self-imposed shackle usually fall away. Their hope of attaining fame and fortune then stands fully revealed to others, perhaps for the first time, and to them-selves. The emergence of naked ambition in Ellen, Anne, and Barbara as they progressed through their twenties and into their early thirties was not only par for the course, it was happening to their male peers as well. Neither sex felt compelled to soft-pedal their desire to be individually acclaimed in order to avoid costing themselves their good standing as members of relaxed and friendly groups.

There were important differences in addition to the similarities. In fact, a significant divergence between the ambitions of men and women emerged between the ages of twenty-five and forty. During this period both became more comfortable about voicing and aggressively pursuing their career goals, but the images put forth by Ellen, Anne, and Barbara had a characteristic that those offered by their male peers did not. Having a partner, being happily married, was accorded a steadily decreasing prior-ity by all three. It was discussed and greatly lamented, yet actually be-came a less pressing issue with each subsequent interview.

AMBITION AND LONELINESS

The women we studied told us time and time again in pained tones throughout the period that, although they were searching for a satisfying personal as well as a successful professional life, they were having little luck finding it. Some complained bitterly about men's fear of involve-ment, while others felt that there were too many gays, workaholics, or men who just wouldn't grow up. It took us a while to realize that even if the powerful historical and psychosocial forces discussed in Chapters 1 and 2 are set aside for the moment, none of these us-versus-them expla-nations could be valid, for two reasons. First, married as well as single women claimed to be hungry for a "real" partner. Apparently, even those who seemed to have one actually didn't. Second, the pressures and opportunities that generated the unhappiness affected the men in our sample as well, though not to the same extent as it did women, for reasons we'll explore shortly.

The argument used by almost all the people we studied to analyze the connection between their own—and everyone else's—work and love lives goes as follows:

1. "Ambition is wonderful, since it gives people the energy and determination to get ahead. Without it, workers stagnate. With it, they can accomplish miracles."

2. "However, there is a price to be paid for having great aspirations: loneliness. People who are ambitious eventually become isolated. It is the inevitable price they pay for success."

Note well the order of events here: ambition comes first, and it leads to ever-greater isolation as people move up the ladder. That this is the way the world works is accepted as an article of faith by virtually the entire sample. Nevertheless, this view is flatly contradicted by the evidence. What we found is that *in adults, isolation comes first, and it generates ambition. An almost panicky sense of involvement with work fills the growing void that is created in people with deteriorating personal relationships or no real partners.*

All the makings of a highly destructive downward spiral are in place here. In the first step, one has a disagreement with an intimate. That could happen to anyone. However, rather than being upset by the dispute and trying to close the gap at the earliest date, they come to see it as an opportunity. It provides them with the chance they were secretly seeking to be in a position one day to stand up and take a bow—as a solo.

A prevailing attitude powerfully colors their judgment. In the United States, it is commonly believed that if something outstanding happens, an outstanding individual made it happen. Praise or blame belongs to just one person, even if the event was accomplished by a group. A prime mover, someone who organized or directed the overall effort or did the most important work, deserves the lion's share of the approval. In short, not only is the nation indivisible, so is any applause its citizens receive. Credit cannot be shared. One must either lay claim to all of it or risk getting none.

Each rift that people have with their partners therefore creates a golden opportunity at the same time that it causes distress. There is a real and continuing reason for them not to heal any rift that develops. As a result, fights tend to be more intense and last longer than they otherwise would, and quiet disagreements may drag on for years, smoldering and unresolved, waiting to once again reignite. Degenerative changes occur even behind what looks like a static marital facade. The initial isolation ends up producing more of the same, as each partner comes to view the marriage in increasingly negative terms. That they are genuinely unhappy, on the one hand, about the deteriorating relationship seems beyond doubt. On the other hand, the deterioration of their marriages is precisely what gave the majority of women we studied the determination they needed to concentrate on nothing but their work.

Most had suspected that achieving success would take total determination. What troubled the few who actually thought about the subject this openly was, "Where will I find that degree of determination in myself? What will I use to generate such strong and consistent self-motivation?"

They could locate only one source, a combination of anger and isolation. Seizing upon it subconsciously, recognizing the power of the mixture, they exploited it fully. As their relationship with a man deteriorated, whether he was their husband or a live-in lover, they became blissfully more energetic. Now, at last, they felt ready to conquer the world.

Needless to say, the world turned out to be immensely more difficult to conquer than they had anticipated. For all their striving, the results were typically meager after a decade on the job. More determination was needed, and it was found. A crumbling marriage or love affair had helped produce the initial burst of ambition, so the same source was tapped again. Besides, what else could be used as high-test fuel? They knew they'd have to do much more than they were doing if they were ever to succeed. That made attaining a still greater level of drive absolutely essential. Although the majority of women we studied did it without realizing why, pushing men away fiercely and repeatedly provided the added thrust required to get into overdrive. As the only viable recipe for success, hating men became mandatory.

STAYING MOTIVATED

Saying that a member of one sex basically dislikes all members of the opposite sex is a strong statement, one that ought to be rejected unless it came be carefully documented. Fortunately, we know from many studies of past episodes of racial, religious, and ethnic stereotyping what to look for. Someone who doesn't like blacks or Jews may vehemently deny that he is using a stereotype of the people in question to build a case against them. But if his repeated criticisms of the behavior and appearance of the target group keep coming back to various features of the stereotype, it is probably sitting in his mind and affecting his thinking, whether he knows it or not.[1]

1. T. W. Adorno et al., *The Authoritarian Personality* (New York: Harper and Row, 1950.

Prejudice is almost always thought of as hostile emotions and acts aimed at a minority by a majority. However, that needn't be the direction of flow, and in the United States, the reverse has more frequently been the case in recent decades. Blue-collar groups in America have had fun for years deriding the lifestyle of upper-middle-class white-collar workers, and artists have been doing it for an even longer time.[2] Those who see themselves as weak or feel that they are viewed as outcasts can "get even" with those in the mainstream by characterizing them in the most unflattering terms.

Undoubtedly, some of this mental jockeying for social status had an effect on the opinions of the women we studied. Many felt like second-class citizens in the business world and therefore made use of the same steady stream of snide remarks that people on the lower rungs of other ladders also voiced. They too were "evening the score," they felt, by verbally cutting down those on the higher rungs.

It would have been comforting in some ways for our study to find that this is all there was to the abundance of animosity being aimed at men by women during the years after 1970. It is normal for the heat of competition to incline people to make biting comments about one another, regardless of gender. Nevertheless, it quickly became apparent that this couldn't be the whole story. In fact, it turned out to be only a small part of it. Women who were doing poorly in business and wanted to do better certainly had something to gripe about. However, women who were doing very well indeed and had little or no contact with men during the business day were also generating plenty of hostility and aiming it at men. This was a fascinating process to monitor, for it made us realize that women were producing it for a psychological reason, not a social one. *Status wasn't the goal of their anger, stamina was.*

Blue-collar workers are the sprinters of the business world. They have to get themselves "up" for a particular project, erecting a building or bridge, and can relax when the job is completed, or celebrate with a beer when each day's labors are through. White-collar workers, on the other hand, are the business world's long-distance runners. It is hardly surprising that as the concept of a career replaced that of a job during the period 1955 to 1985 throughout the United States, with its greater emphasis on continuous dedication, marathon running moved to the fore as a favorite leisure-time activity for those who were doing well, or hoped to. Intuitively, they recognized that this pastime was the physical equivalent of what they had to do emotionally at work.

Knowing that one has to stay highly motivated day in and day out for

2. F. Haskell, *Patrons and Painters: A Study in the Relation Between Art and Society in the Age of the Baroque* (New York: Alfred A. Knopf, 1963).

decades is easy to say and much harder to do than most people recognize. Anger can definitely produce a feeling of being directed and driven. But since it is a powerful emotion, one with great destructive potential, we usually demand that people who expect to be considered civilized explain their reasons for being angry. If they can't, we immediately classify them as deranged. They therefore hasten to come up with an explanation even if it has nothing to do with the facts. They don't want to be labeled insane.

In short, women who were doing well in business and wanted to do even better were increasingly able during the 1970s and 1980s to use any anger they experienced. But they could express it, dwell upon it, and prolong its duration only if they could locate a socially acceptable excuse for its presence. So they borrowed the resentment people stuck on the lower rungs normally feel toward those above.

However, the women we studied weren't stuck on the lower rungs, and they knew it—though, like their male peers, they wanted to be moving up faster than they were. Characterizing themselves repeatedly as having had their upward progress slowed primarily because they had been "victims of sexist attitudes in the workplace" served their purposes anyway. If nothing else, it prevented *them* from becoming the target of the animosity of women stuck in low-level jobs, whose bosses they were in the process of becoming. Pointing to a common enemy helped them go after and get the promotions and pay raises they wanted without, they hoped, having to pay this particular price for success.

WOMEN WHO MARRY THE BOSS

It was apparent in the early years of our study that the attitudes people had at work and the emotions they depended upon while there had a major impact on their personal lives. Even so, we were surprised to see how increasingly rare it was becoming for successful women to pair up with a man they met in the course of their everyday business lives. Slowly but surely it became clear from their comments and actions that they didn't *want* to meet someone at work. In fact, their stance in the 1980s finally became the exact opposite of the one they espoused in the 1950s. Whereas in 1958 nearly two-thirds of the women in our sample between the ages of eighteen and thirty-five felt that one of the best reasons for taking a job was to meet a potential mate ("That's where all the men are"), by 1985 less than 6% of a comparable group held that view.

The prevailing attitude had swung so far in the other direction that, without being aware of it, business and professional women had developed a powerful bias against the possibility of a romantic encounter on the job. Sex, yes; love and marriage, no. Bizarre as it may sound, while in the 1950s it was considered a dream come true by the young women in our sample to land a good job and find a suitable husband as a bonus, by the 1980s it had become an insult to their pride.

It was revealing to see how women who *did* manage to find a mate on the job were viewed by their peers. Since women generally marry a man a few years older than they, the man they married was likely to hold a position senior to theirs at the firm. That was all the ammunition the woman's peers needed, for it allowed them to attribute vicious ulterior motives to her choice of a partner. Without a moment's thought, they labeled it "climbing," and in some cases that is what it turned out to be. Novels and movies during this period played up the theme repeatedly, depicting an attractive woman who ensnared the boss in a romantic pairing, but only so that she might realize her seething ambitions more quickly.

What was so distorted about the film depictions and the real-life comments of the woman's coworkers was that, in more than 80% of the cases we examined, the woman in question was *less* ambitious than her peers. That, in fact, was what allowed her to ignore the prevailing attitude of the time and marry a man she had come to know and love after having worked with him day in and day out.

Her coworkers at the firm couldn't see it. Projecting their own unfulfilled ambitions onto her, they concluded that she had succeeded by trickery, while they maintained their honor and paid a price for being virtuous. Naturally, they disliked her. "I would never do such a thing," many stated self-righteously, "I'm not a *user*." With that, they redoubled their dedication to the purist approach: work is work, and love exists only on weekends, if one can find it.

They couldn't. That struck many business and professional women as odd, for two reasons. First, they prided themselves greatly on their ability to get things done. Given a task, they relished the idea of proving their effectiveness by accomplishing it—and quickly. Yet here was a goal they had set for themselves, pursued diligently, and still they kept coming up empty. The fact that years, and even decades, were passing in the process only added to the distress. Some of the women claimed that a biological dimension was feeding their frustration: "I love children, and want to have some, but time is running out." A more important factor in most cases, however, was the sheer lack of results by people who were used to achieving them, at least on the job. This was one failure they found hard to overlook.

That led them to what they viewed as the second puzzling aspect of all this. "Where are all the worthwhile men?" was a typical question they asked. "I know lots of really terrific women who have no one." Since in their view the problem couldn't in any way have been of their own making—"I'm doing everything possible to try and *solve* it"—they pointed a finger at their male coworkers, who seemed to them either second-rate or unavailable as potential partners. The men they worked with appeared to fall into four distinct categories: marrieds, gays, closet gays, and losers.

No one came out smelling like a rose. That a large proportion of the men they worked with were married struck few women as surprising. Yet their comments about this group clearly reveal a monumental underlying ambivalence. A frequently heard remark was, "Of course he's married, he isn't exciting enough to be single." The speaker explained that she meant to convey the fact that marriage seemed *too* settled, bordering on dull, and she could understand why a truly interesting and active man might not want to be tied down in wedlock. After all, she wasn't. In the very next breath, however, the speaker could be heard to say, "Of course all that's left is junk. All the really attractive men have already been snapped up. They don't stay on the market long, you know."

An outside observer listening to the thousands of such comments we collected might be forgiven for concluding that tall, witty, attractive, educated, and financially secure men are very appealing, if you can find this rare species at all in your vicinity, but once they marry, they are instantly converted into short, dumpy, balding bores who emotionally drain their wives and friends. Apparently, the wedding ceremony somehow converts the likes of Redford, Reynolds, and Newman into humorless versions of Dom deLuise and Bob Newhart.

The bumper crop of gays that seemed to be sprouting up in almost every urban industry during this time brought forth far fewer comments from the women we studied than did closet gays. These "permanent bachelors" were a source of puzzlement because they gave the appearance of being eligible and attractive—"neat" was the word used most often to describe them—yet they had no sex life that anyone could identify. An active social life, perhaps, but intimacy seemed about as appealing to them as cancer. Since they fit into neither the premaritally dashing group nor the now-dumpy marrieds, and instead straddled the two camps, they were an endless target of amusing and acid observations, voiced when they weren't around.

As for the "losers," this label was used to cover an astonishingly wide variety of men, from those with ambition who were nevertheless judged unlikely to succeed to those who displayed little motivation and were said to be "just taking up space" in the office. It was applied to men who focused more on their work than on women, as well as those who were constantly on the make, trying to get somebody, anybody, interested. These "office Lotharios" were readily dismissed as ineffectual and unsuitable partners, even for a brief fling. They were usually compared laughingly to the horny but wimpy characters in TV sitcoms popular during this time. More important, the women we studied came to believe strongly that the real-life losers they saw in their office constituted the vast majority of potential mates they would encounter, both on the job and off.

That made it easy for them eventually to stop searching for partners, after a few disappointing dates and brief relationships let them see what they were up against. Again and again, they claimed that the deadbeats in their office were a microcosm of what existed "out there." Here, in their own backyard, they had looked hard at the available offerings and saw nothing but slim pickings.

The logic of their stand combined well with their unhappy experiences to make the matter seemed closed. Every male in their office fit nicely into at least one of the four categories, which rendered him easily disposable. That made it unnecessary for them to realize how often they were using the approach, how much it meant to them, and why. It was much easier to talk about the inadequacies of every man they knew than to acknowledge their own burning desire to become successful without even the *hint* that someone else—especially a man with whom they worked and were romantically linked—had helped them.

That may seem like an admirable goal; but by the late 1970s and early 1980s it was being carried to such an extreme by the business and professional women we studied that they didn't realize that, in a work setting, no man met their criteria. Why is that important? Because it meant that an after-hours encounter, particularly when their guard was down, had become the only avenue of access for them. In short, *at work, the standards by which they judged potential mates were impossibly harsh, while in their leisure hours the standards became dangerously lax.*

SUMMER ROMANCES

Vacations and travel, even in town, often turned up partners. "How come?" we asked repeatedly. "Because my guard was down," was the candid and most accurate reply. There is good evidence that their lowered level of vigilance was no illusion, since the women in our sample were more than three times as likely to become pregnant on vacation as at home. At first, we thought that that was because they had more sex during the trip, yet they actually had less. What sexual activity there is during any vacation occurs when one's normally high level of alertness and self-protection is reduced, and pregnancy is much more likely to result.

So is love. People who wouldn't have met one's standard in the city become more acceptable in distant settings. The successful women we studied paired up on trips with a variety of partners they would have ignored at home. And once the pair formed, it persisted, even though the vacation came to an end. This was usually presented to friends in an extremely favorable light. A typical comment: "Strange, isn't it? I had to go halfway around the world to meet a guy who lives only four blocks from here." Her friends did indeed consider it strange, since they knew that at home she'd have passed him by without a second thought after she had met and gotten to know him. However, when they were in the same position, the same thing happened to the friends doing the snickering. Each insisted, "*Other* people have fleeting summer romances; the relationship I'm having is real."

It didn't take a journey to the other side of the globe for successful women to lower their guard to the point where someone unacceptable at home became appealing. Men they met at the beach or on weekend ski trips, in health clubs and on supermarket checkout lines, in night courses, passport offices and while jogging, were also able to slide under the wire. The same forces were in operation in all these cases, with a relaxed state of vigilance the most important common theme.

The main result of their standards being too high on the job and too low off was that men whom they would have shunned in the office as unacceptable (this time appropriately) wound up becoming their sexual partners and, in many cases, their husbands. It was only necessary for them to meet such men in a non-business setting. Even then, it was revealing to see that they rarely fell for the people who worked in their firm. Company picnics, unlike those held in Japan, would not have led to mass marriages. Instead, the women in one office frequently became involved with the men that women in another office were labeling losers. And the women in that firm returned the favor, becoming romantically entangled with men they would, at best, have been merely polite to, if they'd had their wits about them.

But they didn't. Developing a rich personal life was actually a secondary goal, relative to the importance they attached to doing their jobs well and moving ahead in their firms and their fields. Such dedication and concentration of attention produces effects of their own. Psychologists often call such a focused approach a *mind-set*. What is fascinating about this ability that all adults possess and make good use of in their everyday lives is that it allows one to overlook a host of appealing distractions that might otherwise deter one from achieving a goal that has temporarily been accorded top priority.

So much for the good news. In a crowded, complex world, an intense mind-set can easily have a number of negative consequences as well. For instance, if people are driving somewhere in town, looking for a drugstore at which they intend to have a prescription filled that they badly need, their attention may wander long enough from the road for them to run through a red light. Mishaps like this one happened to a variety of members of our sample, and in the specific case just mentioned, led to a three-car crash in the intersection. Fortunately, no one was seriously hurt.

We can't say the same for many of the women we studied, whose single-minded focus on attaining success caused them to take detours repeatedly as a result of becoming romantically involved with the wrong partners. What is fascinating is that, in most cases, they barely noticed the involvement begin, and even when they did, they didn't resist it. First, unlike the person looking for the drugstore until the sound of crashing cars disrupted the mind-set, each crash took place quietly and painlessly, at least initially. For that reason alone, the women viewed them as being "natural." Some even went so far as to call it "inevitable, fate." Second, it was obvious that they wanted to be involved and were simply having little luck making it happen.

In the past, when men and women were less likely to spend their days working together, the community created the necessary opportunities for young adults who were looking for a mate to find one. County fairs, church socials, school dances, and neighborhood barbecues helped, but above all, effective aid came from people who were already married, who felt it was their social obligation to assist their peers to find a spouse. Today, this type of behavior is viewed with disdain as being presumptuous and patronizing. But for centuries, it was neither; just a friend trying to lend a helping hand, in a world in which people felt more personal responsibility for those around them than we do today.

One reason such assistance is no longer feasible is that it was often a relative, not a friend, who tried to play the role of matchmaker. That strikes the modern mind as clannish and provincial. In fact, the women we studied are (secretly) rather proud of the fact that not only do they not work for a relative of theirs, which would typically have been the case a few generations ago, they don't even *see* any of their relatives during the course of an ordinary business day. They may talk to one of their parents or to their husband on the phone, but even women who did that at least once a day at the office were still able to take private delight in far how they'd come. Independence meant leaving one's family behind, at least where one's professional activities were concerned, and that they had done.

An important part of the informal matchmaking efforts exerted by both friends and relatives involved finding someone appropriate. Merely coming up with any convenient partner would have been considered a dereliction of duty. The real point was to locate the best potential mate, with special attention paid to the person's background. It had to be similar to and at least as good as that of the person he or she was to marry. That in itself eliminated a considerable number of ne'er-do-wells and unsuitable partners. Although most people found their own spouses anyway, this kind of outside assessment or third-party opinion was still considered worthwhile. The phrase "love is blind" was usually used by interested friends and relatives whose views had been ignored and who were describing the damage people were doing to themselves on this front as a result.

The people who shun such assistance now with remarks such as, "I don't need the charity. What do I look like, Quasimodo?" have not found an effective alternative. They want to cast their nets wide and leave room for an unexpected find. Since no intermediary could be familiar with even a tiny fraction of the potential mates living in a large city, and since computer dating services are useless (the wrong people join them, for one thing), people are left largely to shift for themselves. They have to exercise a great deal of independent judgment, whether they like it or not. Small-town techniques intended to produce a good match no longer work, but it is essential to see precisely why big city catch-as-catch-can devices result in such an appalling number of mismatches, as the people involved later judge such pairings to have been.

In retrospect, most of the single women we studied were unaware that they often were heading for trouble when they found someone on their own. Eager for company, caught in the romantic-erotic "honeymoon phase" that normally accompanies the initial stages of a relationship, they rejoiced at whatever intimacy they were experiencing without asking whether this was someone with whom they could be truly intimate for decades to come.

What criterion did these educated and intelligent women use to decide on the merits of their partner? One word was voiced more often than all the rest combined to signal that the person had passed their meager tests: "He's *nice*," they would say, and that was considered sufficient.

However, in a service society people learn how to be "nice" even if they aren't. Most waiters manage to put at least a half-hearted grin on their faces until the check is paid. Salesmen, especially those who work on commission, do the same. Since the women in our sample were upwardly mobile, and tried to look ready for the next step by dressing as though they were already there, they spent a fair amount of time in salons and shops. Grooming and clothing were matters they took seriously, though few tried to look like something out of the pages of the latest high fashion magazine.

Between the time they spent making work-related and recreational purchases, they encountered a wide variety of men employed in these fields. A service economy brings people from different walks of life into much greater contact than a mining or manufacturing economy does. Men who in a previous era would have been farming or employed in a factory now are found selling such things as stocks, real estate, sporting goods, and cars.

And themselves. This proved to be the most fertile source of partners for the business and professional women in our sample. Our statistic tells the story: for every woman in this group who, while vacationing, met and had sex with a man who could have worked in her office, but didn't, twenty-eight met and ended up in bed with men who were selling them a product or service near the place where they worked or lived. Not that the women anticipated that that would happen. In the vast majority of cases, they insisted that they'd been focusing on what they were shopping for, not on the person selling it to them. Then they noticed that he was nice. Typical comments: "He seemed sweet, not like most salesmen," or, "He took a kind of personal interest in me, and tried hard to find what I was looking for."

That led to some revealing pairings when these women got together with their friends. Before we see what they were, and why they were so revealing, let us look briefly at how the attitudes of the women we studied changed once they had finished school. We mentioned earlier that between the late 1950s and mid–1980s there had been a radical drop in the proportion of women who considered a job primarily a good way to meet a man. In an accompanying shift during these decades, the notion of a career replaced that of a job, and the self-concept of women became dramatically more professionalized.

Nevertheless, it didn't take twenty-five years for the women we studied to change their view of the men around them. Women who were only in their pre-teens in the 1950s made the transition within a few years of the time they graduated college. It was a major change, and meant that they saw their male coworkers in an altogether different way than they had looked at their male classmates only a few years earlier.

While in school, these young women considered it perfectly normal to sift through their classmates and find the most appropriate partner among them. But then again, the problem that was to plague them later hadn't yet arisen—namely, that if they paired up with a man at their firm, especially one who was older and held a senior position, they or their friends couldn't be sure that any success they subsequently achieved was due to their, and not their husband's, efforts. In school, the issue couldn't even be raised seriously, since each student's grade was determined by how well he or she—alone—does on the semester's tests. Pooling grades with a boyfriend, husband, or anyone else is forbidden.

This feature of the academic environment, which everyone takes so much for granted, is precisely what allowed many bright and energetic women to be ambitious both educationally and maritally, trying on campus simultaneously to find the best professional training and the best husbands available to them. If they got help from a boyfriend or husband at all, and 19% did, it was likely to be (in descending frequency) in calculus, statistics, and physics. Yet there was never any doubt in the minds of the 19% or the remaining 81% that their academic record was theirs and theirs alone, a reflection of their own interests and efforts, no one else's.

School, in some sense, spoiled them permanently, for it offered them individual achievement in its purest form—an addicting experience for the driven. Exercise, especially jogging, would later offer them a taste of the same. Although they were unaware of it, nothing like that would be available to them in the business world, where the efforts of many underlie every success. But they would carry the rules of the old arena fiercely and self-protectively into the new.

SEXUAL SLUMMING

Now let us turn to what typically happens when women in our sample in their twenties get together with their friends. If we are talking about two couples chosen at random, what we're likely to discover is that one of the women met her husband while they were both students. The second woman met her boyfriend in a sporting goods store, when he sold her a pair of high-priced sneakers. They went running together in the park that Sunday and have been together for the last seven months.

If the women are a little older, in their thirties now, the odds are good that the couple that had been together since college has broken up. This time, both women show up at dinner with men they met in everyday activities outside the office. The boyfriend of one might have installed some bookcases in her apartment, and himself as well shortly thereafter. The boyfriend of the other, rather than being a "creative carpenter," may be in real estate. He got her to sign a three-year lease on a one-bedroom place that she was thrilled to find, and now he lives there with her.

Since we have learned that such relationships stand little chance of enduring, a year and a half later when the women get together with their current companions as a foursome for dinner, one of the men turns out to be a photographer who developed some pictures for her; the other man is an actor/waiter. He had served the woman he is with at a restaurant she patronizes regularly near her apartment. She thinks he's cute.

What sort of dates have the two women had in the intervening eighteen months? One of the women is a lawyer who doesn't like male lawyers: "I see enough of them at work. The last thing I want is another of them in my home." However, she did go out with one six months ago who had been pursuing her for a while. A few days later she told us that she thought he was a "creep."

The other woman is an executive at a financial services firm. She has met a number of men in the course of her work who hold positions comparable to hers. She found them totally uninteresting. The comment she voiced most frequently about the lot was, "They are boring." With some of them, who were basically business acquaintances, she spent the evening discussing business-related matters. "It was just shoptalk," she said, casually dismissing one such occasion. "I guess it was all right for a few hours. I didn't have anything to do that evening anyway."

If the characterization of these events sounds a little frivolous, there is nevertheless a deadly serious question sitting just beneath the surface (oddly enough, the question seems not to have occurred to the typical woman who finds herself in this position): Why were the men she was willing to have a sexual relationship with acceptable to her even though, by any objective standard, they'd have ranked even higher in the "loser" category than the men she worked with daily?

The answer is that the men she met in retail stores, during local recreational activities, or while on vacation all shared a highly prized feature: they were no threat to her determination to succeed on her own. The encounter could therefore be allowed to proceed rapidly to a more intimate level, especially where sex was concerned. It was with a tremendous sense of relief that she realized subconsciously that here was someone who did not endanger her prospects for self-generated achievement. Such a man could allow her, at last, to feel open and carefree, consumed by love.

Why, then, did these relationships, which flowered so quickly, disappear with even greater speed? Because she had never really gotten to know her partner, never really wanted to. His niceness—as long as she believed in it—was a wonderfully blank slate on which she could create any fantasy she chose. It became a movie screen which reflected her longings for what she wanted to find in a perfect partner. Then, as she got to know him a little better, the lights came back on right in the middle of the show and the lovely image vanished.

Basically, she'd been "slumming," as her friends knew at the time and she herself would later feel. If that sounds terribly snobbish, and makes it seem that these women were merely compensating for being hurt by using elitist rationalizations after having again chosen, partners who weren't right for them, consider a few simple numbers. Many of these encounters led not only to the bedroom, but soon after to the altar. The rate of dissolution of these marriages tells the whole story: 77% of the international (he was from another country), 84% of the interracial, and 61% of the interreligious marriages ended in divorce. So did 71% of those in which her age, income, and education exceeded his, as opposed to 49% for the group as a whole. Each of these figures is 10%–25% higher than would otherwise be expected.

Instead of insulting the men for not being "good enough" for these women, what the figures show is that the men too made a serious mistake. They may have been flattered initially that a women whose standing in the world was a notch above theirs was interested in them, but the other side of that coin soon became evident. It was hardly encouraging for them to hear that they were failures, unable to keep up socioeconomically with the women they'd married, much less able to support her should the couple decide to have children. Unlike the male coworkers of the women in this group, these men were eventually told to their faces that they were losers. We believe that both parties suffered needlessly.

"WHERE ARE ALL THE GOOD MEN?"

To make certain no one misunderstands what the evidence we've accumulated and the conclusions drawn from it indicate, let us summarize briefly the key points covered in this chapter.

First, achievement-oriented business and professional women in their twenties and thirties, acting as trend-setters for their less-motivated peers, generally dismiss the men they work with as unsuitable marital partners. Their conscious argument: the men are married, gay, or worthless. The subconscious reason: they want to prove themselves by becoming outstanding on their own, or at least without help from the men with whom they work.

Second, that forces them to find a personal life after hours. If there were a way for them to meet their male peers who worked at other firms, while still dismissing the ones who work at their own, all would be well. But particularly in cities, there is no such social matching mechanism available. Singles bars interest and are patronized by very few women in this group. Ski trips and beach houses in places where their male peers congregate result in sexual encounters, not romance and marriage, for reasons we will discuss in greater detail in Chapter 5.

Third, living in a society that is increasingly oriented toward services instead of manufacturing, these women encounter during their leisure hours a variety of men trying to sell them goods and services. If their guard is too high in the office, then here, while they are shopping, it is too low. They concentrate on what they have come to buy, not on the person selling it to them. Then, they are pleasantly surprised that the person is "nice."

Fourth, as a result, people who under normal circumstances they would have deemed inappropriate become important in their personal lives. The women are hungry for intimacy, so here, in what began as a commercial transaction, they allow themselves to find it. And for a brief time it is present, but then the sex becomes less exciting, the conversations more repetitive, and their partner's flaws begin to emerge. A little while later, it is over.

That may sound like the end of the story, yet it is merely the beginning. They don't learn from their mistakes, though they certainly try, because the psychosocial pressures that caused this mistake in the first place intensify. Year in and year out, partner after partner, the pattern repeats itself—even when they swear to themselves there will be no further recurrences because there aren't going to be any bedmates at all. Few implement their resolution to remain celibate forever, but even for those who do, it changes nothing. Nor does settling down with someone who seems Mr. Right. The pattern continues because the needs persist—and grow—and clearly aren't being fulfilled.

Finally, it affects their business and professional lives. That was one outcome that neither we nor they anticipated. Over and over again during these years, many stated, usually with an air of resignation, "I may not have much of a love life, but at least things at work are going pretty well." Slowly at first, and then much more rapidly in their forties and fifties, their professional positions deteriorate significantly. How that happens, and why, will be discussed in detail in Part Four. For now, let us note a painful irony: the cause of the difficulties that did such harm to their careers in later years is to be found in the very attitudes we've been describing that they evidenced in their early years on the job. They had unwittingly dug a small pit for themselves in the beginning, and their actions during their late twenties and throughout their thirties steadily made it deeper.

As we'll see, a few minor changes could have made an enormous difference.

5

Romance is
a Career Threat

Deriving inner strength from rebellion is nothing new to adolescents. As long as they have a target to attack, they feel mighty indeed. It is only when the target has been removed that an observer has a chance to see how much structure it gave their lives. With it gone, they become aimless and even lackadaisical. It is a startling and revealing metamorphosis to witness.

Teenagers usually adopt one of two solutions to the problem. Either they find someone else with whom they can do battle or they grow up. Using their own interests as a guide, they bring structure and direction into their lives, without having to be in constant need of an opponent to serve the purpose.

We all have a picture of how a permanently adolescent male behaves. Four main features characterize his approach to life. First, he doesn't take anything seriously. He is a prankster and playboy who wants, above all, to spend his days laughing and taking it easy. Second, he is endlessly self-indulgent. Whatever he wants, he expects to obtain immediately. The whole idea of delayed gratification, of waiting for something, perhaps working for years to attain it, is simply alien to his thinking. Third, he is immensely narcissistic. He wants to be in public settings, out and about, he tells us, because he likes to be with people. Yet what he really wants is to be continually admired by them, and to have them pamper him as well. They aren't to have lives of their own. Only his needs and whims, his desire for attention and adulation, matter.

The fourth and final feature is an immediate consequence of the first three. The personal relationships he forms are unbalanced and empty. Even to speak about such a person having a serious involvement is a joke. In his view, there is no one out there sufficiently worthy of it. There are no candidates for the position.

The male version of eternal adolescence has been a literary staple for centuries, appearing in plays, poems and novels in guises such as Peer Gynt, Peter Pan, Don Juan and Til Eulenspiegel and his merry pranks. However, the female version of eternal adolescence has, by contrast, received almost no attention. That makes her harder for most people to recognize; yet with so many women now in offices instead of the home, it is essential to be able to spot those whose personal growth stopped when their teen years ended. Three questions are central: How does a woman stuck in adolescence behave? How is her behavior different from that displayed by her male counterpart? Third, and most important, what harm is she doing to herself much less those around her?

OUTRAGE—A FUEL INJECTION

The main, and most conspicuous, characteristic of a permanently adolescent woman is that she is chronically angry. Anger makes her—makes anyone—feel stronger, and strength is what she believes is required to get where she wants to go. In that respect, she is the polar opposite of the permanently adolescent male, since he usually doesn't consider anything important enough to get angry about and wants to be everybody's friend. He is of course capable of becoming angry, even enraged, when he doesn't get what he wants, but it is only temporary. If he doesn't get it, he soon forgets it and becomes enamored of something else.

Women who are ambitious need something more suited to the long term. Rage is too exhausting, but outrage is perfect. Rage reactions are mindless outbursts of such intensity that they often result in physical violence, sometimes against blameless bystanders. It is hardly surprising that one speaks of rage as being blind. Outrage, on the other hand, is vastly more rational. Mind is very much involved, since one has to use it to assess the degree to which one has been insulted, a process that may even require consultation with a friend or colleague. In short, whereas rage tends to become physical and may lead to murder or mayhem, outrage is more verbal and literary and usually leads to a lecture or a letter to the editor.

That makes it a convenient form of fuel to be used for stoking the fire in a human locomotive. Taking offense at a remark one might otherwise have dismissed as the words of an ignoramus or a crank allows one to generate an extra burst of determination to stay one's course. As we said at the beginning of the chapter, it is a mechanism that teenagers very commonly use. The trouble, and it is a major one, is that the offending person will soon have to be replaced by another if the fire is to be kept burning. Fools wear out fast, even among people who are suffering them gladly in order to stay all charged up. Also, few outrages are so great that they can be resorted to again and again to boost one's sagging level of determination.

Here we see a second way in which men and women stuck in adolescence differ importantly. The dependence of the male on the people around him is visible to all. He needs them to feed his ego and cater to his whims. Small wonder that some observers think of him as an infant rather than an adolescent. The dependence of adolescent women, however, is equally great, though not nearly as visible.

Whom is she dependent upon? *The adolescent woman is dependent upon her enemies.* She must have at least one, lest she lose her bearings. As real adolescents know, without an opponent, life loses much of its spark, its meaning. However, not all opponents serve the purpose equally. Some are much more suitable than others, and therefore it is essential to choose one's enemies carefully.

Adolescents don't sit down and consciously determine who the best adversary for them would be. They simply leave the choice to an internal emotional barometer that tells them who gets them all fired up and who doesn't. The winner by far turns out to be their parents. Adolescent working women don't consciously select who the most effective adversary would be, either. Like teenagers, they trust to instinct and merely monitor their own emotions to see who gets them the most incensed. That person serves their motivational purposes best and hence they seize upon him or her every bit as firmly as someone drowning might clutch at a life preserver. In their case, the winner by far turns out to be their husbands. If the women aren't married, the men they work with or men in general will do.

It seems paradoxical at first that teenagers and adolescent women end up hating the very people they need most in the various stages of their lives. However, exploring the apparent paradox a bit further brings us to the heart of the matter and allows us to understand why these women wind up doing so much damage to their personal and professional lives.

No long-term goal is more important to teenagers than to lessen their degree of dependence upon their parents. Regardless of what it takes to achieve this goal, somehow they sense that it is essential. Sooner or later their parents will die and they will have to fend for themselves. The earlier they learn how, while still getting the emotional sustenance they need, the better. Even if their parents outlive them, they recognize that their lives will never be their own, will never have been lived fully, unless they first impose some distance. Only after they have separated themselves will they finally be in a position to sense their own needs and wants, likes and dislikes, rather than exist as a mere extension of those of their parents.

Adolescent women use the same line of thought, but they aim their animosity at their husbands instead of their mothers and fathers. A key question is this: Why is the person to whom they feel closest the most suitable target, both during their teen years and once they are married? There are two main reasons. The first is that "out of sight, out of mind" applies to hatred as well as to love. It is much easier to keep hostile feelings alive if one receives regular reminders of the despised person's existence, thanks to frequent encounters with him or her.

The second and more important reason teenagers and adolescent women choose as targets the very people to whom they feel closest can best be grasped by thinking for a moment about war. It has been observed for centuries that soldiers fight best when they are on their home soil. Familiarity with the terrain and the support of the local civilian populace helps somewhat, but more critical is the desire to protect what is one's own. Fighting in a foreign country always makes soldiers who have been sent there eventually ask, "What are we fighting and dying for here? What, if anything, is so valuable about this place?"

Once the enemy invades their own shores, however, the question is no longer heard. The battle literally turns into an all-or-nothing conflict. This time, the defending soldiers and civilians have no place left to run, and they are emotionally connected to what they are fighting for as well. The conflict is likely to become intense.

Teenagers didn't consciously decide to become so attached during their childhood years to their parents. It just happened. Similarly, adolescent women didn't say to themselves, "Here is someone I think I'll fall in love with." It too just happened. But once it does, once the person has found his or her way into their affections and become an important part of their lives, the effort to expel that parent or partner is likely to become intense.

That makes the situation ideal if one of the goals all along has been to find someone who angers one sufficiently to generate the resolve needed to propel oneself in the desired direction. With a battle cry constructed out of phrases such as, "I won't be your pawn" and "I'm not your puppet," the determination to go forward on one's own is finally present in abundance.

Susan Johnson's experiences are typical of those of the more than 3,400 women in our sample.

"WHAT DOES HE SEE IN ME?"

When she described her face and figure during her teen years, Susan said repeatedly that she had disliked her skinny legs as long as she could remember. She didn't notice her boyish body taking on womanly curves in her late teens and early twenties, but she was relieved to find her calves acquiring shape. Susan also wasn't quite happy with what she called her "pre-Raphaelite frizz," the auburn hair haloing her face. Yet it was her most memorable feature, one that gave her a drama of sorts and set her apart in crowded rooms. When she was engrossed in her work, she simply tied it back, off her face, as if to reinforce the seriousness with which she attacked her tasks. It was the only time she forgot herself; it was also when the people who knew Susan told us they found her to be most attractive. Releasing her hair after finishing the job was a sign of celebration, the time to play.

Susan went through her teens and twenties not sure of anything about herself. Was she smart, pretty, talented, well-liked, sexy, and classy? She wasn't certain about any of these things. From time to time Susan received confirmation that she was indeed what she wanted to be in one department or another, but the sense of certainty was soon erased by her alleged deficiency in some other area. If she felt smart, she didn't feel sexy. And when someone made her feel sexy, she began to wonder whether she was sufficiently classy.

The only constant in her life, once she finished school, was her work. Here the rules were simpler than anything she had ever encountered before. The fact that she spent hours trying to make herself alluring to her peers didn't necessarily mean that even one of them found her so. Frequently, none did. The fact that she sometimes devoted whole days to shopping for the latest status symbols, so as to project an undeniable image of class, didn't mean anyone had to view her as chic. However, on the job there was a more direct connection between effort and reward. When Susan worked hard, she got a raise, and when she learned the ropes, she got promoted.

Much to her surprise, that gave her a high that lasted longer than anything she had received in her personal life. Here at last she felt she was in control of the compliments that eventually would come her way. Susan had finally found what she considered her real self. Her work no longer seemed like something she merely *did*; it was something she *was*.

It is small wonder that she subconsciously came to view personal relationships with men as a threat. The fragile self that she had carefully nurtured into existence over many years stood too great a chance of being swallowed up in any intimacy that consumed her. In seeking to protect her ability to work—her desire to *strive* at work—she was trying to protect the only real sense of self she had ever had.

Two incidents brought all the underlying tensions to the surface. When Susan was twenty-seven and had been out of school long enough to be nearly finished with her transition from campus to corporate life, she met Brian Wilson at a party one Friday night. He was a twenty-eight-year-old marketing manager at a small but rapidly growing electronics firm. She and Brian spent almost three hours together at the party and went out, and to bed, the next night. Susan was deriving an increasing measure of self-assurance from her work by this time, yet here, in her after-work hours, many of the old self-doubts were still active. "What does he see in me?" she asked tensely, and immediately proceeded to answer her own question with, "Not that I don't think I'm special. I am. But he could probably have a thousand women."

What she considered her good luck continued, as the two started seeing one another regularly. Within four months, she no longer thought of their get-togethers in terms of luck. "I kind of take it for granted now, especially on weekends," she said, "and am very happy about it. He makes me feel like no one else ever has." Susan was visibly more peaceful when she was spending time with Brian than when she had been with anyone else or alone, something her friends commented upon and of which she was well aware. That doesn't mean they never fought. They did, but the tiffs were minor and seem to have been resolved completely by the time they finished making love.

Fifteen months after they met, they were married. Susan had always thought that, as she'd seen in Hollywood movies, she would enter a prolonged state of ecstasy during the honeymoon months after her wedding. It didn't happen. She was very pleased about having a partner, someone whom she loved and who clearly loved her, but she didn't think about it much anymore. She was living it instead, and that gave it less luster in her mind than it had the many times she had watched it on the screen.

By the end of their second year of marriage, a singularly important shift took place. Ever since our first interview with Susan when she was fourteen, and in every subsequent interview until she was twenty-eight and married, she had always managed to get at least one self-critical comment into the conversation. Susan discussed many other topics during those years, but her insecurities evidenced themselves each time in a self-doubting remark. Now, married only a little over a year and a half, it was her partner who became the target of her criticisms. Whereas in previous years Susan had been able to dwell endlessly on her own flaws, now she dwelt endlessly on his.

Scrutinizing his every action and comment, just as she had always scrutinized her own, she found much to criticize. However, nothing caught her eye so readily and moved her to upbraid him so much as what she called his immaturity. When Brian was at work, he dressed neatly and liked doing so. "I think of my suit as a ticket of admission to my office," he said lightheartedly. "I feel uncomfortable there when I'm not wearing a tie." At home, on the other hand, he was likely to wear a pair of old but comfortable blue jeans, a sports shirt and sneakers. On short notice, a friend of Susan's from work came over one Saturday to pick up some papers needed for a report due on Monday morning. After the coworker left, Susan began badgering Brian about his clothes. "I'll bet she thought you were the building super, not my husband," she commented sarcastically. It was said as a joke, she later insisted, but it had too much bite for either of them to believe that it really was.

On another weekend afternoon five weeks later, the two decided to have dinner at a restaurant that required reservations. Susan went shopping briefly and it was agreed that Brian would make the reservation. She returned a half hour later and asked whether he had made the call. He hadn't, although he intended to once the game he was watching reached its half-time break in about ten minutes. Susan suddenly began to mimic his words angrily. Surprised by the hostility, he asked, "What are you getting so steamed up about? It's only 1:30. There's plenty of time." She replied, "You're such a baby, always expecting me to do everything for you."

What Brian found striking about the reply was that Susan was doing less for him with each passing month, something he had been only vaguely aware of before but now found hard to overlook. For example, the first of the two incidents that changed the course of their relationship involved the little errands they normally ran for one another. Since they had no children ("We want to hold off for a few years," Susan said a year after they were married), and they ate out frequently, their household chores were relatively simple. They usually shopped together on Saturday mornings for the week's groceries. "We get there early," Brian said, "pioneers, before the wagon trains [multiple carts being pushed to the registers by families with a number of children] arrive." Susan would drop off Brian's shirts at the laundry once a week on the way to work. Brian would pick them up on Saturday. The first time he found no shirts to pick up, he thought the cleaner lost them and was upset until he found them at home in the hamper. The following week, when Susan again didn't make her usual stop at the laundry, he asked her about it. "Why do *I* have to take *your* shirts to be cleaned?" she answered acidly. Brian became furious and said, "Dropping them off was your idea in the first place, remember? You told me that this was the best cleaner." They argued bitterly for twenty minutes, after which Brian said, "Don't touch my shirts again. I'll take care of it myself from now on." The rift caused Brian to start monitoring Susan's behavior every bit as intently as she had been monitoring his. Things he would previously have dismissed he now made careful mental notes of. That later led to fights much worse than this one.

Susan's job with a major retail chain, where she was a merchandise manager, paid well and had proved a rapid route to executive positions for some of her women friends. Not for her. She had done well by any measure, but not nearly as well as she wanted—and expected—to do. Referring to her peers, she said, "They're no better than I am. What's their secret, their trick?"

Here, in her early thirties, Susan was as irritable and unhappy as we had ever seen her. She was satisfied with neither her personal nor her professional life; in fact, every setback in one sphere only seemed to make matters worse in the other. A coworker who had taken a job at another chain labeled her "hyper." Yet an ex-supervisor volunteered the opinion that Susan was frequently depressed. "I'm no expert on the subject," he said without any malice in his voice, "but she's not exactly what I would call a picture of stability. She doesn't react, she overreacts." Susan heard neither of these opinions, at least to our knowledge, and instead she continued to concentrate on the tasks immediately before her. At work, that meant trying to hold her own against talented contemporaries, some of whom were moving up the ladder significantly faster than she. At home, the problem was different, though in many ways it seemed the same.

The second incident that took place between Susan and her husband and caused the underlying pressures in her life to burst to the surface concerned her in-laws. Susan had never liked Brian's father and mother. "They're plain people," she said, attempting to be upbeat. "You know, colorless." That was the kindest remark we heard her voice about them, and she voiced many. For the first few years Brian was spared the remarks, but during their third and fourth year of marriage he began to hear them more frequently. Still, without expecting any complications he asked her what time on Sunday they would be driving out to see his folks. She responded with, "Why do we have to go at all? I don't feel like seeing them just now. They're boring." Brian may not have been anticipating so negative a reply, but he had a quick comeback ready. "Two weeks ago we were at *your* parents' house," he said coldly. "Let me tell you that that was no bowl of cherries. Talk about boring." That Sunday, he drove to his parents' house alone.

"I HAVE A LIFE OF MY OWN"

What Susan, Ellen, Anne and Barbara, as well as the majority of other career women in our sample, have in common is that between the ages of twenty-five and forty they became increasingly uncooperative where their partners were concerned. At work, they could be and often were flexible beyond belief, willing to adapt to new situations and supervisors on a daily basis if need be. At home, however, they had unwittingly adopted a no-concessions stance.

That is not how they saw it. Their view of themselves was that they were constantly being put upon. "Why am I the one who always has to do everything?" was the question they found themselves frequently asking, not always out loud. Since that was their view of themselves, not surprisingly they viewed their partners as the opposite. "Won't you ever grow up?" they asked repeatedly. Since they were intent upon seeing themselves as excessively burdened, someone close to them had to be doing the burdening—someone who wasn't entitled to be imposing upon them.

Why was it necessary for them to see themselves as being put upon unjustly? So that they could get mad—and hence stay highly motivated. Success required nothing less, as far as they could see. They needed an adversary at home to keep themselves aggressive and determined at work.

Their partners sensed none of the underlying self-motivational reasons for the hostility, noticing instead only that their partner had become more stubborn and uncooperative, less of a partner in every respect. The state of obstinacy was soon superseded by one of open hostility. Something was encouraging these otherwise intelligent women to ignore the fact that their marriages had entered a destructive slide from which few would recover. After we witnessed enough cases to see what the general pattern of development was, it became possible to accurately predict not only that other women in this position would ignore the obvious signs of deterioration, but also that they would quietly be pleased by their presence. In spite of their surface dissatisfaction with the troubled status of their marriages, they were secretly satisfied with the progress they were making toward a more important goal: keeping themselves striving.

The justification they consciously used for overlooking and even smiling at the damage being done to their relationships was contained in just a few sentences. Most of the women we studied used them continually, in a variety of different forms. Of the more than 12,000 comments we collected, approximately four from each member of the sample during the fifteen-year span when she was between the ages of twenty-five and forty, nine were voiced more often than the rest. They were:

"I don't have to do your bidding."

"You can't tell me what to do."

"I have a life of my own."

"I don't need you—or anyone else."

"If I don't feel like doing it, I don't have to."
"Since when am I your slave?"
"I am not your housekeeper."
"You'll have to do it yourself."
"I am not your mother."

Not only did the women almost stand up and cheer when they themselves said the words, they usually applauded openly when someone else voiced them. The sentences sound like a declaration of independence, and in a country which dates its birth to a similar declaration more than two centuries ago, such sentences almost had to be seen in a positive and even laudatory light.

Yet when one watched what the words and associated actions later led to in these women's lives, both at home and on the job, it became clear that they were doing something quite self-destructive. They saw themselves as nothing if not mature, and their partners as nothing if not adolescent. Yet the fact remains that the quantity of adolescent behavior displayed by these women increased substantially by any measure as they passed from age twenty-five to the end of their thirties. At a time in their lives when one might have expected to see the emergence of a more adult perspective on themselves, their jobs, and their love lives, what one witnessed instead was a slow but steady increase in immature behavior. Pouting and outrage became the emotional polarities between which they painfully bounced painfully back and forth.

The nine sentences that they used most often, and that were quoted above, should have told us where the real trouble lay. Nevertheless, as Americans studying other Americans, it took us a while to set aside our cultural biases and realize the true meaning of the words. Especially during the ten-year period between the ages of twenty-five and thirty-five, these women were basically returning to adolescence, with its angry and often stubborn rebelliousness, but they were doing so in a way that made it look as though they were moving resolutely forward on every front. No steps backward were involved, or so we thought. Moreover, we initially believed that their stance was that of an adult.

Eventually we recognized that their anger was masking their immaturity—and producing more of it, since it was causing their adult relationships to collapse. A downward spiral became almost inevitable, since they were actively destroying the only setting in which mature attitudes and actions can be either learned or lived.

It was revealing to see that they repeatedly labeled what they wanted as "good" and what their husbands wanted as "bad," even when both wanted the same things. For example, in a dangerously self-deluding bit of rhetoric, a woman who was seeking some parenting from her husband would claim she was looking for "supportiveness." However, a similar request from her husband was resentfully branded a search for "mothering."

BINGES OF ALL SORTS

What really told the story was that these women were powerfully attracted toward any man who insulted them. It was immensely revealing to see the typical woman in our sample literally gravitate toward the very people who had the least respect for her. Subconsciously, she knew she had no other choice. She needed to use them as a source of outrage and hence motivation. Success required nothing less.

An item in the newspaper in which a well-known male political or sports figure said something derogatory about women was relished rather than relegated to the trash can. The comment was circulated rapidly— "Did you hear what so-and-so said?"—and with evident excitement (cloaked, of course, in a sneer). Here was more fuel for the fire, a lift for those whose determination was flagging. Best of all, it could be shared. In fact, the more women who heard and became indignant about it, the larger a lump of coal it became. Rebroadcasting every insult would seem to be doing only one's enemies a favor, yet it is worthwhile to keep in mind that the main fuel being used by these women wasn't rage, but outrage.

Anxiety served the purpose almost as well as anger. Women who were convinced that they were falling behind because they weren't trying hard enough could push themselves still more by using internally generated doses of adrenalin. Scaring themselves any way they could appeared to them a natural route to travel, and most did so without giving the journey much thought. Their rationalization went this way: "Just worrying about the fact that I'm not doing as well as I'd like will help me solve the problem and make greater progress. For the anxiety, in and of itself, will heighten my vigilance and improve my performance on the job." As we'll later see, it did no such thing and instead merely caused their personal lives to deteriorate more rapidly. The chronically high levels of anger and anxiety seen in many women in our sample often ruled out serious relationships altogether.

Anger and anxiety were widely used as potent sources of self-stimulation, performance enhancers. Nonetheless, as those who were using it were only too well aware, that wasn't enough. They hadn't yet become a success in anyone else's eyes, much less their own. Caffeine and nicotine were called upon to help fill the gap. Not one of the women who smoked had any doubt that the habit was harmful and that it increased significantly the chances that she would die of lung cancer. The most popular justification for continuing to do so nevertheless was that, "if I stop smoking, I'll eat." Meaning it's better to stuff one's face with smoke than food and end up being a fat failure. The real reason they continued smoking, in addition to the habit-forming action of the chemicals involved, was that death was in the future, probably decades away even if lung cancer did get them, and they needed something *now* to keep them on edge and to give them an edge as well.

These four pillars—anger, anxiety, caffeine, and nicotine—were expected to support a high enough level of output daily to guarantee that professional goals were attained. It still wasn't enough, as their agonizingly slow rate of pay raises and promotions made clear. Jogging and chocolate, binges of all sorts, soon entered the picture. The focus of headlines and magazine stories quickly became the binges themselves, rather than the underlying pressures which were generating one binge after another in the first place, all fruitlessly. The stories might as well have been about the shapes of various scabs, rather than the hidden obstacles causing so many seemingly healthy people to fall down and hurt themselves.

6

Fear of Success and Other Bogus Nightmares

People are always interested in knowing how their own abilities and performance stack up against those of others. Nevertheless, they want to believe that forces that spring from within determine how well they do. Richard Easterlin, in *Birth and Fortune*,[1] argues that numbers are destiny; the size of one's generation, relative to the ones before and after it, really determines how well one does. If one's generation happens to be the record-setting post-war baby boom—the seventy-six million children born in the United States between 1946 and 1964—then competition at every level will be intense throughout life for its members and the number of people who fail to prosper inevitably becomes disproportionately large.

Easterlin's thesis has its strengths and weaknesses, yet it struck the women in our sample who knew about it as too impersonal. It placed the fate of the individual in the hands of large-scale forces over which the individual has no control. In Asia the argument might have seemed perfectly logical and acceptable, but in the United States it contradicted one of our most important beliefs: namely, that the individual is the prime mover and can always do something to modify the tide sweeping over him or her.

The notion that there is always "room to maneuver," even for people allegedly caught in the straitjacket of history, can be both a blessing and a curse. It has been largely a blessing for Americans because it says to them, in no uncertain terms, "You are the master of your own destiny." The implication is, "Your present situation is a result of your past actions

---

1. R. A. Easterlin, *Birth and Fortune: The Impact of Numbers on Personal Welfare* (New York: Basic Books, 1980) (op. cit.).

and attitudes—and your future situation depends on your current actions and attitudes."

As people who have used this approach for many years are well aware, it is a self-fulfilling prophecy. Individual initiative has repeatedly demonstrated its worth. People with fewer advantages than their peers have been able to overtake those with a headstart, thanks to hard work and a determination to excel. Accepting that "All is fate, and nothing can be done about any of it," would have guaranteed the status quo. Those who were left behind would never have known what the outcome *could* have been, since they made no attempt to influence it.

"YOU SHOULD THINK BETTER OF YOURSELF"

There is a flip side to this story. While the notion that "Your fate is in your own hands" has undoubtedly been a boon to Americans for the most part, it has at times proved a self-defeating belief. The women we studied were an ambitious and educated group, and they were doing everything in their power to make great strides professionally. With only meager rewards for their prolonged efforts, they were finally forced to assume that they were doing something drastically wrong. The fault, they concluded, lay not in their stars but in themselves.

Where had they gone astray? The most satisfactory answer they could find was that they were afraid of the very thing they claimed to want most; they were suffering from a condition grandly named Fear of Success. Make no mistake about it, this was a very satisfying disease in its own way. No sweeping historical force held them in its grip and decided their fate. Instead, like all good Americans, they looked within themselves to locate the source of their painfully slow progress up the ladder.

The logic of the argument was impeccable. If they were responsible for their triumphs, they must be equally responsible for their failures. Since, as we've seen, they were already generating a fair amount of anxiety each day, they came to believe that it was due to their drawing nearer the goal—and being afraid of achieving it. Psychologists call this *misattribution*, for it involves attributing to one source an emotion or event that actually derives from another source, perhaps in no way connected to the first.[2] The anxiety was subconsciously being produced as a way of keeping themselves motivated. In that sense, it was a self-generated extra push intended to speed their forward progress. Yet they now interpreted their

2. J. Jaspers, ed. *Attribution Theory and Research* (New York: Academic Press, 1983).

persistent anxiety as a fear of the goal toward which they were rushing. In that sense, they saw it as a force that was holding them back.

Their conscious thoughts about the subject were much more concrete than this. What made Fear of Success an appealing explanation was that more than 92% reported that the prospect of having to get up and address a large audience made them nervous. Fear of public speaking struck them as a telling bit of discomfort. Their reasoning went as follows: "The more successful I am, the more visible I will become in my firm, my field, and the nation. People who have never heard of me before will then know my name and want me to make a public appearance at a luncheon, at a conference, or on a TV show." The natural conclusion that flowed from such misgivings was, "If I am afraid of public speaking, I obviously must be frightened of becoming a real achiever."

However naturally it may seem that Fear of Success flows from Fear of Public Speaking, the two have nothing to do with one another. Professionals in the public relations field are well aware, and our own results confirm, that most people need practice before a live audience in order to become good at public speaking. Teachers get more such practice than business people usually do. Few rising young executives, male or female, have a chance in the course of their ordinary business day to obtain the needed experience, so the fear remains when the demand for a speech arises.

It is interesting to note that the women in our sample who were not afraid of speaking publicly, and who felt quite comfortable doing so, did not find Fear of Success a satisfactory explanation for the limited degree of career advancement they had experienced. Instead, they were more than three times as likely as their peers to conclude that their failure was due to another factor—male bias against women—even if they worked at a firm whose top executives all were women.

The trouble with diagnosing an ailment incorrectly is two-fold. To begin with, it prevents those who have it from searching further and discovering the right explanation. Second, it allows them to take the wrong medicine with real assurance. That may help them, quite by accident, or it may worsen their condition substantially. In this case, those who came to believe that they were suffering from the dreaded mental malady, Fear of Success, proceeded to jump out of the frying pan and into the fire.

People who were afflicted by Fear of Success were told, first and foremost, that they had a negative self-image. Professional recognition would be theirs just as soon as they came to view themselves in a distinctly more positive light. Each woman in our sample had heard the words so often that they had become a mere cliché to her. That they were familiar didn't mean they were wrong—only that she hadn't done anything about them lately. Concentration on boosting her own self-esteem seemed a reasonable and useful goal.

However, there are few psychological phrases that are emptier than "You should think better of yourself." A physician might as well tell the dying, "You should live longer." Without a thorough understanding of what was causing these women to think so little of themselves, the words of advice were irritatingly glib.

What was being overlooked by people dispensing the advice, and even more so by the women taking it, was that there was a very good reason for the feelings of inadequacy. It had taken a number of years for these women to re-orient their aspirations and come to think of the business world as the arena in which they should excel. That in itself was no small feat. As we saw in Chapter 3, women who chose a liberal arts, social or natural sciences major in college tended to make this switch more readily than their male peers. Having made the transition, the women came to identify themselves closely with their work. That doesn't mean they loved every minute of it; there was often tension in the air, conflicts and rivalries were common, and much of what they did during a typical day on the job struck them as silly. Nevertheless, their view of themselves as worthwhile and attractive beings, people who had a right to smile in public and hold their heads high, had come to rest squarely on the degree of success they had attained in their professions.

To tell such a woman that she should think better of herself, just like that, when she could plainly see that the real-world results for which she was striving were nowhere in sight, was a nonsense prescription. The advice sounded familiar, so she tried to take it. And tried again, with no more luck than she had had the first time. The well-intentioned people who were telling her to concentrate on boosting her self-esteem weren't helping her, they were turning her into a permanent patient.

Only 12% of the women in our sample handed themselves over to a therapist. The rest attempted to do the job on their own. Both groups failed, of necessity, since the high level of self-esteem each woman was seeking actually depended on her first becoming a high achiever, and (at least in her own eyes), she wasn't. No inspiring words or reassuring lectures from others, comforting though they were in their own way, could erase that fact. The advice couldn't be ignored altogether, in spite of the difficulty she was having implementing it, for thinking well of oneself is obviously desirable. So self-therapy on the run became a common phenomenon.

The women started talking to themselves. Everyone does that to some extent each day, but people in therapy usually do it more. Those who are their own therapists do it most of all, since they never get a respite from their shrink's probing and badgering. Mumbling to themselves, distracted from the important tasks they had to do each day, these women began to second-guess their every move. Yet when all was said and done, they were treating themselves for a condition they did not have.

Far from being shy and retiring types, the women who worried most that they were suffering from Fear of Success, and who were most likely to seek help for it, were precisely those who had previously been highly confident. Pursuing success diligently, they had long had every reason to believe that their quest would not be in vain. It was only when these brighter-than-average, capable, and energetic women became aware of how little career progress they had made, relative to the amount they were seeking, that they looked for and found an internal reason for their failure.

That made them distort substantially the histories they gave both themselves and their therapists. Barbara told the psychiatrist she saw twice a week for nearly three years in her late twenties and early thirties that she had always had doubts about herself. First of all, doubts are normal; only megalomaniacs don't have them. Second, and more important, our records show that by any measure she had far fewer of them than most of her peers had during the prior eleven years. Not until she was in her mid-twenties and had come to evaluate herself strictly in terms of her work-related achievements did her self-confidence begin to erode. This was a strange affliction indeed, affecting the memories and work performance of previously confident women. Revealingly, the cures being attempted only worsened the alleged illness.

Professionals who were prescribing remedies for the dreaded affliction they had invented, Fear of Success, didn't stop just with the dictum, "Boost your self-esteem and the rest of your problems will vanish." They went on to state in a number of books and a much larger number of magazine and journal articles that the condition was based on a very real fear. Women, it was said, were afraid that once they became truly successful, they would be alone. "It's lonely at the top," one psychologist said during a radio interview, with enough artificial emotion to match an entire afternoon of TV soap operas. "I don't blame them for having grave misgivings about what will happen to them once they get there." Not to worry. Anyone who spent as much time as this therapist's patients agonizing about the subject was never going to be in a position to find out.

Here again the most important point about the damage these women would allegedly be doing themselves once they were occupying top slots is that therapists ignored their actual case histories altogether. They didn't have to wait until they were senior executives before they could wreck their love lives. As the four cases covered in the previous chapters indicate (and they are entirely representative in this regard), these women had *already* destroyed their personal lives. For years they had unwittingly been attacking the very person to whom they felt closest so that they'd be in a better position to scale the heights of the business world unburdened by excess baggage.

They didn't want anything, especially their love lives, to distract them from what seemed a realizable goal, at least for these talented and educated women. For them to believe that (1) they were afraid of success, and (2) the fear stemmed from the harm they might do their personal lives in the future, was truly absurd.

KEEPING PACE WITH THE PACK

What, then, were they afraid of, if not success?

Passivity. They feared that they would be too lethargic and inactive relative to the large number of men—and other women—in the business world who were moving ahead briskly. The women in our sample didn't doubt their own intelligence, nor did they question their ability to handle any task that came their way. As Susan often commented, "Just give me the job; I'll find a way to get it done." However, they had great doubts about their ability to function like tireless robots in high gear, putting forth the maximum effort each and every day without flagging. In any race, the leaders set the pace, and what distinguished both the male and female front-runners in this quest for success is that they seemed indefatigable. Willing to work ten hours a day, even on weekends, these human machines set a pace that the rest of the pack had no choice but to keep up with, if they could.

Once war breaks out between two countries, the citizens of both are pressured to take sides. No one is allowed to remain neutral. The same kind of polarization takes place in the minds of women between the ages of twenty-five and forty. Their desire to achieve success is often characterized as a race, with all contestants lined up at an imaginary starting point and turned loose. In terms of how each woman perceives the contest, however, she might as well be in a war. For her picture of the options available to her becomes equally polarized.

The vast majority of women we studied eventually came to believe that there were only two possible outcomes to their actions. Either they would somehow manage to force themselves to run at top speed all day, every day, or they would lose so badly that they might as well not have entered the race to begin with. What would happen to any woman who lost? How did she visualize in her own mind this embarrassing outcome?

It was, she felt, going to turn her into a cow. When she was shown, on film, scenes from the everyday lives of such women, she didn't think of *them* as cows. When she encountered such women in her round of daily activities she didn't view them in such a demeaning light. She called them homemakers and hard-working mothers, and wouldn't have thought to add to the burden they were already carrying by abusing them verbally either to their faces or behind their backs. No, this was one insult she reserved solely for herself.

She had never really put her fears into so many words, never really explored them in depth. Nevertheless, she was convinced that in entering the race for success in the business world, and taking each step with deadly seriousness, she had no choice but to emerge a winner or a loser. There was nothing in between. The prospect of victory was exciting, and since she was among the most qualified entrants, it occupied her attention most of the time. The flip side, the possibility of defeat, was there too, but it was thought about very little—in realistic terms, not at all. But when the thought did cross her mind, it made her squirm. "If I do this for twenty years and I don't get anywhere," Barbara said at thirty-one, when she was down, "I'll see myself as a *zero*." Anne and Susan depicted their situation in equally graphic, all-or-nothing terms. As Anne put it at thirty-two, "I say to myself, 'Should this not work out for me, I can always get married,' but I'm not sure I believe that anymore." Susan, at thirty-one: "I like doing this—I don't want to do anything else." Then she added, "I wouldn't know *what* to do with myself if I weren't working. I'd go crazy. I really would, especially if the only other person in the house all day besides me was a two-year-old." Nightmares are revealing, much more so than ordinary dreams. Some things scare all of us from time to time in our sleep—for instance, disease or impending death. Other nightmares belong to a private hell we each create for ourselves, based on what we see as our own inadequacies. Outsiders who hear about such inner agonies may make light of them, but to us they remain all too real. So to protect ourselves from ridicule, we stay silent or make light of them ourselves.

The women we studied chose the former route and said next to nothing about the fate they felt would befall them if their most important dream in life failed to come true. Not too many more years could pass by before they would reluctantly have to admit that all their effort had been in vain. There were only two categories, success and failure, and they'd no longer be able to escape the realization that they belonged in the latter, not the former. Then their nightmares would emerge from the shadows and seize them.

What made the prospect of being turned into a cow the most widely shared private nightmare? Why was this insulting self-description added to the injury they would already have suffered as a result of losing in the race for success? Because it embodied all the public risks of the race. Cows are stupid; these women were bright. Cows are slow almost to the point of being inert; these women wanted to be fleet of foot, agile in body and mind. Cows stare at the world blankly, oblivious even to the threat of impending harm; these women wanted to see danger at a distance and react to it effectively, long before it threw them down. Cows are led around by a ring through their noses or rope around their necks; these women wanted to be independent and decide for themselves what to say and do. Last but by no means least, cows are for milking; the women were horrified at the thought of being used and discarded, and they wanted to be more, much more, than full udders for calves. As Barbara put it, "Even lionesses and mama bears look like they're having more fun with their cubs."

Particularly throughout the 1970s and early 1980s, women saw themselves as primarily in competition with men. Male versus female seemed the key issue. For those with partners, "Who wears the pants in the family?" often seemed the key question. However, a close look at the nightmares the women in our sample were having during these years indicates that a different and deeper dimension, of crucial importance to both sexes, was gnawing away at them: activity versus passivity. As these women subconsciously knew, it was their position on the active-passive spectrum that would decide their fate. If they could stay maximally productive day in and day out, all would be well. If not, the roof would cave in, and in their own eyes they might as well be cows.

Anyone who took their words at face value during these years would have concluded that the primary battle these women were waging was external and being fought with the opposite sex. A more careful analysis shows that the primary battle was internal and being fought with their own level of motivation, not with men.

In that sense, it resembled most their attempts at dieting. There, they tried to keep their weight low. Here, they tried to keep their level of drive high. In both cases, the real menace lay within.

THE RACE FOR SUCCESS

Having an inner enemy makes most people very uncomfortable. To relieve the tension, they seek an excuse to let themselves off the hook. It is always easier to point a finger at someone else as the source of the problem. In this case, that also helps them produce the *sustained* energy they consider essential. The best way to see why it does so is to think about something easier: motivating oneself to do well by thinking continually about how well one's enemy is doing.

The large majority of women we studied found the second way of spurring themselves on much more natural and easier, even liberating. Instead of being at war with themselves, they were now at war with someone else. They were no longer engaged in a lonely struggle; it had become social instead. They had (women) friends everywhere in their mutual battle against a common enemy (men).

Two serious flaws in this stance slowly emerged. First, not only were their male peers passing them by in the race for success, so were a considerable number of women. Susan, at thirty, was one of the first to notice that focusing only on the men who were outdistancing her at work provided at best a partial picture of what was really occurring there. Susan had taken up jogging in her late twenties and quickly became a devotee of the sport. While twenty-six-mile marathons seemed a bit much to her, and she participated in them only rarely, she entered many ten- and, especially, five-mile events. Her comments about the contests clearly telegraphed her view of the world. As she put it, smiling after a race, "I should only care about my own time, but I watch everyone else too. I don't care how many women beat me, I count the men *I* beat and the number who finish ahead of me."

She didn't know the exact number in either category, but in the race she had just run it was 255 women and 2,161 men. Not surprisingly, a few minutes later she said, "Did you know that women now run a marathon faster than men who once won *gold medals* in the Olympics for running at that speed?" It wasn't a question, it was a victory song without music, making her feel that she (and her allies) were waging a battle against men, and winning.

Although she tried hard to take the same attitude with her to work, she couldn't. When a coworker of hers was promoted and she wasn't, Susan was incensed. "I should've gotten that promotion, not her," she said, visibly upset. Six weeks before that, Robert, a man her age with whom she had been working for over a year, received a substantial raise for a demanding project he had successfully completed. Since Susan considered herself smarter and more capable than he was, that annoyed her as well. Now she was having trouble deciding what her current status was: "I'd like to say only one person has passed me by—Robert—but I can't get it out of my mind that *two* did."

Susan frequently commented that a unisex world, in which all vestiges of gender had been erased among humans, would be best. Yet one major disadvantage of such a world now struck her. "I would have to count *everyone* who beat me out," she said, not at all pleased at the thought, "not just the men who did."

Worse still, a unisex world would have deprived her of a key source of fuel, since men who had been declared enemies in order to serve the purpose would have vanished. She would have found other opponents, that much is certain, but the race for success would have been far lonelier. The self-serving nature of the quest would also become more apparent. She would no longer have been able to hide her personal ambitions by claiming that she was merely part of a movement.

Some readers may feel that it can't possibly make a difference how one motivates oneself to get a job done just so long as one gets it done. Maybe for a job it doesn't matter, but it certainly does for a career. The word "job" here means a specific task that takes a limited amount of time to complete; making a set of bookshelves, for example, or writing a term paper. However, a career is another matter entirely, and continuity is its central theme. Most white-collar professionals realize early on that their "work is never through," in the sense that one task flows into another, with any number of projects overlapping.

People who hope to have a career need a different kind of motivation than do those who are merely doing a job. Anger or anxiety may serve as useful fuel for those who have to accomplish a specific task—let's say, knock a door down with their shoulder (in the case of anger), or study hard for a final exam (in the case of anxiety). The key question is: How suitable are such intense emotions as fuel for one's daily efforts as part of a career? Sustained output may be crucial to success, but feelings as intense as anger and anxiety aren't likely to produce it. They are too exhausting, more likely to lead to fatigue than a steady stream of top quality work.

Unfortunately, the women in our sample who were using these intense emotions for motivational purposes didn't realize that. They did top quality work anyway, but at what cost? The main source they were tapping for fuel, anger in the form of outrage, was the most expensive of the lot. Predictably, they often found themselves frazzled and on edge. Nevertheless, the prospect of struggling as a solo against inner resistances seemed to them downright depressing when compared with struggling side by side with millions of other women *against* men. That felt more upbeat.

If they had adopted that approach merely to get a particular job done, the problem would probably not have become severe. Football players and boxers often tell interviewers that they hate their opponents prior to and during an event, in order to whip up a bit more determination, yet once the event is finished they turn off the animosity. Since they consciously activated it, it remains in their control. With the brief extra spurt no longer needed, the taxing emotions are forgotten.

Those who embark on a business career and unwittingly make use of the same self-propulsion techniques do themselves serious harm in the long run, and it is important to spell out precisely how. The animosity that adolescents use to free themselves from their parents is supposed to be merely a prelude to a less angry life of their own. The anger imposes distance and creates a space for them that, if all goes well, should end up being filled by their own interests. Thereafter, the *pull* exerted by these interests is supposed to prevent them from relying on a *push* away from their parents.

Adolescents may feel very original when they take each of their parents' beliefs and stand it on its head, yet truly original thought usually requires the rebelliousness of this phase of their lives first to lessen dramatically. Then, with less dust in the air and an inner peace needed to see the world clearly, they can come up with something that is uniquely their own. The point is so pivotal it is worth noting that teenagers who are tied to their parents evidence the dependence in one of two ways: if they feel comfortable with the bond, the youngsters mimic what they consider best about their parents' attitudes and actions. If the bond is resented, the youngsters try to mold themselves into the opposite of what they see at home. That doesn't mean they are any less bonded than the ones who copy openly. In fact, often the tie is stronger when there is rebellion visible than when outward compliance is seen, since in the latter case it may be accompanied by an inner distance and even indifference. Many children are remarkably skilled, every bit as much so as adults, at going through the motions.

Neither route, becoming a carbon copy or a photographic negative of one's parents, achieves the prerequisite state of independence for creative thought and behavior to take place. Oddly, most of the ambitious young women we studied tried to do both at the same time: copy and reject. How is that possible? Call it *hate-and-emulate*, and it can be seen in such everyday examples as people who view themselves as artists ("I must be, I despise technology") who nevertheless love to use the advanced technology of camera and film to make movies mocking the technical aspects of modern life. Similar are people who see themselves as revolutionaries ("I must be, I despise the business world"), yet who do their preaching in designer jeans and expensive boots.

Hate-and-emulate is even exciting as a strategy, since one is the sole judge of when to do which. Be that as it may, for all the attractions it offers, hate-and-emulate still represents a stunted stage of development, one that hampers both one's personal *and* professional growth. Let's look briefly at the occupational sphere first. The damage done here is that one feels compelled to copy what the most successful people are doing—without necessarily admiring what one is copying and, even worse, disliking the fact that one is indeed copying. Ellen, Anne, Barbara, and Susan from time to time found themselves imitating the successful women they knew at work or saw depicted in the movies. As Barbara put it, and she was one of the few who realized the extent to which she was doing it, "I model myself after Joan a lot because she's going places. Everyone already looks up to her and I think her star is going to rise much farther." That Barbara mimicked her actions didn't mean that she had to like her—or what she copied—and she voiced a number of bitingly sarcastic comments about Joan. Barbara was too old to comfortably copy openly.

What was being overlooked in Barbara's attempts to be either the same as or the reverse of Joan is that she was not developing a style of her own. Barbara possessed substantial theatrical abilities, so if someone had so much as hinted that she didn't have her own style, she'd have concocted something right then and there that looked appropriate. Consciously avoiding being Joan's duplicate or her opposite, Barbara would have synthesized a persona that no one would have identified with Joan.

The point is that that should have been happening automatically by this time (Barbara was thirty-two), and it wasn't. The most destructive thing about the chronic anger and irritability ambitious women such as Barbara were using to keep themselves motivated was that it was costing them the chance to develop their own individuality.

Exploring one's own tastes and sense of direction takes time. Also, coming to terms with the intricacies of one's own personality and the effect they have on one's professional and personal life can't be done when there is animosity constantly in the air. The anger and anxiety that Barbara was generating daily in order to stay in high gear forced her to spend most of her time comparing herself to everyone else around her. She kept trying to decide whether each was better or worse than she was in some important respect.

A CHANGE OF FACE

Why did that affect her personal life? The problem with copying someone at the office is that in most cases one doesn't know what that person is like after hours, and hence one is left without a script to follow in the evening. The frantic search for a leisure-time personality produces confusion. Trying to tie up with a partner, or make intimate contact with an existing one, becomes a tension-filled exercise in impromptu impersonation.

Switching focus for a moment from Barbara to all the professional women her age in our sample, two variations on the theme of mimicry emerged. The first was that, having worn the face all day in the office, they were reluctant to take it off at home even though it wasn't theirs. They were trying hard to make it real, so that it might do for them what it was doing for its original owner. If they shed it at the door and slipped into something more comfortable, they were afraid they wouldn't be able to put it on again convincingly the next morning. Better not to take it off in the first place.

The reason this did such damage to their personal lives is that, instead of taking their work home with them, they were taking their business posture home, which is far worse. It prevented them from relaxing. The face's real owner, who at times took home the work but never the posture, had no such trouble. It surprised and even stunned the mimics to hear their partners eventually refer to them as "cold," "hard" and "fake."

Others attempted to leave their managerial stance at the office but found nothing to take its place at home. Even if they were able to make the switch, they didn't want to bother. Work came first in their minds and was never taken for granted, whereas their partner was theirs and was supposed to love them regardless of how they acted. These women too were surprised that both they and their partners soon came to view the relationship as lifeless.

Many women in our study made no effort to repair the damage they saw developing, but that was much more likely to be the case when the women were in their twenties. Once they entered their thirties, a different attitude generally prevailed. They considered personal relationships less disposable, more difficult to establish with someone new. As Susan put in at thirty-three, "I'm too tired to keep on doing this: finding someone and getting to the point where we're functioning as a pair." Barbara, who was divorced at thirty-one, when her son was six, said, "It's a big investment—and tons of time down the drain—when things don't work out."

In spite of their very real desire to breathe new life into the relationships they formed in their thirties, little improvement was to be seen. Barbara remarried, and Susan and her boyfriend decided to live together. These pairings too soon wound down and became more of a drain than a relief. Both women felt that it must be something in the air, and that their unhappiness wasn't any of their own doing. Yet they were paying the price, more so now than before, for not having developed their interests and personalities. Success meant everything to them, more than they realized. Since they hadn't yet achieved it, they were spending too much time copying people who were undeniably successful, so they frequently came home irritable and out of sorts. Why? Because the very act of having to decide who and what to be, when they were supposed to be relaxing instead, was a continuing strain. Nevertheless, they felt that dressing for success meant wearing the right mood and manner even more than sporting the right clothes.

Barbara finally concluded, "There's just not enough of me to go

around." Her successful and happily married boss Joan, on the other
hand, said, "There aren't enough hours in the day for me to get everything done and I'm under a lot of pressure on the job." But it was precisely because of that pressure that she was so relieved at the end of the
day to come home and find something different but equally rewarding.

CHASING THE LIMELIGHT

In summary, there are events in couples' lives that take place independent of historical decades, and that arise instead as part of the stages of
psychosexual maturation. A complete picture of the pressures upon these
individuals, and the golden opportunities they see as being dangled before them, requires us to look at the combination of these internal and
external, local and national sets of forces.

In Chapter 3, we saw that women's preferences in men—and, to a
significantly lesser extent, men's preferences in women—usually undergo
an initial three-stage evolution. However, we also saw that, after 1960,
the nation offered first one group of young professionals, then another,
the opportunity to reach for the brass ring. At any given time, the number
of young men and women who were eligible to make the leap into the
national limelight was small. It still is. Making matters worse is that the
limelight keeps moving. Without their being aware of it, that happened
again just when Ellen, Anne, Barbara, and Susan were convinced that it
was finally time for them to stand up and take a bow.

The fact that the majority of women we studied never got to take
that bow irked them when they were part of a couple. But the key point
is that it irked them much more once they became single and work was
now the hook on which they had hung all their hopes for professional and
emotional satisfaction. Could they even have found a personal life with
this lethal combination of historical and psychological forces working
against them? We hoped so. But as we'll see in Part Three, when the
camera moves a little closer and many important aspects of their lives
stand out clearly, their pain and frustration only led to more of the same
instead of ultimate triumph over the obstacles to a satisfying personal life.

7

Women's Magazines

For centuries, it was common for intellectually gifted people to want to sit down and write their philosophy of life, hoping that others would find it a suitable guide for them. Unlike celebrity autobiographies now, which are devoid of philosophy and could hardly serve as a master plan for anyone else's conduct, many of these historic works were aimed primarily at affecting the way people lived or thought. Kant, Locke, Hume, Spinoza, Hegel, Spencer, Spengler, and Marx were setting forth what they saw as a system of truths to which they hoped people would adhere. Telling the story of their own private lives interested them little, if at all. Promulgating gospel, not gossip, was their main goal.

In the 1950s, when we first began our study, it puzzled us that so few people still yearned to write such works, and that even fewer adults wanted to read them. When we asked the members of our sample why, a typical reply was, "I waded through Marx and Locke in one of my history [or philosophy or political science] courses." The books seemed fitting to these recent graduates as assigned readings for a course, but they had no appetite for them at the time and certainly didn't think of them as useful guides to contemporary life. Nor would updating the works have changed their view, they insisted. We should add the authors of the Old and New Testaments to the list cited above, since the Bible, the original work of its kind that these later books were trying to supplement or supplant, had also ceased to be a guide for the daily behavior of the vast majority of people we studied.

THE ARROGANCE OF SPECIAL-INTEREST MAGAZINES

What, if anything, had taken the place of these books? Most of the more than 6,000 people we asked that question replied, "Nothing, we don't need them anymore." As far as they could see, they were totally on their own, picking up an idea here, another there, each person piecing together his or her own attitudes and lifestyle. At first glance, that seemed to be the case. If any outside influence was given grudging acknowledgment as having an effect on them, it was television. "How about movies?" we inquired. Their response was, "No, movies used to have that kind of influence, but now it's television."

If that answer was once valid, it has become less so with each passing year of our study. What has taken television's place is magazines. Not just any magazines; those that are called "special interest." The distinguishing characteristic of such publications is that they limit themselves to a particular product (for example, computers or cars), sex (women), or age group (children or retirees). The formula works. By the mid–1980s, magazine circulation figures had reached record levels, with 90% of all Americans reading them regularly, averaging eight each month. By contrast, the prime-time network audience, a hotly pursued group, had shrunk by nearly 20% in the previous nine years.

None of this was happening in a vacuum. The work world was becoming more specialized each year, with each field feeling the pressure. Especially after 1959, its members were expected to become expert in a smaller and smaller segment of the profession. Physicians and lawyers, for instance, complained bitterly that they not only had to pick a specialty, they subsequently had to repeat the process and select a *sub*specialty once they had been in practice for a few years. "I'm no longer an ophthalmologist," said one with an air of resignation, "I do [laser] surgery to reattach retinas, and that's *it*." A brilliant attorney commented, "I dreamed of doing it all; everything from corporate and matrimonial to negligence and tax law. But all I handle now is corporate. If I developed a reputation as someone who did a little of everything, I'd make *less* than I do now."

To professionals with specialized interests it made perfect sense that everywhere they turned were people and publications that were equally specialized. If they were looking for a car, they reached for a magazine devoted solely to the subject, figuring that if anyone knew what the best current offerings were, its writers would. As far as readers were concerned, the more specialized the magazine, the better. They reported themselves wary of single magazines that covered cars, trucks, vans, and motorcycles. "These really ought to be separate magazines," they stated firmly. Soon each was. The pressure on publications to become and stay specialized in an era of specialists came from advertisers as well as the public. They repeatedly told us they wanted to advertise a client's product in the magazine that was most successful at reaching people already interested in the product area. "For us," one ad agency executive stated, "it's all a matter of demographics: if a magazine has managed to gather the right readers, we're interested. Otherwise, we're not." Said another official, at the nation's largest ad agency, "The magazine's *focus* is as important to us as the demographics. It tells us if this is a suitable setting for our ad."

The end result of the combination of intense pressures was the creation of thousands of special-interest magazines. It was almost as if general-interest publications such as *Life* and *The Saturday Evening Post* had exploded, and each little piece had managed not only to survive, but to thrive. More than one million additional jobs were created, since the new publications had to be staffed with everyone from writers, editors and artists to production and salespeople.

The striking thing about these specialized publications was that they deliberately assumed that the rest of the world did not exist. They had no choice; finding a niche for themselves made it mandatory for them to look at the world with blinders on. Whether they liked it or not, they had to view everyday life in an extremely one-dimensional way. Each fragment was forced to present itself, arrogantly, as though it were the whole.

HELPING READERS—TO FAIL

With so many hundreds of varieties available even in a relatively small magazine store, readers gravitated only toward the ones in which they had a fair amount of interest to begin with. That was unfortunate, for it made it much more difficult for them to see the pattern each publication displayed. Its editorial content, the articles and commentary, *and* the advertisements it carried were all cut from the same mold. The one-dimensional view of life each magazine offered was spelled out by its articles and underlined by its advertisers. Both might as well have been shouting in unison, "This is all there is to life!"

Someone who picked up a copy of *PC*, *Byte*, or *PC World*, highly successful magazines in the mid–1980s devoted to personal computers, would see no advertisements for retirement villages. Old people don't exist in the magazine's pages. Nor do babies. Only people interested in computers—*so* interested that it's all right to think of them as "computer freaks"—are assumed to be real. Everything and everyone else has become fictional.

The same holds true in a copy of *Ski* or *Skiing*. Readers don't have any other hobbies or favorite sports—unless they are using such athletic activities to get in shape for skiing or because, alas, the ski season is over and there is no snow on the ground. Note well that the only people assumed in the magazine's pages to exist are "ski freaks." That makes it perfectly understandable, even acceptable, to have a sentence in a feature story read, "The snow was so beautiful that morning you wouldn't have waited for your wife even if it meant divorce."

Road and Track, *Car and Driver* and *Road Test* present the same narrow illusion. Could people who are reading these magazines really have any other interests? Maybe in a new radial-ply tire or electronic ignition, or perhaps in a new stereo for the dashboard. Other than things of this sort, they can't be interested in anything else, because *there isn't anything else.* The assumption is that the reader is a "car freak."

It should be clearer now, without going through dozens of additional examples which point to the same conclusion, what attitude each of these magazines takes toward its readers. Under the guise of, "My God, our readers are overflowing with *enthusiasm* for this subject," it presents a severely restricted view of the world in which nothing else exists, or if it does, it is insignificant by comparison. What is important to keep in mind is that this self-serving approach is essential if the magazine is to find a place on the shelf. The assumption that the reader is (or can be converted into) an enthusiast, a "freak" about the topic, is a key ingredient of each magazine's success.

"Where is the harm in any of this?" some readers may be wondering. "I'll bet that even subscribers don't take these magazines all that seriously. They're mainly for browsing and picking up tidbits of information." We agree, in most cases, and think the publications mentioned above do a good job of covering their limited terrain. However, the reason for analyzing this entire phenomenon, of which these magazines are merely examples, is to discover the hidden guidelines that shape their content. Also, and more to the point, it allows us to understand what happens to readers who unwittingly swallow the simplistic message being peddled. The most important question to ask about such people is: What do they lose when they come to believe that the pages of a particular special-interest magazine contain "all there is to life?"

Which brings us to women's magazines. It is impossible to understand the personal lives of women without paying some attention to these publications, because—unfortunately, for many women—these magazines *are* their personal lives. During evenings and weekends, and on the job as well, they form a constant reminder of the world each would like to live in if only she were able.

A great deal of abuse during the past fifteen years has been heaped upon magazines such as Vogue, Bazaar, Mademoiselle, Cosmopolitan, Family Circle, Women's Day, Glamour, and Ladies Home Journal by militant women's groups who complained that the picture of life usually presented was not only a fantasy—and an expensive one, at that—but it also made women "pawns of men." The lifestyle depicted depended on there being a man in the picture, sooner or later. *Ms*, and many others, adopted the opposite stance. No man was necessary, they insisted. It was better, it was more *effective*, to go it alone.

We saw in Chapters 1 and 2 that the time was ripe for this particular view to find a place on the rack. The proportion of working women was rising; the divorce rate was climbing rapidly; women were marrying later; the birth rate was declining; and a large number of women who said that they were interested in getting married told us repeatedly that they could find no eligible men. Under the circumstances, enshrining the idea of "going it alone" in the glossy pages and snappy prose of a monthly magazine seemed like a good one, since, if nothing else, it made a virtue of what was often an unavoidable reality.

Nevertheless, it is one thing for a hostile attitude to be comfortable to adopt during a given era and—quite another to assert that it will aid the people who adopt it to realize their aspirations. The claim that it will help them get where they want to go needs to be carefully scrutinized, since, as it turns out, the people so stating have no basis for the assertion. They make the claim anyway, and keep on making it, because of commercial necessity: it gives their magazine the uniqueness it must have if it's to distinguish itself from numerous competitors. Although loyal readers are always distressed to hear it, a magazine is a business enterprise, not a scientific one, and it isn't about to do anything that might decrease its circulation. The claim that it is helping its readers will therefore be asserted endlessly, whether it is true or false.

FEELING LIBERATED

Each special-interest magazine, then, tries very hard to create the illusion that there is nothing else in life except the topic which it covers. It does this not because it wants to, but because it has to. This constricted approach is precisely what allows it to find a place on the magazine rack.

To further the illusion, it pretends that its readers aren't merely interested in the subject, but that they are fanatics who think about nothing else. Their monomaniacal involvement with the topic is seen as deriving from a twenty-four-hour-a-day fascination with and enthusiasm about it. The word "freak" is used approvingly to describe the positive emotions that pour out of such people for the subject.

Since humans are a social breed, common interests readily bring them together. It is hardly surprising that people who are wild about a subject often start or join car clubs, user groups (in the case of computer hardware and software), and ski clubs. Revealingly, those who do, no matter how shy they may be in other settings, feel emboldened to insist that the magazine give some space (usually in the letters column or the back pages) to club activities. Some threaten to cancel their subscriptions if such space isn't granted, at least occasionally. Without having examined the logic of it all, they know that they are acting well within their rights. As "assumed maniacs about the subject," they sense that it is acceptable to demand space for social aspects as well as the purely literary and photographic form into which the whole subject is converted in each month's issue.

Women's magazines fit the general pattern and fall into two categories. Magazines in the first category concentrate on positive emotions— love, affection, interest, and enthusiasm. Their readers are "fashion and home decorating freaks." The second category of magazines concentrates on negative emotions, and keeps its readers anxious and, even more, angry. Just as skiers, runners and computer owners are depicted by their respective special-interest magazines as being constantly enthusiastic, women's magazines that have adopted a hostile stand toward men assume their readers are constantly angry at men. It is the constant excitement of the skier stood on its head to produce an allegedly endless stream of hatred and resentment.

Many of the women in our sample at one time or another adopted this severely constricting view, and came to think of it as "all there is to life." It had the expected effect. Women who were devoted readers of these magazines and also developed an interest in men, told us that at times they felt apologetic for deviating from the foaming-at-the-mouth picture of themselves portrayed in the magazine. Since a magazine that concentrated on whipping up negative emotions could not call its readers freaks, it had to find a different name for the same thing. It called them feminists.

When we switch our focus from the magazines themselves to the behavior of people reading them, something fascinating emerges. Some people who stumble upon a particular special-interest magazine start to believe that it, and others like it in the field, portray "all there is" to reality, and they become evangelistic. As outside observers, we know that they are seeing the world in a very narrow way. They, on the other hand, begin to act as if they are Columbus discovering America, or Archimedes shouting "Eureka!" after coming up with a major scientific breakthrough. Apparently, everyday life in all its glory is difficult for anyone to grasp any longer; hence there is something profoundly pleasing about having it suddenly rendered simple.

There is a paradox here of enormous importance. People who become lost in the world presented in the pages of a special-interest magazine experience a sizable outpouring of energy. Previously, they felt themselves being pulled in dozens of different directions. They had a host of daily responsibilities and chores to attend to, most of which seemed routine, unproductive, and a little annoying—everything from paying rent, taxes, and the phone bill to going to the dentist and dry cleaner, commuting to and from work, and shopping for food. Hardly uplifting activities. However, having discovered how satisfying the world of, say, running, skiing or computers can be, everything else vanishes. Rendered secondary, relegated to marginal significance, all these petty aspects of life are swept away while one focuses on the only thing that matters.

Most people find the magazine to be at least as important as participating in the activity, because the activity frequently looks and feels even better as depicted on nice, clear pages than it does in reality. Unfortunately, one's favorite activity too has its share of routine, unproductive, and mildly annoying details, as any running, skiing, or computer enthusiast knows. The magazine neatly sweeps away these messy or inconvenient aspects—bruises, reluctances, and frustrations—and presents the simplified world of one's special interest in a still more satisfying simple manner. The paradox that emerges from studying how people react to special-interest magazines is this: they feel *liberated* only when they have actually had their world *reduced* to a mere sliver of what it formerly was.

Call it runner's, skier's, or women's liberation; the feeling depends on discarding most of everyday life. Only an extremely pinched view of the world will produce it. In spite of the many differences between magazines that cater to positive versus negative emotions, this aspect—the readers' behavior—is something they have in common initially.

Once again, a skeptic might inquire, "Where is the harm in any of this? If people feel excited and energized by adopting a highly constricted view of life, why not let them enjoy it? Maybe it helps them in the long run."

We hoped it would, and in the beginning, at least, we thought it did. Seeing them energized instead of lethargic clearly seemed a plus. Nevertheless, since special-interest magazines were mushrooming during an era of highly specialized professions, the real test of how helpful or harmful the resulting self-constriction was would be applied on the job. Did working women find themselves aided or hindered by adopting so narrow a focus for years on end—especially when the activity that formed the basis for the magazine was far removed from their profession? In some fields, where the reading and the women's profession were closely allied, the answer was that its members found the pinched approach to life quite helpful.

A biochemist in our sample who believed that nothing in the universe mattered except her research on enzymes was able to concentrate morning, noon, and night on her work. Scientific journals, the ultimate special-interest publications (so specialized, indeed, that other people in the field, but not in the subspecialty, are usually unable to understand them), were her only reading. Even newspapers were dismissed as "irrelevant." A friend of hers, a woman who worked nine-to-five in the same subspecialty and then happily went home to her husband and two children seemed less likely to become outstanding in the field. In science, total immersion has shown itself for decades to be worthwhile for the profession, if not the professional. Advances have often come at the expense of the innovator's personal life.

However, very few of the women we studied (37 out of 3,466) were doing anything resembling scientific research as a livelihood, and that number decreased as the decades passed, just as it did for the men in our sample. The vast majority were, or soon wound up, in the business world, and they very much wanted a satisfying personal life in addition to a successful career. Specialization proved necessary in this arena as well, but since business inevitably involves dealing with people rather than test tubes and microscopes there was a limit to how specialized anyone could become—and remain—and still go on to become a success. Other skills, social in nature, were just as essential. In part that was so precisely because of the bumper crop of specialists with whom those moving into top slots had to learn how to deal.

It took us a while to see which women, if any, were being harmed by an extremely narrow approach, and why. Those who were the most adversely affected were women who adopted a highly constricted view *filled with hostile feelings*. They found their work situations steadily deteriorating. The cause was obvious. They were not expanding their social skills, their ability to work with men and women, perhaps none of whom they liked. Thanks to the powerful encouragement they received during the 1970s and early 1980s, they had a sizable chip on their shoulders regarding men; and, as it turned out, they weren't all that friendly toward women at work, either. Their chronic hostility could not be switched on and off quickly enough to prevent numerous spillovers. These women's coworkers, both male and female, considered them unpredictable and unpleasant to be around. Their career progress slowed and, in many cases, was reversed.

"AT LEAST MY CAREER WILL FLOWER"

To some women, that was a shock from which they still haven't recovered. To others, it was an outcome for which they had secretly hoped. They had fallen into the pages of a special-interest magazine, the way Alice fell into Wonderland, and they really didn't want to come back. They liked the new world they had discovered. Things happened almost automatically after that. Workers who wouldn't deliberately have gotten up, walked into their boss' office and said, "I'm quitting so I can go skiing [or running] all day, every day," achieved the same goal in a less direct manner. Their jobs became secondary in their minds, and soon the attitude was reflected in the way they did their work. The skiers to whom that happened became ski bums; the runners who became true enthusiasts started structuring their day around their running, not their work. In fact, their work had become little more than a nuisance, an impediment to immersing themselves in the new special-interest world they saw portrayed so appealingly in the pages of the magazine.

The important point here is that women who adopted the chronically hostile stance of women's magazines in the negative category did *not* think they had suddenly relegated work to a secondary position in their lives. They would have contended that the sense of outrage and indignation fostered by the magazine was adding to, not subtracting from, their commitment to their work. They were wrong. Women who came to think of themselves as feminists were every bit as detached from their everyday profession as were jogging and computer freaks. Feminists, in fact, were more remote, since their coworkers had stepped away from them (consciously) at the same time that they stepped away from their coworkers (subconsciously). The distance that resulted from these actions taking place almost simultaneously was substantial. A wall had come down and separated these workers from their work.

For one thing, their outside interests were all they wanted to talk about now. In our regular interviews with them, they kept bringing the conversation back to the flashy new model ski on the market, or a snazzy new microcomputer, or yet another insult from male chauvinists. They could have been monomaniacally involved with their new special interest even if there had been no special-interest magazine around. But this way, with the magazine waiting for them at home or tucked away neatly in their attache case, their alternative world had even more reality. "It isn't just in my mind," many said when they needed a bit of reassurance.

It was clear to everyone but the people caught up in a special interest that their connection to work had changed. The sense of distance these people were unwittingly imposing between themselves and their coworkers quietly eroded their chances for success. Why couldn't they see it? They thought they had actually drawn closer to their coworkers. They hadn't, but they convinced themselves they had because they'd written off their superiors and found at least one other person who shared their special interest. Computer freaks located someone else who owned a microcomputer, preferably of the same brand, while skiing or jogging freaks found someone else at the firm who knew about Rossignols or Adidas and places where the moguls were high or the running fun.

In some measure, every worker does this. Common interests help hold friendships together. However, we aren't talking about people who did this in a small way. We are focusing upon those who swallowed the message of a special-interest magazine hook, line and sinker, even if the emergence of the interest preceded their seizing upon the magazine (which was usually the case). We are particularly interested in seeing what happened to workers who seized upon a women's magazine in the negative category—a publication whose main goal was to make its readers continually feel resentful and outraged. Common interests didn't hold these readers together (their anger would quickly have forced them apart); only common enemies could.

The bond all these people had previously had with their work suffered significantly in the process. The key point is that hobbyists often knew that. They were aware that they'd rather spend their time doing something else. Feminists, who were usually more detached from their work, did not know it. They truly believed that their hostile stance and nonexistent personal life would help rather than hinder their rise. They would have been stunned to find that the women who realized that they were competing against other women, as well as men, did best. These individuals put their own *work-related* interests first, and were aware that, as one of the most successful women in our sample put it, "Laboring for the women's movement is a detour, a distraction, from what I want to accomplish." Far from feeling guilty about letting her "sisters" down, she recognized that huge differences exist among women. In her words, "They're not all the same, you know. The talented and hard-working ones will make it. The others only *think* they deserve to."

There is a painful irony here. Women who got caught up in the mentality of the time, and liked all the animosity being aimed at men during the 1970s and early 1980s, at first felt very "with it." The fact that that made it impossible for them to have stable, much less satisfying, personal lives seems to have escaped their notice. Those who did notice the connection often said, "So what, at least my career will flower." But once their hostility solidified and became chronic, thanks to what they were reading in issue after issue of the special-interest women's magazines in the negative category, their relationship with their work also deteriorated. Then they really had something to rail about. If they thought they were being held back before, now they felt doubly so. What they couldn't see is how far removed they had become from a fondness for the nuts and bolts of their jobs and from wanting to win the approval of their superiors. They had a new focus, much simpler and more appealing than the old one, and it neatly guaranteed that they would do less well than their peers. It was a distressing, self-fulfilling prophecy: A woman who previously blamed men for the slow pace of her career progress wound up, years later, with even more frustration and failure to blame them for.

What disconnected these women from their work, and hence set in motion so damaging a sequence of events? Aiming animosity at the men they saw daily became as much of a consuming hobby for them as running and computers were for others. They had no intention of cooperating fully with the men they worked with and resented even being asked by them to do anything. Not one stated that she "hated all men," and they always denied it whenever a friend accused them of harboring that view. Instead, they hated men one at a time, but the result was the same.

Complaints were voiced about every man with whom they worked or became even moderately familiar; none could pass muster. To protect themselves from criticism for issuing a steady stream of harsh comments, these women claimed to be waiting and yearning for Mr. Right, a man so successful and secure within himself that he wouldn't find an allegedly career-obsessed woman a threat. Mr. Right never appeared. Was it really her career he found a threat, as she'd like to have believed, or was it her chronic hostility? There was a fascinating reason why these women kept misinterpreting how men were reacting to them. *Women who resented men seemed more obsessed with their careers, yet were actually less involved with their work.* They were on the outside of it, looking in.

TURNING A HOBBY INTO A PROFESSION

The conviction that one is right and everyone else wrong has a power all its own. Without our being aware of it, we may find ourselves pushed by the logic of a stand we have taken into a position that is not in our best interests. Not wanting to appear inconsistent, we end up taking the next step, even if we are reluctant.

The skiers, runners, and computer freaks in our sample often found their lives changing inexorably. Having burned their bridges behind them, thanks to their evident loss of interest in their work, they had no alternative but to take one more step, and then another, down the road on which they were traveling. The general conclusion that emerged from monitoring hundreds of such examples is the following: *People who become caught up in what was once a hobby may have no choice but to try and turn it into a profession.*

For the computer freaks we studied that rarely led to harm, and it made millionaires of a handful. Jogging and ski freaks who made a similar switch to full-time involvement in what was once their hobby found their incomes taking a beating. They had expected that to happen, and at least they had the satisfaction of doing precisely what they wanted. They were on their own, behaving as they pleased—no small boost to their pride, even though it stunted their personal growth.

Not many of the chronically hostile women in our sample switched to working full time for women's causes (only 18 out of 3,466 did), and in many ways that is too bad. For they too had burned their bridges behind them, without being aware of it, yet had little interest in joining any organization, women's or otherwise. They occupied a "no-man's land," one that wasn't so wonderful for women either.

The limbo in which they found themselves produced neither the high incomes computer freaks often found nor the psychic satisfactions that runners and skiers who gave their hobby top priority usually experienced. What blinded these women to the unproductive situation they were in was that, as we've seen, an outpouring of energy typically results when one's world is voluntarily reduced to the dimensions of a special-interest magazine. New readers frequently become exhilarated and evangelistic. These women also did, and it made them feel they had discovered a new region to inhabit.

Enthusiasm is contagious, as computer and ski freaks soon recognized, and the same thing applies to magazines that are purveyors of negative emotions. Outrage and indignation are contagious too, especially when the social climate is right, and it made these women think they had plenty of company. But the outrage they were experiencing on a daily basis was experienced only occasionally by those who concentrated on their work first and foremost. Women who became evangelistic about the severely restricted, resentful view of the world they had just adopted didn't have nearly the number of compatriots they thought. When all is said and done, by unwittingly taking themselves out of the race they were merely making it easier for their female peers to beat them out in the competition for the top positions and professional eminence for which both were striving.

Men who served in Vietnam in the 1960s learned the bitter lesson that solders who fight in a popular war come home heroes, while those who fight in an unpopular one come home invisible. They don't have to wait until they grow old and die before they fade away and are forgotten. Women in the 1970s had a parallel experience on our own shores. Many imagined themselves to be fighting bravely for women's rights while holding full-time jobs in the business world. Thanks to the ease with which people can convince themselves they are right by limiting the amount of information they look at or hear, the women convinced themselves that what they were doing was productive and that "every woman is standing together with me, shoulder to shoulder."

When the 1980s arrived, these women came to the same dismaying realization that returning Vietnam veterans had a decade before. Most of their "sisters" never even entered limbo land, much less joined militant women's groups. They devoted themselves to their careers and families instead and were now miles ahead of warriors who had been keeping themselves in an outraged state either part time or full time.

One key that allowed the most successful women we studied to move ahead was readily switching from one magazine to another, not treating any as a serialized bible. That stopped them from becoming permanently lost in the overly simplistic world each magazine conveyed. Culling their information and insights from a wide variety of sources turned out to be the best way for these women to guarantee their freedom. For two centuries, the diversity that resulted from a free press in America prevented people from falling for any one party line.

In short, those who feel that it is worthwhile to make sacrifices for a cause should do so. Nothing written here is intended to diminish in any way their willingness to give their lives, if need be, for something in which they strongly believe. Our point is that the vast majority of women we studied were never offered such a choice. No one asked them, "Are you willing to reduce substantially your chances of career success and the possibility of having a satisfying marriage in return for joining a militant women's group?"

Had they been offered that choice, some undoubtedly would have decided it was indeed worth it. However, the overwhelming majority made it clear to us that they expected *nothing but benefits* from being "in favor of women's causes and doing something about them." There was no warning label on magazines that were devoted to whipping up outrage and resentment stating that "The attitudes fostered by this magazine will jeopardize your job performance and your marriage." The readers viewed themselves as subscribers, not soldiers. They were convinced that the stance they were strongly being encouraged to take would *help* them, at least in their careers, rather than merely guarantee the magazine's existence. It did no such thing.

PART THREE

Regular interviews with women who were twenty-five to forty and single for any length of time between 1970 and 1985 produced a perplexing result. The majority said they had few dates and fewer partners, and further claimed that worthwhile men were hard to find. Comments about the shortage of attractive and available men were frequently heard, and the speakers seemed sincere. However, the fact remains that these women did have dates, "one-night stands," long-term lovers, and live-in boyfriends during the fifteen years under discussion. In the majority of cases, they even found someone they wanted to marry—and did. For many it was their second marriage.

The disparity between their words and behavior was sizable and striking. On the one hand, their remarks made it appear as though they had no partners at all, yet a succession of partners rolled through their lives—most for a brief time, others for an extended period. The men may not have been all that they'd hoped for, and were usually substantially less. But they were indeed there. Who the men were, and what kinds of relationships the women formed with them, are important questions, particularly when the pairing did not result in a trip to the altar. Four major categories emerged, and it is revealing to examine each one separately. For not only did these relationships occupy a considerable amount of time and energy without making the women feel fulfilled, but they also prevented them from becoming involved with a partner whom they'd have found more to their liking.

Gresham's Law in economics states, in essence, that "bad money drives out good." That is, if people have a choice of using two currencies, both with the same dollar amount per unit (for instance, a $100 bill and a $100 gold coin), they hoard the one with the higher intrinsic worth and circulate the other. In that sense, paper drives gold out of circulation. Odd as it may sound at first, a similar principle operates in the love lives of single women between the ages of twenty-five and forty. Unfortunately, it produces the reverse result. The men they tied up with but whom they viewed as substandard turned out to be "paper" partners who ended up driving away those who were more analogous to gold.

The women we studied simply didn't have time for both, and since they were caught up in the relationship, they unwittingly stopped looking for something better. Even when it crossed their paths, they were oblivious to the possibilities inherent in the situation—at least while they were still involved with a partner whom they later acknowledged was substandard.

Our goal in the next four chapters is to understand not only why these inherently troubled relationships formed in the first place, but also why they endured. Their longevity was a real mystery, not only to professional observers but to well-meaning amateurs as well. The vast majority of women we will be discussing were told by close friends, sometimes harshly, to "dump the bum," yet such advice consistently fell on deaf ears. A flood of magazine articles and popular books offered similar advice that was equally ignored. As we'll soon see, there was good reason for the deafness. The advice was superficial and, in most cases, missed the point entirely. Nevertheless, this is too important a topic to brush aside, since such relationships, which are becoming more common, squandered what many of these women now view as their best years.

8

Fran: Love 'em and Leave 'em

It is very easy for a cynical observer to say about any man or woman who has had hundreds of sexual partners that that must have been the person's intention all along. Since a number that high could hardly have been reached by accident, the cynic immediately shifts attention to the other end of the spectrum and assumes that it was deliberate, all part of a planned campaign from the start. "He's got something to prove," is a typical judgment one hears, or, "She's nothing but a nympho."

The labels sometimes turn out to be valid. There are indeed men and women in our sample with something to prove, and they have been using sex for that purpose above all for decades. However, they represent less than 4% of the total. A much larger proportion who have run up sizable numbers of sexual partners aren't out to prove anything—and ironically, they would have outdistanced the male and female Don Juans by a considerable margin, had a sexual marathon been going on.

Monitoring such individuals on a regular basis, starting in their teenage years, allows one to see an entirely different explanation for their game of musical beds. Each relationship *seems* very real in the beginning, at least to them. Outsiders may snicker and call the feelings mere self-delusion, yet to the person who has them they are as palpable as a piece of furniture. The central question, then, shouldn't be whether the passionate feelings are present. They are. The critical issue is how these emotions, which seem so exaggerated and empty to outside observers, come to seem so real *time after time* to the person experiencing them.

The reason they do, as we'll see throughout the next few chapters, involves the concept of *inventorying*. A woman who unwittingly walks around at work with a chip on her shoulder toward men, as a way of keeping herself motivated, is not thereby freed of her desire to be involved with a man. The desire is merely masked. Needs that aren't satisfied don't vanish, they accumulate. And it is these pent-up desires, carried as it were in inventory, that finally affect the way a woman reacts to the men she meets and becomes interested in.

How do the desires influence her responses to these men? The growing backlog of her needs causes her to overreact romantically to the first even moderately acceptable partner she meets. Rather than chocolate or cookies, the binge this time involves love and lust, but the damage done is much worse. Dieting is a snap by comparison with trying to forget an involvement that, in retrospect, one realizes was hollow and hopeless. And the time the relationship and its aftermath take are lost forever.

The intense, unfulfilled needs she has in inventory blind her to the self-interest that would—and should—normally be there during the tentative early stages of intimacy. Instead of a period of testing and exploring, while she gets to know and assess her partner, the dam breaks, forcing her to rush the process. Excessively hungry for contact at any cost, she is overly trusting, leaving herself wide open to the possibility of being hurt.

Somehow sensing the danger, many successful women try to prevent the process from ever beginning. In this chapter we will see the most important strategies they employ to hold themselves in check. Unfortunately, this only magnifies the inventorying process. One popular technique, the Ostrich Strategy, is for them to bury themselves in their work. Ask about their personal lives and they are likely to reply, "I don't have time for one." Women using this approach don't even have to dine alone, since they can usually arrange dinner dates with coworkers, business associates or female friends.

A BRIEF BUT INTENSE AFFAIR

It isn't fair to begin the story of Fran Weber during her thirty-eighth year. By then, she had slept with enough men to be an easy target for anyone who wanted to describe her as sex-starved. She was nothing of the kind. The men with whom she had had intercourse exhausted her interest in them after only a few minutes in bed, often well before she and her partner had even removed all their clothes. And when the act did take place, little changed; she was repeatedly left unsatisfied. "Most men are lousy lovers," she said in a matter-of-fact tone of voice. "They are looking for a quick climax, not to do something for the woman they're with. Or else they try too damned hard to please you in bed, in which case you feel you *have* to come, just as a way of saying 'thank you.'"

Fran voiced comments similar to these sufficiently often, and to enough different people, for them to think of her as worldly wise. Her own view was that she had barely begun to see the world of affectionate and erotic feelings because the right man hadn't yet been in her arms. As she put it, two weeks after her thirty-eighth birthday, "I've had a lot of sex, with a lot of different guys, but it was difficult to tell them apart. The same dull routine was there each time. They'd take me to dinner, get me back to my apartment, sit with me on the couch and kiss for a few minutes—and then we'd head for the bedroom. I hope it was ecstasy for them. For me, it was only mildly amusing."

Some of the pairings lasted for a night or a weekend, others longer. But few lasted for years. If they did, Fran commented between tense puffs on her cigarette, "they were just taking a long time to die." To see how Fran found her way to such a jaded view of love and life, we need to turn the clock back twenty years. At eighteen, Fran was another story altogether.

An English major in college, Fran knew she wanted to write. For some of the women in her class the idea was appealing in the abstract—being a writer combined artistic and intellectual features, was dirt-free, and had prestige. To Fran it meant something more private and organic. She envisioned her involvement with writing to be steamy and agonizing, with results that would be special and profoundly personal. The inner struggle would allow her to dredge from her inner depths experiences and emotions she was certain others would want to read about.

That was the ideal, as she herself would have spelled it out any time between the ages of eighteen and twenty-two. But her parents weren't rich and she wasn't prepared to live in poverty while trying to write. So, after graduation, she took a job in the marketing department of a consumer goods company. Interestingly, it was her literary skills that her employer liked most. Her supervisor, now at another firm, told us that her way with words got her the position, even though many of the other applicants had taken more courses in the subject area. She was given one of the company's products, a skin care lotion, and asked to write a few paragraphs about it as part of the interview. Fran later said it felt as though she were applying for a job at an ad agency, but she went along good-naturedly and got the job.

Fran realized that the wardrobe of penny loafers and jeans that got her through college wouldn't do in the work world but that the fashionable clothes featured by *Vogue* and *Bazaar* weren't quite her. She settled on dressing her 5'6" frame in turtlenecks and pleated skirts in muted colors that blended with her sandy hair. "I'm not into jewelry at all," she told us at twenty-four, "though my mother offered me some of her 'treasures.' I do wish I was better with makeup." As it was, she didn't wear much of it and didn't need to.

When she spoke seriously, wanting to be believed, Fran would lower her head slightly and look *up* at the person to whom she was speaking. It was something she did subconsciously, and which conveyed a picture of wide-eyed innocence, as though she were simply too naive to ever tell a lie. Although her face and body changed considerably during the next twenty years, this habit remained unchanged.

The first boyfriend of Fran's who had a major impact on her feelings was Walter Sloane, whom Fran met through a friend in her junior year of college. There had been other men in her life before Walt, and she had had sex with one of them when she was sixteen, yet she was aware that none had "consumed" her the way she had so often read about in novels or seen in films. This one did. "It sounds self-centered," Fran said at twenty, as the realization dawned on her, "but this is the only man I've known whose name floats across my mind all through the day. The others never mattered enough to me, I guess, for that to happen. I could take them or leave them."

Walt and Fran looked like a couple when they were together. Four inches taller than Fran, with dark hair, an expressive face, and a slightly stocky build, Walt could usually be seen in animated conversation with Fran, whether the two were sitting or walking. Many people in love almost automatically slip into speaking in subdued tones with their partners. This pair, though no less in love, would have found that artificial. When Walt was on his own he played volleyball or swam. While not much of an athlete, he preferred a combination of exercise and conversation to merely sitting around and talking.

The first hint we had that this relationship might not last a lifetime came approximately four months after it began. Fran and Walt each had a circle of friends prior to pairing up, but once the two found each other, the rest of the world might as well have vanished. Initially, such behavior is par for the course, and none of their companions protested. After a period during which the couple cements their union it is typical for them to turn to the outside world once again, seeking contact with friends, though to a lesser extent than before and perhaps with new ones altogether.

Sparks started flying as these two began bringing old friends into the picture. Walt wasn't too fond of Fran's sidekicks, but he found them bearable. Fran, on the other hand, considered Walt's cronies objectionable on every count. For one thing, they were loud. For another, they drank beer, which Fran viewed as irretrievably lower class. "I don't want to associate with that sort of people," Fran told him irritably. Walt replied, "They aren't *that* sort of people."

Perhaps an outsider could have explained to Fran that what she was seeing was basically an affectation by college men who would doubtless go on to bigger and better things once school was through. Indeed, the friend of Walt's whom Fran was most critical of is now a respected New York physician. Another, about whom Fran had only slightly less harsh things to say, is currently vice president of an electronics firm in the Southwest. At the time Fran would never have believed it, even if someone had suggested such an outcome (at that stage, all it could have been was a hypothesis, since she was convinced that the whole group, except for Walt, would wind up unemployed or in jail for repeatedly disturbing the peace).

The basic elements of this incident formed a pattern that would recur over the years. It was common for Fran to make up her mind and then stick with her conclusion regardless of subsequent information that contradicted it. "I don't like those jerks," she told Walt, "and that's all there is to it." It was clear to Walt that Fran wouldn't budge, but just when we thought he might, he decided to become equally stubborn. "I'm going to the auto show—with them," he told her, "and you're welcome to come." She wouldn't.

With this molehill rapidly turning into a mountain, it was inevitable that other similar incidents would start cropping up regularly (one was connected with where to study together in the library), and it soon became clear that this was a tug-of-war neither side was going to win. Soon they stopped sleeping together, and when Fran found herself attracted to a classmate named Lenny, she started seeing him instead. News travels fast on campus, and although Walt heard about it within days, he never responded. That he could shut her out so quickly, and not even call, puzzled and offended Fran.

"Did I mean so *little* to him?" she asked rhetorically, not knowing whether to cry or get mad. "Poof, just like that, I'm not in his life anymore." That wasn't exactly the way it happened, and Fran's slide into the role of victim didn't yet have the practiced ease it would twenty years later. The sense of shock was real, and to this day she wonders what Walt's thoughts were in the final days. She never called to find out. When the term ended a few weeks later, he graduated with a degree in economics and got a job at an oil company. The relationship had lasted seven intense months.

INEXHAUSTIBLE PARTNERS

During Fran's senior year she had a number of partners, but none serious enough to last more than a few weeks. That was also the case during her first year on the job, when she seemed to have other things on her mind. Fran liked her work, but since it was still so new to her and wasn't what she had imagined she'd end up doing for a living, she hadn't yet made it her own. To some extent, she was still on the outside looking in at herself and her on-the-job activities. That would apply to the next few years as well, though less so with each succeeding year.

During her second year at work she was introduced to Ron Harper, who was walking with a friend of hers. Fran was very interested in him on the basis of the ten minutes or so that the three spent chatting. She did nothing about it, however, as she assumed that her friend and Ron, who were on their way to lunch together, were a couple. They weren't, but she didn't learn that until some weeks later because at the time she didn't want her interest to show by asking too many questions.

During a subsequent encounter with her friend, Fran learned that the two were just old acquaintances. "Old lovers?" Fran asked in her openly inquisitive manner. "Or old acquaintances?" The reply she got to her question thrilled her: "Oh, Fran, cut it out. He used to live in my building, that's all." Fran then volunteered that she found him appealing. "He's very good looking," she said excitedly. Her friend responded with, "He liked you too." That was all Fran needed to hear. Wasting no time she added, "God, I wish he'd call me."

Ron did, and the relationship matured quickly. They didn't end their first evening together in bed, but as Fran said about their second date a week later, "I could hardly wait for the dumb movie to end. I wanted to get home, get our clothes off and have him next to me all night." That night turned into a weekend.

The same inclination to make instant decisions that helped sink Fran's relationship with Walt helped start the relationship with Ron. The men and women she liked, she liked very much, and she often referred to them as "my favorite people." Those she disliked, she disliked greatly; there didn't seem to be many slots in between. Her shoot-first-and-ask-questions-later style, where opinions were concerned, was classified by some coworkers (now at other firms) in a positive light: "She is very quick, very bright," and, "Fran immediately grasps whatever you're telling her." Others who had worked with her felt exactly the reverse. One said, "It never takes her more than ten seconds to make up her mind—even if she would need fifteen minutes to hear all the facts."

There could be no doubt about the vigor and tenacity with which Fran went after something she wanted. She jogged, and even ran in a marathon, but emotionally she was a sprinter. (That, we believe, is why she pushed herself to run long distances; it was a subconscious attempt to use physical means to modify a fundamental aspect of her personality.) Fran would throw every bit of herself into the contest, ignoring other tasks that needed to be done, hoping for results before she had exhausted her supply of energy.

The relationship with Ron blossomed quickly not only as a result of

Fran's approach, but also because of the similarity of their interests. During the next eleven months they became constant companions and seemed to have less trouble than most couples at this stage finding things to do together that they truly enjoyed. The transition from college to work had stripped both of their circle of school friends, but, unlike the case with Walt, this never became a thorny issue with Ron. Nevertheless, it was revealing to see how mild her reactions were to those of Ron's friends that she did meet, a striking contrast to her behavior only three years before.

It took us a while to realize that the key, in these two instances and others to come, had to do with how much of a claim the friends were making on each man. Ron's made almost none, nor could they; they were basically neighbors or business associates, past or present. Fran's intense feeling of possessiveness had no real opposition. Walt, on the other hand, seemed so embedded in his social circle, it was hardly surprising that Fran was constantly left wondering how much, if any, of him was available to her.

A little over a year after they met, they married. Ron, at twenty-six, two years older than Fran, worked for a commercial real estate firm as a salesman and very much looked the part. He was tall and thin, with an easy smile and straight brown hair, usually (though not always) kept short. His oval face was highlighted by brown eyes, and he expressed emotion almost as much with his eyebrows as with his mouth. Dark blue suits were his favorite, and he had four of them. A year into their marriage, with Fran settling further into her work and Ron's earnings beginning to climb, they looked like the perfect couple: attractive, happy, and doing well in their careers.

We didn't know it at the time, but beneath this pleasant exterior trouble was developing. By the third year of their marriage, Ron and Fran had been together for many thousands of hours and had discussed nearly every topic imaginable. For the good couples we studied, that never became a problem because new events were always occurring, and these pairs rarely seemed to run out of things to say, at least to one another. Indeed, for them conversation was usually just an excuse for contact, so the specific sentences used didn't matter all that much.

They did to Fran. From her late teen years on, she had found small talk difficult, which we took to be a consequence of her above-average intelligence and much-above-average impatience. As she put it at age twenty-two, "I want to *learn* something from every conversation I have." That was an admirable desire in its own way, but it clearly contained the potential for serious problems. Not every conversation can be thought-provoking.

When she and Ron became a pair, this desire seemed to have vanished. She neither spoke about it again nor acted upon it. "Fran is mellowing," we wrote, after she and Ron had been seeing one another steadily for eight months. We might as well have written, "The *Titanic* is unsinkable," because after Fran had been married to Ron for a little over two years the desire was back, stronger than ever. Apparently, it had merely been shoved aside temporarily by the cloud of affection that swirled around these two, making then interested primarily in one another.

Once it lifted, Fran again was determined to walk away with something concrete from each conversation. That is all but impossible to do with one's mate; this unrealistic expectation stood almost no chance of being fulfilled. Perhaps with a different husband, the odds might not have been stacked so severely against her, but Fran was significantly smarter than Ron (each had commented upon it good-naturedly to us at least once), and that flaw now became fatal. Although Fran had known it all along, she hadn't anticipated that it would make much difference to the happiness of their marriage.

The reason it did is that Fran found herself increasingly bored. We know from other case histories that a brighter husband—one brighter than she—might have struck her restless mind as inexhaustible. This one no longer did. Almost thirty-one months into the marriage, she commented, "He hasn't said anything in weeks that I haven't heard at least ten times already." It was a chilling remark. Here, as with other couples from whom such words were heard, it almost certainly meant the beginning of the end. Fran accidentally hastened that end by finishing a few too many of Ron's sentences for him. That surprised and angered him, finally causing him to retort, "Well, do stop me next time, if you've heard this one before." Fran couldn't help but taunt him more and more as the months passed. "I wish he'd stop me," she said, visibly tense. "I really do. I'm out of control. He says something stupid or stale, and I attack."

Five months later, after a number of heated disputes about everything and nothing, they agreed to get a divorce.

"I DON'T NEED A MAN"

Fran was relieved, though she was also sad. At twenty-seven, doing well in her job and with a few good friends (mostly at work), she couldn't decide whether the best part of her life had already occurred or was yet to come. "I'm not sure where I'm going," she said. Then, abruptly, she added, "Maybe I should stop thinking about it so much."

Without reflecting on the matter consciously, she apparently concluded that men should play a smaller part in her personal life. It was the spring of 1974, and the theme had been very much in the air in those years. Fran had no trouble finding support for her new strategy of "I don't need a man." Selecting the right women's magazines allowed her to create a mental world for herself in which everyone seemed to agree with her view. That didn't stop friends from asking, as the months rolled by, whether she was interested in meeting and marrying someone else. When they did, Fran had a ready reply: "Why would I want a husband? I've already had one."

That line did the trick and stopped short any further inquiries. Its humor lay in the implication that having a partner is like trying exotic food or seeing an exhibit at the local museum. Once is enough. For Fran's sake, we hoped so, and her actions during the next few years confirmed that she was trying to live, not merely espouse, her new philosophy. After avoiding men almost completely in her leisure hours for the next four months, something fascinating happened, a harbinger of the future. She ran into an old friend from college named Ben, someone she and Walt had known on campus. Ben too had been an economics major. He had worked for a few years after graduating and was now studying full time for an MBA. She had never thought much about him one way or the other. "Ben didn't turn me on, or off, while we were in school," she said. "He was just *there*, like a piece of the scenery, if you know what I mean."

They had dinner that evening, and by the time they got through their appetizers, Fran had decided to take him home. "Don't ask me why," she said a few weeks afterward. "I still didn't find him much of a turn on. But *I* was turned on." They spent the night together, and did the same three days later. By then, Fran had obviously had enough. "I'm not going for three," she commented with a smile and a wave of her hand. "If he calls, I'll tell him I'm busy. I don't care if he thinks I'm fickle."

Even during the four months when she had no lovers, Fran certainly hadn't sworn off having relations or relationships with men—"Celibacy isn't for me," she stated more than once after her divorce—she simply wanted the topic to be moved to a back burner. Having casual sexual encounters seemed a good way to minimize the matter, and she discussed it in the same terms as a homeowner might discuss the services of a plumber or an electrician. "When I *want* someone," she said, two months after the episode with Ben, "I'll find someone. Otherwise, I'd just as soon not have them around."

Finding someone proved more difficult than she had anticipated. Women who were still single or recently divorced had warned her that this was no easy task, but Fran viewed herself as more resourceful than the rest and was certain she'd be able to handle it better than they. She did, and had seven new lovers during the next five months. Then she decided that in addition to sex she wanted some romance in the picture.

"I've almost forgotten what it's like," she said with exaggerated sarcasm, "to climax with someone I really care for."

On a flight to Dallas a few months later, Fran met Allen Jennings. Two months after her twenty-eighth birthday she had transferred to a new firm in the market research field, gotten a good raise and a promotion, and was being sent to a convention at which the firm wanted to be represented. When Allen was about to sit down in the seat next to hers, she gave him the once-over while pretending to look for the stewardess, and thought to herself, "Not bad." After an hour in the air, during which the two had talked non-stop, she proceeded to the next step, which for her was, "He'll do." There was little doubt in her mind that if he was willing, so was she. When it turned out that they were staying at the same hotel, "We might as well have checked into the same room as Mr. and Mrs.," as Fran said when she returned. Fran enjoyed the sex thoroughly because she was convinced that Allen had "more substance and sex appeal than the last half-dozen rolled into one. There was so much love in the air you could taste it." They saw one another for nearly two months when they got back, after which the feelings waned almost as quickly as they had arisen. "I guess he really wasn't all that different from the others," she concluded soon afterward.

That was eleven years ago. Rather than examine the development and dissolution of all forty-one relationships and one-night stands that took place during the interim, let us see what they had in common. Fran was no ordinary woman. Better educated and more energetic than most, she was also more impatient and impulsive. That enabled her to make decisions at work quickly, and it would have inclined her, even under ordinary circumstances, to pick partners a bit hastily.

The point is that Fran's life during the decade after her divorce has been anything but ordinary. When she had no bedmates, and hadn't had any for weeks on end, she was convinced that her need for male companionship, sex, intimacy, and affection were dormant. In her words, "If I don't *think* about a man, I don't need one." That was probably the falsest statement we have heard this intelligent and attractive woman make in the past quarter of a century. What made the attitude a dangerous self-delusion is that her desires accumulated steadily without her being aware that they were. Then, in settings in which she would have wished those feelings gone, and with men in whom she would otherwise have had no interest, they asserted themselves. They had become sufficiently intense by that time to have a will of their own.

Fran therefore has unwittingly gone through the same sequence of emotional states dozens of times during the past eleven years. Having just finished an overnight stand or longer love affair, she felt satisfied and self-contained. "I got what I was looking for," she said, in an instance typical of all the others, after spending a weekend with a man she met near the beach house she rented with friends one summer. "Do you have plans to see him again?" we inquired. "No," she replied, shaking her head, "there isn't enough there to bother. It was what it was. I feel very good." She added almost mechanically that she was still looking for some- one to have a more serious relationship with but there didn't seem to be anyone around.

Fran always assumed that this state of contentment lasted far longer than it actually did. In fact, she was convinced that as long as she could vividly remember what the good times were like, they would magically continue to exert their soothing effect on her. It was mind over matter, or so it appeared. Fran might as well have remembered what the sun felt like on her bikini-clad body and thereby expected to suntan later, in- doors. This was yet another example of the approach she had been using when she went jogging, and assuming the exercise would somehow bring about the changes she wanted to make in her personality.

While Fran purred about the good times she had recently had, her hunger for more of the same slowly continued to grow. Unfortunately, her increasing appetite for an encore—and then some—escaped her notice. What she eventually *did* become aware of was her dissatisfaction with both her work and her personal life. At such moments, she would stuff her face with too many snacks and meals that were too big. While doing so she would casually avoid looking at the cake, ice cream, cookies, or pile of junk food that she was wolfing down, as though it magically be- came smaller if she prevented herself from peering directly at it. Her daily coffee and cigarette consumption also jumped, the latter to a pack and a half from half a pack, which only served to make her more tense and irritable than she had already been. She immediately projected this inner discomfort onto the people around her and assumed it to be *their* feelings, not her own. "They are so crabby and uncooperative," she would say about her coworkers, "a really moody group." The more than two dozen coworkers whom we interviewed during these eleven years had their own version of what was going on, and we'll hear what they had to say shortly.

When she wasn't on the lookout for partners—wasn't thinking about men at all—she would suddenly run into one who seemed like a dream come true. Even before she told them, the people Fran worked with could usually guess whether she had begun or planned to begin an affair with someone new. The contrast between the bristling of yesterday—and the days before—and the sweet mannner of today were a bit hard to miss.

Those in whom Fran did confide (there was always at least one, typically a subordinate) got to see yet again the abundance of romantic feelings such encounters generated in her.

What was striking to them, and even more so to us, was the similarity of the initial descriptions she gave of most of these men. It seems that almost all were polite, presentable, fun-loving, warm, and sexy. No one who met any of them shared her view, and Fran herself certainly held a different opinion about them later, so it is fair to say that she was seeing what she wanted to see.

However, the question that stumped everyone who knew Fran well was how she could produce such an apparently genuine Niagara of affection after knowing each man so briefly—and do so time after time. As one of her subordinates, now at another firm, put it, "It was the same story with each and every guy: 'Oh, he's so wonderful and charming.' I don't know why she never got tired of it. *I* sure as hell did. It was like listening to a tape recorder."

Nevertheless, Fran was living it day to day, not looking at it calmly from afar and noticing the inevitable pattern. She'd have vigorously denied there *was* one. To her, the feelings were all too real and she felt as though she were caught firmly in their grip. Far from treating these affairs as mere diversions with which to keep herself entertained (an accusation made by some of her coworkers, which she never heard), she complained bitterly at times that they were making a mess of her life. "If he calls, I'm happy," she said, in the midst of one passionate three-week involvement. "And if he doesn't, I feel blue." In fact, it was precisely because she was so often distressed about how a current relationship was faring that, in desperation, she used subordinates as sounding boards and sources of reassurance. To her, each relationship felt like the only real one she'd ever had.

THE LOOK OF INNOCENCE

Condensing eleven years of a vibrant, successful woman's personal life into a handful of pages may make the pattern painfully obvious. Yet, as we said, it wasn't apparent to Fran, and if it *had* been, she'd certainly have attempted to do something about it, especially for the sake of her work. Without realizing it, this was becoming a more pressing matter each year. Her superiors, both male and female, had finally arrived at the view that Fran's chaotic love life *and* temperamental behavior in the office sprang from the same source. "She's just a very emotional person," said one ex-boss. Others expressed similar sentiments in a much less tolerant and forgiving manner. Her immediate superior, now active in another field, told us, "I didn't like working with her. No one else does, either. She's too tense—although she tries to look relaxed—and it forces her to make snap judgments."

"Snap judgments" was a phrase used by the majority of people who were trying to describe what made it so difficult to work with her. Fran, on the other hand, thought of this as one of her greatest strengths. "It takes some of the clowns around here *weeks* to make up their minds," she said in utter disbelief. "I keep wanting to say to them, 'Why don't we cut the crap and get on with it?'" She didn't say it, nor did she have to actually voice the words; her reactions communicated the message loud and clear. Indeed, this behavior was a central feature of her personality, one that had been present ever since she was a teenager but which her unstable personal life had now dangerously magnified.

On a Friday two months after her thirty-fourth birthday she was fired without prior notice, and given two weeks severance pay. The details of the firing, as we pieced it together from interviews with the three parties involved, are revealing. Fran was in her office working when Gregg, one of her superiors, came in to discuss some of the projects the two were trying to complete. As we stated earlier, one of Fran's main idiosyncracies, also present since her teen years, was that she would lower her head slightly and look up innocently at someone she hoped to impress with her sincerity. It was done subconsciously and was effective. People who talked to Fran only once, briefly, when she was doing this, came away with the very impression of youthful directness that she was trying to project.

While Gregg was in Fran's office, Norma, another of Fran's superiors, stopped by, looking for Gregg. Norma had been with the firm only four months and hadn't yet gotten to know Fran. As Norma later put it, "We would exchange hellos, but that's about it." Norma let Fran finish her thought and then asked Gregg the question to which she was seeking an answer (it had to do with moving the copier into the hallway and using the copier space as another office, since space was in short supply). Gregg got out two words of his reply when Fran, presuming he was through, suddenly said, "I think the idea stinks."

Norma was offended by the unsolicited opinion, rudely offered. But what shocked her more was that it emerged from what, until a moment ago, had been an angelic face, speaking softly. After Norma and Gregg left together and walked to Norma's office, she said to Gregg, "That woman is a real bitch." Gregg's response was, "I guess she is, isn't she?" Two and a half weeks later, Fran was fired as part of a "corporate reorganization." She wasn't let go because she had insulted Norma but because her haphazard personal life repeatedly lowered the quality and consistency of her work. That cost Fran the good will of her superiors just when she needed it most. The amount of time executives are willing to allow someone's personal problems to interfere with that person's on-the-job performance has been shrinking in recent decades and is now much shorter than is commonly thought.

The abrupt dismissal jolted Fran, but she managed to land on her feet. After six weeks of searching, she got a job at a nearby firm in the same field and got a pay raise in the process, to more than $50,000 per annum. She didn't have to see the entire pattern we've been discussing to sense that her troubled personal life was jeopardizing her job stability—and therefore contributing in its own way to her nervousness when day was done. "I can't unwind on weekends," she said uneasily one Sunday, "if I think I'm going to get canned again soon." Without another word from us, a minute later she remarked, "Men are going to be my undoing."

Since that is how she saw her problem, what she did next should come as no surprise. Between 1976 and 1984 dozens of articles advising masturbation appeared in magazines aimed primarily at women. In some instances, the article was devoted solely to the subject; in most, it was merely mentioned in a positive light. For women like Fran, the suggestion seemed a natural way out of their plight.

These clearly promotional pieces presented their case in a very persuasive manner. "No one else knows your body as well as *you* do," said one. Another stated, "Why wait for someone else to touch you the right way, in the right places?" What was being promised in all these articles was freedom. In essence the pieces were proclaiming, "You can end your dependence on men. Their bodies are different from yours, so they're never going to understand what feels good to you. Forget them. You can do it better by yourself, and have more satisfaction than you've ever had before."

What is interesting is that when electronic vibrators first appeared in drugstore windows in the late 1960s, they were greeted with a giggle by most of the women in our sample. Some (241 out of 3,466, approximately 7%) bought them anyway, primarily those over thirty. Younger women, a group we thought would be more adventurous, shunned them, since they viewed the item as "too defeatist" and "an admission of failure." The more than 650 drugstores we surveyed nationwide estimated that one-fourth of the purchasers of vibrators were gay men; the other three-quarters were women. Their most frequent rationale, if they offered one, was, "I'm going to use it for a massage." Basically it was a new toy, an erotic entertainment, with no philosophy attached. Technology, for the moment, was a step ahead of ideology.

Scientists and engineers have known for centuries that such imbalances rarely last long. One German missile expert, whose professed first love was rockets, not war, heard that a missile he helped design had landed on London with devastating effect. "Oops, it landed on the wrong planet," he remarked. Analogously, as the 1970s progressed, some of the more radical women's groups tried to find still more ways not only to turn women against men, but even to sever completely the bond between them. Such heavy-handed appeals to turn straight women into lesbians ("Put yourself in the hands of someone who *really* knows a woman's body," one article preached) produced little success. Turning women into masturbators seemed the next best thing. Like Fran, many had bounced back and forth between stuffing themselves with, as one put it, "junk food and junk partners," all the while trying hard to further their careers. They too wanted some peace, so that at least their professional lives might flower. They began masturbating regularly.

STARVED FOR AFFECTION

Did it help? For all the differences between male and female sexuality, if these women had questioned men who had already been down this road they would have learned some very useful insights. We asked the nearly 3,000 men in our sample what effect they thought restricting their sex lives to masturbation would have. For many, this wasn't a subject about which they had to speculate. They had already experienced it for prolonged periods, usually because of military service. Others had had isolating jobs, such as work on offshore oil rigs, that made them vividly aware of the answer. If their reactions were similar to the one these women expected to find, the men should have reported that they were content. Autoerotic behavior should have made them feel self-sufficient and, especially, independent of women.

The vast majority (2,398 of 2,704, or approximately 88%) were of the opinion that a steady diet of masturbation would only *increase* their appetite for a female partner. Moreover, they were convinced that that would be the outcome even if the restriction on their sexual behavior had been voluntarily imposed, rather than involuntarily, as it had been for those in the armed forces. The word used more often than any other by these men to describe their mental state after an extended period of autoeroticism was "crazed." The most typical replies: "I'd be sex-starved," and, "At that point, anything wearing a skirt would look good to me."

Women who were masturbating wound up feeling the same way— and not knowing it. Remember, for them masturbation wasn't merely solo sex. In the 1970s and early 1980s it had been burdened with a hefty load of ideological baggage. The act was supposed to free women of their need for men, not just relieve sexual desires. It had been touted as an effective escape.

What it accomplished instead for the women we studied was to starve them for affection. More than anything else, they realized now how much they wanted to be held. Whatever means they employed, the climaxes simply weren't enough. "I want a man's arms around me," was the most common reply from the few who accurately sensed what was missing. "I long to be loved." The problem—and it quickly became a major one—was that most women, like most men in this situation, were hungry for contact but unaware of it. They truly believed that the escape route they had taken was working.

Slowly but surely, unequivocal proof emerged that it wasn't. Women who had acted in a more restrained fashion than Fran, with fewer lovers and longer times spent with each, eventually began to behave like her. They started impulsively seizing upon almost any man who was available. The selectivity they had displayed for decades about lovers and friends became conspicuous by its absence. The needs they hoped would vanish had instead been accumulating, disrupting their ability to make important distinctions once men were near. The result was that they wound up becoming involved with men to whom, under ordinary circumstances, they might not have even said hello.

Americans are uncomfortable with the idea of hidden or subconscious forces guiding their behavior, preferring instead to view their own actions as the result of conscious and rational decisions they have made. In this case, the inclination only added insult to injury, since the women were forced to conclude that they knew what they were doing all along and therefore must have had good reasons for becoming involved with partners who would otherwise have been unacceptable to them. Most of the relationships were brief, but some led to marriages, troubled ones, which were usually brief as well. Nowhere was the much-ballyhooed improvement in their on-the-job emotional state to be seen. In the estimation of their coworkers, the reverse was typically the case.

What is now clear is that the people who were allegedly seeking to aid these women couldn't have been less helpful. When the relative handful (less than one in seven) woke up to what was happening to them and realized that autoeroticism was making matters worse rather than acting as an effective substitute, they were cross with themselves. "How did I manage to take such a giant step backward?" one asked. She had obviously forgotten the high-pressure "assistance" she had received. As it turned out, telling her to retreat into the self-absorbed world of masturbation nearly guaranteed that she would unwittingly fall for the first marginally passable man she met.

What we wanted to know next was: once that happened, would she be able to free herself? And if not, why not?

9

Karen: "My Lover, the Loser"

High school confused the women we studied. Most attended a school in which the numbers of boys and girls were approximately the same. A similar situation prevailed at the colleges they chose. That made them subconsciously conclude that their chances of finding a partner once school was through would be almost as good as they had been during their student years. As one put it at the beginning of her senior year at Princeton, "I'm not ready to get married yet, but there are plenty of guys here who feel that way too, and I'll run into them again in the city—when we're both more ready."

She didn't. What she and her peers encountered instead was a large number of men who had come to the city with something other than marriage on their minds. Two important forces made the reassuring balance of men and women in high school and college become a frustrating imbalance once school was through and work began. Had men really disappeared? Was there actually a shortage of men in cities?

The two pressures which made it seem that way had to do with entertainment and money. Monitoring the migratory routes followed by randomly selected members of the graduating classes of more than seventy high schools and colleges between 1958 and 1985, we discovered that young men and women who wanted to find a place for themselves in such fields as acting, singing, dance, or design, headed for the major cities at the earliest opportunity. "New York [or Los Angeles, San Francisco, Dallas, Cleveland, Chicago, Boston, Denver, or Washington] is where it's at," they told us, without a moment's hesitation. "You can't become a great concert pianist in East Podunk." The total number of male hopefuls in these fields making the migration exceeded by a substantial margin the number of female hopefuls, so no problem should have arisen. People who didn't pair up on campus could do so once they were in the city. The difficulty, as the women we studied were well aware, was that a disproportionate number of men in these fields turned out to be gay. In fact, between 1960 and 1985, for every heterosexual woman who made the journey to the city, approximately 2.7 homosexual men did so. Most wanted to become performing artists, or art or design professionals.

The modest income of heterosexual men in these fields was a problem that loomed almost as large. "He can't even support *himself*," many young women told us, when thinking about the life they'd have with men they met in their fields. "My landlord isn't much of a romantic," one aspiring actress told us. "He makes it kind of hard for me to believe that my boyfriend and I can really live on love." For young women whose fondest dream was to be in a Broadway play, TV sitcom or Hollywood movie, making financial sacrifices and living less well than their parents had quickly became second nature. However, they expected marriage to alleviate that state, not make it permanent. We surveyed more than 3,700 such women at various open auditions between 1958 and 1985. A steadily increasing proportion rated marrying an actor, singer, dancer, or musician as a bad idea. In their view, it was "important for my potential partner to be able to earn a decent living." Less than 36% felt that way in 1964, nearly 51% did in 1974, and by 1984 more than 60% held that view.

There were mounting pressures upon the tens of thousands of heterosexual young men who drifted into major American cities each year hoping to succeed in the performing or creative arts, photography, or as poets or novelists. "No place is cheap anymore," they complained. "Greenwich Village and SoHo [in New York] and Sausalito and Big Sur [in California] have become ridiculously expensive. Middle-class couples live in lofts now. Artists can no longer afford to." Earning enough money to cover rent, utilities, and basic living expenses compelled artists and performers to take a wide variety of jobs. Many of these men waited on tables, while others found positions as sales clerks. They deliberately sought work that was *not* meaningful to them so that they could keep their minds on their quest, and also so that they could quit on a moment's notice if they got an offer to perform or their paintings began to sell.

The variety of aspiring professionals doing this kind of work became apparent when we examined annually, from 1971 to 1985, the applications received by more than 230 restaurants in New York and California when they advertised for additional staff. Questions were inserted at our request, when they weren't already part of the application, dealing with the applicant's profession and the need for flexible working hours or days off to facilitate further progress in the his field. More than 41%—3,591 of 8,624—of the applicants were, or wanted to be, in the performing or creative arts. A healthy theater/movie industry in each city was clearly doing wonders for the restaurants in the area. After being waited on at dinner by aspiring performers who hadn't yet made it, theatergoers could see on stage those who had.

Few of these men thought of themselves as social climbers. In fact, they usually insisted that their "total artistic dedication" prevented them from giving financial considerations even a moderate place in their everyday decisions. "I want to write great literature," said one who had had all seven of his novels rejected by more than fifty publishers. At age thirty-four, he said, "Money isn't very important to me." He worked in a clothing store to supplement his income. Another, who was a waiter, commented at thirty-one, "One day, I'll be a famous photographer." Both may find that their dreams will come true eventually, but what interests us more for the moment about the large number of such ambitious men in major cities is the relationships they formed with successful women.

It used to be that men had money, and the women they married did not. Now, in a growing number of cases, it is the woman's income that is high and the man she pairs up with whose earnings are low. That happens because women subconsciously avoid romantic relationships with their male peers, wanting to prove to the world that they have made it, or soon will make it, on their own. It also happens because the men they meet during typical commercial transactions often don't care about their work and so can afford to be more jovial on the job than the men these women see in their own offices. The bouncy and even devil-may-care attitude these men have strikes the women as refreshingly different and appealing, especially since they suffer from the same excessive seriousness for which they unwittingly fault their male coworkers. The fun-loving demeanor of the waiter or salesman with whom they have a chance encounter during a business transaction melts their resistance, even if they end up not buying his product (and, sometimes, *because* they didn't buy it).

Are such men opportunists? Are such women "slumming"? What happens before, during and after such "invisible" (*i.e.*, even the women themselves downplay them to friends) relationships currently taking place in every sizable United States city?

Karen Sherman knows, and we found her experiences to be characteristic of thousands of other women in her position.

LIVELY BUT LONELY

Karen was born and raised in Connecticut. Her father was an engineer and her mother a homemaker who raised two other children besides Karen—her older brother and younger sister. The family gave the appearance of being tightly knit, and they were an attractive fivesome when they went anywhere together. However, emotions were rarely discussed in the house and were, in fact, expected to be repressed. This prohibition had the effect of turning the children into mind readers; each was somehow assumed to know, without being told, what the others were feeling.

Karen was the most responsive of the three and was also a good student. By the time she was fourteen she had already made a crucial decision that would affect her decades later, but, as is typical of adolescent boys and girls, she made it without talking about it with others or thinking consciously about it herself. The decision she made was that if she had to choose between work and play, she would choose work. That pleasantly surprised her parents, but they would have been equally pleased had she gotten only Bs instead of As in school and spent a bit more time socializing. That was what her sister, two years younger than she, did, and her parents found the mixture just as appealing.

Although Karen wanted very much to be liked by the boys in her high school, she did little about it. That she was one of the brightest girls in her class interfered to some extent with her psychosocial development, for the boys and girls she saw each day were usually more involved with flirting and fun than with their studies. They didn't dislike Karen as a result, but they also didn't make much of an effort to include her in their after-school activities or social circles. That puzzled and hurt Karen more than she was ready to admit at the time, since she had merely carried into the school setting the central assumption in her home: namely, that she knew what her peers were thinking, or so she thought, and hence it was reasonable to presume that they could read her mind as well. She wanted to join them, though she never said so or made the desire evident. Her attitude was that she wasn't repressed; rather, she preferred to intuit other people's feelings, and have them intuit hers, thereby insuring that no messy emotions need poison the air. Since she assumed they could read her mind—but nevertheless weren't acting on her desires—she felt sure she had been explicitly rejected. The isolation, always covered by a quick smile, had the effect of causing her to redouble her dedication to her studies. There, at least, her efforts produced a visible reward.

By the time Karen was in her senior year, her face and figure had attained the form they still have today, twenty-three years later. She was thin, with straight brown hair, and she had brown eyes that kept glancing briefly at anyone to whom she spoke. Some of her fidgeting was normal for adolescents her age, yet together with the body tension she evidenced, it made her seem more nervous than most. How did her friends see it? As liveliness. If something dropped and she was seated, she would gladly jump up and get it. Whenever someone suggested something active while she and her friends were sitting or standing around, she would immediately second the motion. The liveliness was real, not just nervous energy, but it had the peculiar effect of making her see herself as a leader without anyone else in her group agreeing. "I'm always the one who wants to *do* things," she told us, at fifteen, seventeen, eighteen, and twenty. "Everybody I know would rather be like a bump on a log."

Karen chose biology as a college major and, as in high school, had no trouble being a nearly straight-A student for the four years (her cumulative average was 3.73). The emphasis in her upper-middle-class suburban high school on looks and popularity made Karen feel "out of it," as she commented a few weeks after graduation, but college was a different story. The men she had the most contact with each day in her biology courses were also science majors, and she ran into them repeatedly in other classes she was taking, such as chemistry, statistics and English. Although they could be playful and boyish, and liked puns and board games, they tended not to be drawn to the women whom Karen had greatly envied in high school as "ideal partners." These men, at least, usually found such women a bit superficial, preferring the ones who looked more like Karen.

The first time she heard that, on a date with a fellow named Rick, she was stunned. Karen had long been lobbying her friends against "the cheerleader type," as she labeled women she considered pretty and sexy but brainless. In fact, she had been doing it for so long, it disoriented her at first to hear someone else voicing her own words. When she heard them from other men as well during the next few years, her shock turned into delight. She still had trouble believing that men really found her attractive, although they did. Their actions conveyed their true feelings better than their words, and they gravitated toward women who looked more like Karen than like a Dallas Cowboys cheerleader.

Karen's uncertainty about what she viewed as her sudden good fortune prevented her from putting the attention she was getting to good use. Her behavior with men was still too awkward and intellectual. As long as they just talked, she felt comfortable with her date. This was the situation she could handle best. Otherwise she would automatically find herself suggesting something active—walking, jogging, ice or roller skating—anything to relieve the tension, just as she had done with boys and girls throughout high school. Her date usually went along, reluctantly, aware that it was a ruse, and then didn't ask her out again. The pattern continued until her junior year in college.

Ed Petersen wasn't so easily put off. He liked her very much and good-naturedly refused when she suggested they go jogging, yet another attempt to avoid the sexual tension in the air. "We did enough of that this afternoon," he said calmly. "At 10 p.m. on a Saturday I don't think it's such a good idea." As Karen commented on a few occasions, she loved hugging Ed. "He seems to need it as much as I do," she said revealingly. However, whenever he tried for more sexual intimacy, "I tense up," she remarked. "I know I should relax and like it, and I kind of do, but I get very tense." The tension lessened over the weeks, as they repeated their petting, but when he finally brought her to climax manually (with their clothes more on than off), Karen decided that she had had enough. Few of the thoughts that went into her decision were conscious, but the conclusion she reached and found sufficient was, "He's too needy," and resolved not to see him again.

LOOKING FOR AN EXCUSE TO FIGHT

She was rid of Ed and back in control, but much to her surprise Karen found herself attracted during the fall term of her senior year to an even more aggressive man in her class named William Howard. Tall and lean, like Karen, Bill had a long, loping stride and athletic agility, though he participated in no organized sports, nor did he exercise regularly. His face bore a remarkable resemblance to TV newsman Dan Rather's. Bill's lower lip was usually chapped, not from the weather but because he would chew on it when he was thinking or readying a response while someone else was speaking.

Karen had already made up her mind to attend medical school, and although the prospect scared her, she was convinced that this was one graduate curriculum her studious habits and undeniable intelligence would enable her to manage. Confident about little else, Karen jokingly remarked, "I can memorize as well as the next person—and pass." Later, Karen's friends would say that she had become a doctor because she liked helping people, and that was certainly so. Yet in terms of her thoughts about the matter beforehand, the decision was based primarily on her academic abilities. She was going with what she felt was her only strong suit.

Bill had also decided to attend medical school. He had chosen premed as a major during his freshman year, and his father was a physician. Whether it was the fact that Karen and Bill had similar family backgrounds and were accepted at the same medical school; that she was emotionally drawn to him more than she had been to any other potential husband; or that he was indeed the most aggressive partner she had ever allowed herself to have, we don't know, but Bill became her first lover. The two began to have sexual relations regularly, and decided during their spring term to get married that summer. The trouble was (we didn't find this out until years later) that Karen found herself unable to let go with Bill. She couldn't climax and, more important, didn't feel comfortable with him while they were having sex. In retrospect, but only in retrospect, she understood why: "He was no more relaxed than I was."

Then she added, "He was a very determined man, that much I have to say for him."

It is interesting that the very determination that allowed Bill initially to break through the many layers of repression surrounding Karen's sexual feelings eventually caused her to become even more repressed. Revealingly, Karen herself once envisioned him in a dream as a can opener, and symbolically that was what she needed, since she wasn't yet ready to acknowledge her interest in sex. Yet his aggressive approach to almost everything he did scared her, making her feel that, as she later put it, "the dam would break and I would go irretrievably insane."

Bill knew no other approach and was doing the best he could to bring peace to them both. Their degree of medical sophistication, and lack of time once medical school began, reduced their inclination to seek help for what both realized was a tension-filled marriage. It was more convenient for them to view the chronic anxiety both were experiencing as having arisen from their demanding curriculum rather than from anything amiss between them. With the pressing issue of passing tests constantly before them, they put behind them any doubts they had about the state of their marriage. It worked. Each got good grades, with Bill attracted to surgery and Karen to radiology.

As medical school came to an end, so did their relationship. The marriage continued because both had been raised in families that strongly believed in one spouse for a lifetime, so divorce wasn't something to be undertaken lightly. They did their residencies together, Bill in surgery and Karen in radiology, as planned, and since they still had so much more in common with one another than with anyone else they knew, they stayed together and continued to make progress professionally. Talk replaced sex as their most important form of interchange, and the frequency of intercourse fell to approximately once a week. When their residencies were through, the marriage outlived whatever usefulness it had once had, and the two began to argue openly.

Bill, it seemed, wanted to settle in one city, while Karen favored another. Bitter disputes erupted about the relative merits of the two towns and then quickly proceeded to become finger-pointing tirades about who was more selfish. "You think only about your own career," Karen told Bill angrily. "Well, I have to worry about mine too." Bill considered the accusation baseless because Karen was unwilling to discuss the matter calmly. "You bristle the minute we raise the subject of where to live and practice," he said. "What kind of conversation is that?"

Their disagreements escalated and prevented them even from having a pizza as their Friday night dinner, a tradition that extended back to their freshman year in medical school. If one wanted a pizza, the other was suddenly ravenous for French food—which only made that pizza look all the more delicious to the first. Having watched hundreds of couples at this stage of their relationship go through a seemingly endless series of squabbles about where to work, live, or eat, we feel safe in asserting that these two were *looking* for an excuse to fight. They had been together long enough so that it would have appeared too cold and cavalier for one to just get up and say to the other, "Thanks for being my roommate all these years while I was a student, but it's time for me to move on to bigger and better things."

However, if they could have found an issue that smacked of "irreconcilable differences," as the divorce lawyer Bill eventually retained labeled it, then they would have had grounds for calling it quits that were personally and publicly acceptable. Finding a good excuse wasn't only a matter of maintaining appearances and seeming like a nice person. They had grown on one another, a process that British psychiatrist John Bowlby describes by the appropriately simple name "attachment."[1] After so many years as a pair, they had each incorporated the other's thoughts, habits, and preferences. An emotional interweaving of the two had taken place in spite of their many differences and disagreements. A rational-sounding scissors was needed to help cut the remaining ties that bound them. Arguments about careers served the purpose nicely. People throughout the United States were taking the subject seriously enough in the early 1970s to deem it sufficient cause for a rift that could lead to divorce. Yet the fact remains that had this been a religious era, for instance, instead of a secular one that prizes business or professional success more than domestic stability, the two would almost certainly have had a fight about God that would have been viewed as the fatal blow to their union.

The many comments their friends made about Bill's potential earning power versus Karen's, and about his preference for city living, said far more about contemporary attitudes than about the outlook for this particular relationship. It was over. All it was waiting for was a publicly condoned rationalization, to serve as an epitaph, for the corpse to be laid to rest. The lesson we as researchers learned from these events was to be reminded once again how enduring an unhappy marriage can be—until the right (that is, socially acceptable) excuse for ending it comes along.

FORBIDDEN FEELINGS

Karen moved to a major city, while Bill chose a small town. (Years later, we discovered that Bill would have preferred a large city and subsequently moved to one. But since, at the time, Karen had chosen a city,

---

1. J. Bowlby, *Attachment* (New York: Harper & Row, 1972).

he didn't feel that he could too.) Exaggeration of differences in order to terminate the relationship overrode the self-interest that would otherwise have motivated each at this point. This often happened with couples we studied. In hundreds of instances, they took positions primarily to provoke a fight, and then got locked into their respective positions long after the fight, not to mention the relationship, had ended.

Although she often missed Bill during the first year, and found herself holding imaginary conversations—and arguments—with him, Karen put her abundance of energy to good use. She commented at the time, "You can be as alone as you want in a big city, or as busy." She chose to be busy, making friends at work, at a health club she joined, and during the sailing and tennis lessons she signed up for. By any measure, Karen seemed more optimistic and outgoing than we had ever seen her. The question in our minds was: Would she have a personal life, and if so, with whom?

Most of the women Karen met and became friends with were, like her, in their thirties and divorced. Most of the men she met and became friends with were married and not interested in getting a divorce, but they responded sexually to something that she was radiating without realizing it. Three times during the first year, attractive but married professionals or businessmen she had come to know at work or through playing tennis discreetly propositioned her. One told her that a large part of her appeal was that, as he put it, "You don't come on strong. I like that. The ones who are too hungry turn me off." Karen gently brushed aside all three offers.

We aren't certain when she decided that being a little hungry wasn't such a bad idea after all. It happened some time during her first eighteen months in the city. The lifestyle was certainly more open and aggressive than anything she had encountered before, a fact that was slowly making a permanent impact on her. She measured the distance that she herself had traveled emotionally since her childhood by telling us repeatedly how shocked her parents would be at what she saw daily all around her. It no longer shocked her, that much was clear, and she was rapidly coming to terms (at least intellectually) with her own erotic impulses. Her desire to make progress on this front had long been present, but only now did it become conscious. Somehow she sensed that she could more effectively remove the shackles restraining her sexuality if she had a series of partners, not just one who, like Bill, would doubtless treat her like an emotionally constipated patient.

The number of men who were Karen's sexual partners during the next four years, between her twenty-ninth and thirty-third birthdays, was large, and they were a diverse lot. They were other doctors she met at work, lawyers, stockbrokers and business executives she met playing tennis and going sailing—twenty-two of them in all, most of whom were married or who had no intention of ever being so, if they could help it. Rather than being a cause of complaint, the unavailability of these men as potential husbands didn't bother Karen in the least because she was making up for lost time where her psychosexual development was concerned. Women a decade younger than she was at this point often acted the same way, experimenting with a variety of lovers, not necessarily to find the right man, but to find themselves.

By the time she was thirty-three, Karen had definitely become more comfortable with her erotic impulses. In fact, it once shocked her to realize that she had had sex three times in one day, once in the morning and twice that evening, climaxing each time; she would gladly have done the same the next day had her partner not had to work. "Have I been burying these desires all these years?" she asked herself on a number of occasions. Karen would have been less amazed by the powerful feelings that were surfacing if she had understood an important general rule about repression. To paraphrase a lyric of singer Janis Joplin: "When you've got nothing, you've got nothing to hide."

Karen had plenty to hide, though she had no idea what it might be. Moreover, she was hiding it so well, she would have insisted that she wasn't hiding anything at all. That is the central paradox about repression: people who are harboring what they think of as a forbidden desire usually erect a wall around it so thick that they come to think there's nothing inside. At that point, their condition starts to deteriorate seriously. For if the desire is one as primitive and powerful as sexual desire, it doesn't go away. It merely accumulates as each day's new forbidden feelings are added to those from yesterday and the day before. The condition feeds on itself. Excessive self-restraint leads to the need for more of the same.

Eventually, the need to shore up the walls and hold back a tidal wave of forbidden feelings consumes most of the person's supply of energy. The inner demand for an ever-increasing quantity of repression sapped the strength of Karen's positive emotions, forcing her to fake them. She had been behaving in this manner for so long by the time she got married, she had good reason to worry that the dam might break with Bill and that she would go crazy. If craziness is taken to indicate totally inconsistent behavior in the eyes of one's audience, then Karen would indeed have been judged insane. After decades as a prude, she had begun almost overnight to live in a way that she herself would formerly have labeled nymphomaniacal. In short, the amount of self-repressing she did daily matched—had to match, since it was geared to—the intensity of her appetite for lovemaking. That appetite steadily increased (and hence the repression did as well) because she never allowed it to be satisfied.

SEXUAL SELF-ADVERTISEMENTS

After 1960, there weren't supposed to be any women such as Karen left in America. Society was allegedly free forever of repression, or so we were told in such widely read books as *Eros and Civilization* by Herbert Marcuse. The trouble with this popular theory is that it was put forth by ivory tower philosophers who did no research into the real-life experiences of the people in question and swallowed whole the impression that young people had learned to convey, that they were sexually and emotionally liberated. Nevertheless, in the vast majority of cases, it turned out to be little more than a sham, and a very convincing one at that. Karen, in particular, had learned how to seem carefree because she was anything but. No one who really was as casual as she wanted people to believe she was, would have had to spend so much time perfecting this bit of theater for public presentation.

Many of the most rigid young women in our sample—painfully self-conscious, chronically tense and artificially calm—had had at least 10 lovers by the time they were 25. However, the key point here is that for every such women, more than a dozen others who fit that description didn't begin acting similarly until they were past the age of 25 and divorced. That led women in both groups to be considered "free spirits," a label that seemed logical given the double-digit number of partners some had each year. Yet they themselves couldn't escape the feeling that something was awry, since they still didn't view their own experiences as normal. The sex acts took place, all right, but no sex act ever made them feel treasured or free, though they'd gladly have settled for either one.

An analogy from the world of sports may help illuminate the underlying dynamics. Surround someone with peers who are outstanding at a particular sport, and the person in question is likely to stop playing the sport altogether, unless he or she is outstanding too or almost so. If the gap between this person's level of ability and that of the group's is high, the distance is usually perceived by the person as too great a bridge. Competitive-comparative beings that we all are, the gap demoralizes rather than inspires. (Remember, we are talking about how our *peers* are doing, not athletes a decade or more older than we, whom we can adopt as heroes and aspire to match once we are their age.) Similarly defeatist reactions are seen in other areas of activity as well. For instance, one of the young men in our sample wanted one day to be a concert pianist, and seemed well on his way to becoming one. At a friend's house one weekend, he heard a recording of Vladimir Horowitz playing the piece he himself had been practicing for three of four hours a day, every day, Schumann's "Toccata." That was the last time he played the piano. "I'll never be able to play that well," he told us, trying to mask his horror. Even the fact that Horowitz at the time the recording was made was decades older than this young man didn't prevent the damage from being done to his desire to persist and hope one day to match his idol.

Since people don't get to watch what other couples do in the privacy of their own bedrooms, they base their picture of the sex lives of others on the demeanor the others display in their everyday lives. People who look loose and laid back are assumed to have no trouble becoming unabashedly aroused when they are in bed with a partner. And if they appear somewhat aggressive as well, the assumption is that such people are able to attain full satisfaction each time by doing what feels good enough to achieve the desired results.

Appearances are deceiving, though, and nowhere is that more true than in the area of sexual behavior. We found that men and women who presented an explicitly erotic image of themselves were usually unable to back it up once they were in the arms of a partner who had accepted the image at face value. "If you've got it, flaunt it," seems not to apply in this area. In fact, it was people who'd been turned on by the flaunting, only to be disappointed once the much-advertised genital gymnastics began, who alerted us to what they labeled "all sizzle, no steak."

Nevertheless, during her teen years Karen accepted uncritically the picture of her peers, puffed though it was with self-advertisement, and used it to measure her own comfort with sex. She couldn't match what she saw. As an adolescent, her response had been the same as that of many young athletes and musicians who felt badly outclassed: she quit the race altogether. In this case, that had the unfortunate effect of making her still more inhibited. Since she would not allow herself to stay in the social swim as best she could, and so develop the interpersonal skills needed to meet and befriend the boys who interested her, her deeper needs continued to accumulate. That made befriending men in later years a doubly dangerous event.

To spell out the steps involved, excessive inhibition in adult women begins in adolescence as a *social failure*, an inability to keep up with their more extroverted and overtly erotic peers. Then, as a result of their withdrawal from the competition, the inventory of unmet emotional and sexual needs increases. *Psychosocial* pressures take over and make them feel like even greater failures when they attempt to remedy the situation. For they sense that they may well inundate with their backlog men with whom they become intimate. Worse still, they fear that the sheer intensity of their demands will turn them into a beggar. The thought of being seen by others as this needy horrifies them. The final stage is an almost purely *psychological* one, even though it appears to have social dimensions, particularly for career women. They become lost in an inner civil war, continually attempting to shore up defenses against the forces seeking to burst through. The repression of self (and others, as we'll see shortly) steadily increases, in order to hold in the ever-growing inventory of need.

It would never have occurred to this bright and energetic young woman to drop out of school, yet Karen dropped out of the self-schooling through which psychosexual development takes place among American adolescents. It may be a more informal type of education, conducted under the learner's direction and at his or her own pace, but in Karen's case quitting was to prove every bit as costly as leaving school at the age of sixteen would have been. When her formal schooling was finished and she was finally ready to attempt to remedy what she knew was a serious, even crippling deficiency, Karen felt compelled to turn to strangers for help. They hadn't known her for decades as a prude, so she could be sexually more aggressive with them. As she put it at age thirty-three, talking about a man she had recently met and slept with twice, "He likes my horniness. He says it gets him aroused too."

THE TROUBLE WITH MARRIED MEN

By the time Karen was thirty-three, her (mostly subconscious) efforts to become comfortable with her erotic impulses had begun to yield results. At no point did she say to herself or to us, "My intellectual and professional development have been going well, but now I have to concentrate on my personal and sex life." Instead, her conscious view of what she was doing was that her actions were steps toward finding a potential husband and remarrying. When a friend of hers pointed out that the men she had been seeing during the past four years weren't interested in being married, or already had wives, Karen had an uncharacteristically flip reply ready. "You never know," she said, raising her eyebrows, trying to look mischievous. "I might get one of them to change his mind and take the plunge."

The line got her friend to drop the subject, but the number of men Karen was meeting who were available for even a brief fling seemed to be dwindling. That didn't bother her nearly as much as we thought it might, because some time during her thirty-third year she apparently came to the conclusion that she wanted a permanent partner. As she put it, "The trouble with married men is that they're not around when you really want them. They're home with their wives."

That made her more responsive to Paul Heller when she first met him than she would have been even two years before. Although Karen kept some of her medical journals and books in her office, the bulk of them were in her apartment, along with classic novels and contemporary best-sellers. As they began to pile up, she decided to buy a bookcase she had seen in a do-it-yourself furniture store window. The shelves looked good empty, and assembling the inexpensive unit herself wasn't a problem. However, when she went to put books on the second shelf from the top, after the top one was already full, the sides of the unit bowed and the whole thing collapsed with a roar. She badly bruised the thumb and index finger on her left hand, which got caught between the two shelves as they crashed into the third. For nearly three weeks she had little use of her left hand, and normal function returned slowly.

Karen had had enough of do-it-yourself furniture and decided to let a professional carpenter install some built-in bookcases along one wall of her apartment. The one she chose happened to be good at self-promotion as well as carpentry and asked Karen to let a free-lance photographer, Paul Heller, photograph the wall "before," so that the picture could be used in conjunction with an "after" in advertisements for additional carpentry business. She agreed, and when Paul came over on a Thursday afternoon (which she had off), they spent two hours talking, twenty minutes photographing the wall, and then went to dinner together. Paul paid. It was the last time he did.

The next time they saw one another was the following Saturday when the two planned to go to a movie after Karen fixed a light meal for them both. They spent the night and most of the next day in bed together, going out only to get the Sunday paper and some croissants. Karen hadn't evidenced any of her own arousal with Paul when they first met, and that pleased her. For instead of her horniness turning him on, his evident sexual interest in her helped turn *her* on. That was the kind of subtle compliment from an attractive man that she had wanted all her life, it seemed, but had rarely received. Shouts and obscene gestures from construction workers and other men in the street did nothing for her self-esteem, but she was flattered by the erotic attention paid to her by Paul and questioned it no further. "He's very good looking," she said a few days later. He was, but there was more to this encounter than met the eye.

Paul was two years older than Karen. Although he still had high hopes of becoming, as he put it, "the next Steichen or Avedon," he had had little enough success since entering the field to become more realistic. According to his friends at the carpentry store, "Paul wasn't always as big on money as he has been lately. He asks us for [free-lance] jobs now. We used to have to ask him." By the end of their fourth week together, Paul was complaining openly to Karen about how difficult it was for him to try to accomplish "something significant" in his chosen field and still make ends meet. "I'd like to have a really nice studio and color lab of my own," he told her, "but I don't see how I can possibly afford it on what *I* make." In spite of the greater attention he had paid to financial matters in recent years, Paul continued to see himself as being far above the petty concerns of commerce. Twice in their first three months together, when Paul discussed having to take jobs such as photographing Karen's wall, he compared himself to a "fine musician who is forced to play at weddings and bar mitzvahs in order to earn a living."

Let us pause for a moment and consider what this relationship offered both parties. One thing is certain: each was seeking something entirely different from what the other wanted most. Paul bragged more than once to his friends at the carpentry store that it was nice "not to have to worry about money anymore—there isn't *anything* that doctors can't afford." That wasn't quite so in Karen's case since, unbeknown to Paul, *this* physician's earnings were lower, on average, than those of other medical specialists. Moreover, unlike Paul's income, which usually came to him in cash (and which he did not declare for tax purposes), Karen received a fixed annual salary of $43,000 from which city, state and federal income taxes, as well as social security, were deducted. That left her with a net income of approximately $25,000. To Paul, that seemed like a lot of money, since he was paid $50 in cash for the "before" and "after" shots he took of Karen's apartment. His earnings were about $1,000 a month, mostly in cash. One number that made a real impact on him was that Karen spent nearly $5,000 having bookcases installed. "I don't understand people who throw away that kind of money for some shelves," he told a friend, adding, "It must be sweet to have that much bread."

What Karen wanted most, on the other hand, was the seemingly endless stream of flattering remarks that Paul voiced. He complimented her when she cooked dinner and was equally full of praise when she picked up the tab in a restaurant. If she was his meal ticket, he was doing a good job of singing for his supper. "He *never* criticizes me," she said, delighted to realize how different her relationship with Paul was from her marriage to Bill. She also derived real pleasure from seeing how "flexible" Paul was, a word Karen used about him with envy and admiration. She was unaware, though his friends were not, that his flexibility was primarily the result of indifference. His comments, taken collectively, indicate a marked alienation from the mainstream of American life, to which Karen did and always would belong. His mildly anti-capitalist remarks entertained rather than offended her, since she viewed her field as public-spirited, not mercenary, and she liked the vicarious sense of rebellion they offered her. Paul's opinions weren't intense enough to be a threat to the values she held dear. So the two talked up a storm that both enjoyed. Finally, as Karen reminded us even years later, "the sex was good, consistently good."

When Paul quietly asked her for a $500 loan "toward" his much-discussed studio, Karen didn't give the matter a second thought, either then or later. She said yes and wrote him a check. No visible results of the loan were expected immediately, since the amount fell far short of the $15,000 Paul estimated it would cost him to do it right. Four months later he borrowed another $500. Karen saw no reason to be hesitant in the least about saying yes again, because she was thoroughly convinced by this time that once he got his studio set up, his earnings would increase dramatically. As she put it, "He'll have enough to pay me back many times over."

The relationship slowly wound down after that, from a mutual loss of interest, and the two drifted apart. They saw one another only four more times after the second check changed hands, with the gap between visits growing steadily longer. The last time she saw him was just before her thirty-fifth birthday. Nearly six years later, Karen still hasn't gotten her $1,000 back, and Paul doesn't yet have his studio.

MARRYING FOR MONEY

Relationships similar to the one Karen had with Paul followed. During the past six years there have been five men like Paul in Karen's life. Two were actors (one of whom, at thirty-seven, had never acted professionally); another, the chubbiest fellow of the bunch, with a body type to which Karen had not before been attracted, was an aspiring opera star; the fourth was the manager of a movie theater who dreamed of writing screenplays; the fifth had nothing to do, at first glance, with the world of entertainment, but was maitre d' of a well-known midtown restaurant. However, it turned out that he had once wanted to be an actor and had actually made a living at it in his twenties. Now, in his forties, he was putting the skills to good use each evening as customers arrived.

If nothing else, the five brought a certain amount of "culture" to Karen's life. These men, although unsuccessful in their own eyes, usually had friends who were in a position to admit them without charge to various performances around town. Often Karen and her current boyfriend went to a show merely because they could enter for free. That allowed them to say, on the many occasions when they witnessed a real flop, "We got precisely what we paid for." If the saying is applied to Karen's personal as well as her cultural life, then it is clear she was badly shortchanged by the events of these years. She was paying dearly, in terms of money and time, but receiving precious little in return—except erotic compliments from men who, in many cases, openly acknowledged to friends that they were hustling her.

One question that may have occurred to the reader (it did so repeatedly to our staff in cases like this one) is: Why were these attractive and articulate men pursuing Karen when none of them previously rated women who looked like her as having any sex appeal? To put the question another way, which may be more revealing and less insulting to Karen (to whom we mean no insult whatever): Why didn't these men automatically chase women who more closely resembled Marilyn Monroe or Bo Derek? Wouldn't women such as these have been a more natural choice?

In the beginning we were certain they would be, and so made it a point to monitor the fortunes of every girl in our sample who was rated "Best Looking" by her high school classmates. The result: over the course of the next two decades (and with all other factors, such as socio-economic status and grade point average, held constant), these women turned out to be underachievers. The "gorgeous hothouse flowers," as a number of men referred to them, needed to be supported. They had not been successful enough occupationally to be in a position to do the supporting. That would have made perfect sense to Karen, who told us in high school and again in college that, "God gives some of us looks and the rest brains. It's only fair. No one gets an abundance of both." There was no question in her mind about which category she belonged in, though she commented more than once that she would "gladly trade a little of my brains for a sexier face and body."

Since such trades couldn't be made—and, more important, men like the ones we're discussing couldn't find an exceptionally beautiful woman who also had a high income—they decided to go for the latter. In doing so, they were unwittingly acting in accordance with a guideline that many of the women we studied had been offered by their mothers. More than 20% of the mothers had told their daughters, "It's just as easy to fall in love with a rich man as a poor one." That is, all other things being equal, you might as well find someone with money and make your life a little easier.

However, for the ambitious but basically lazy men we are talking about, other things were not equal. Since beautiful young women turned out, on average, to be significant underachievers, these men were forced to make a choice, and did. They increasingly became involved with women who were only moderately attractive but whose incomes were well above average. And the more above average a woman's earnings were, the more appealing she apparently became. The men were readily able to find a place for themselves in the lives of such women because ever since high school the women had been comparing themselves to the hothouse flowers whom they had long since outdistanced occupationally. This picture of themselves was an afterimage of adolescence, but it continued to make them think of themselves as ugly ducklings by comparison. That created a market for men who wanted to share the women's incomes and didn't mind paying them compliments on a regular basis to get it.

In some sense, the practices of prior generations of young men and women had finally come full circle by the mid–1980s. Women had previously been encouraged by their mothers to make some compromises, if necessary, to marry a man with money. As one put it sarcastically to her eighteen-year-old daughter, "He doesn't have to look like Paul Newman, you know, if he has the bank balance of a Rockefeller." Suddenly a large number of men, without similar suggestions from either of their parents, were acting the same way. In fact, more men than women were. Surprisingly few young women took their mother's advice—which resulted in some intense quarrels, with mothers saying, "I'm older than you and there *are* some things I know that you don't." Nevertheless, the vast majority of daughters we studied said that they married for love, not money. However, an alarming number of men paired up with—but only infrequently married—women who, if all else stayed the same but their sex were changed, would have been considered highly eligible bachelors earlier in the century.

From the mid–1950s to the mid–1980s in the United States there was a steadily increasing emphasis on careers; the subject became all-consuming for many women in their twenties and thirties. That had the effect of accidentally producing a bumper crop of working women who were vulnerable to the blandishments of the kinds of men we've been discussing. Since these women had been encouraged (far more strongly and subtly than they realized) to devote themselves primarily to their work, many had neglected their social and psychosexual development until they were in their late twenties or early thirties. Professional education and occupational attainments came first. But once these had been given top priority for a number of years and had produced results, more personal needs pushed their way to the surface. Delayed marriages to appropriate partners often took place. However, in a larger number of cases, particularly after a divorce, inappropriate pairings with low-income partners—"paid flatterers," one woman called them—were seen repeatedly.

THE SEXUAL PROWESS OF AGING ATHLETES

Who, specifically, was involved in these pairings? Just radiologists and photographers? Hardly, although it is worth noting that female physicians like Karen were prime targets of these men. This largely introverted and intelligent group of women, whose earnings were typically high and whose level of social skills was just as typically low, were more vulnerable than most, for reasons which Karen's case makes clear. Fully 39% of the 121 female physicians we studied who had never been married had at least one such boyfriend when she was between the ages of twenty-five and forty. The percentage was much higher for women in this category who were divorced: 51% had at least one such boyfriend, and 38% had two or more. Less than 1% of these relationships led to marriage for those who'd never been wed or remarriage for those who'd previously been divorced.

Some readers may be wondering whether male physicians who were these women's peers were forming the same kind of liaisons. They weren't, and the main reason was that the men frequently paired up with nurses they had come to know on the job. Approximately 18% of these pairings resulted in marriage. Female physicians had no access to a similarly convenient arrangement, since the majority of male nurses they worked with acknowledged to us openly during interviews that they were gay. The women therefore had to find—during their leisure hours, if they could—acceptable lovers and potential husbands. That was an especially difficult task for this group, if for no other reason than the long hours they worked, with sixty hours per week not uncommon and weekends "on call" an accepted part of their positions.

Women in the medical field were by no means the only ones engaging regularly in such relationships. They were even more common in the fields of law and management. Confining our attention to women who were law school graduates or who held an MBA, we found that 42% of the attorneys and 41% of the MBAs had such partners while single and between the ages of twenty-five and forty. After divorce, the percentages jumped to 55% and 52%, respectively, with more than 43% and 29% of lawyers and MBAs, respectively, reporting more than one such relationship.

Women in less glamorous professions, and particularly in sales, had remarkably similar experiences between the ages of twenty-five and forty, even though many weren't even college graduates. (This shouldn't be too surprising, since the men we are discussing tended to boast to friends, and to us, about either the woman's earnings *or* the prestige of her profession.) Successful saleswomen, especially in the securities and real estate fields, often had six-figure incomes, though few had them on a steady basis. Earnings normally fluctuate significantly in these fields, for both men and women, in conjunction with the phases of the nation's economic cycle. Nearly 28% of the women in our sample who were in sales had such a relationship while single. However, 61% had at least one such pairing after a divorce and 50% had more than one.

Let us focus for a moment on the other half of these relationships, so that we have a better picture of the kinds of men involved. The range was wide. Not only were they men who aspired to success in the fields of art, literature, and the performing arts, there were those who hoped one day to become famous athletes. Some even looked like Bruce Jenner. However, unlike Jenner, they had won no Olympic gold medals and hence had no lucrative commercials to make or breakfast cereals to endorse. In fact, contrary to what they told us, they hadn't even come close to qualifying for the United States Olympic team in any of the winter or summer events. A careful check revealed that only 11 out of 312 had told us the truth about even the modest degree of success they had actually enjoyed as athletes in high school and college. Still less reality was found among the stories of those who had told us, in essence, "To hell with this amateur Olympic stuff, I almost had a contract to play *professional* football [baseball, basketball, hockey, or tennis]."

Not wanting to separate themselves completely from the field in which they had once hoped to attain world renown, many took jobs in sporting goods stores, selling sneakers, skis, and tennis rackets. They were (or once had been) more serious athletes than most of their customers, and so they felt comfortable saying such things as, "Well, personally, I've always preferred [brand X]," and "When I'm really going all out, I use [brand Y]." The sense of superiority they felt relative to the store's typical customer was some compensation for the low level of pay they were receiving. Although turnover rates at these stores were high, as employees looked for greener pastures elsewhere (rates on the order of 20% to 40% per annum were common), the situation was no better elsewhere. It made the men uncomfortably aware that they were having trouble supporting themselves—at an age at which many of their peers, with a lesser interest in sports, were becoming well established in better-paying professions.

To make certain we don't accidentally insult anyone here, let us repeat what we said in the Preface. No one can tell just by looking at a particular person, either on the job or off, that the person's future occupational prospects are minimal. Even extensive interviews conducted by a team of experienced professionals will not reveal that information. It becomes clear only as the years roll by, and opportunity after opportunity for these individuals to better themselves is permitted to pass. Then, and only then, does a pattern begin to emerge, one that must include the sexual partners with whom these individuals have either fleeting or enduring contact.

After a minimum of a decade spent assembling the information needed to see if a pattern exists—and, if so, what it indicates—one has the basis for hazarding a guess as to the person's future prospects. Even then, the guesses often turn out to be wide of the mark. One of the most satisfying aspects of doing long-term research is the chance to see a man or woman who had been coasting or treading water for years suddenly come to life and start to make real headway. At least in the United States, nothing about the marginal financial and psychological status of men and women in the age range of twenty-five to forty is carved in stone.

Having said that, it is worth noting that there *is* one characteristic which most of the men we've been discussing in this chapter shared. And when it was present, it did indeed bode ill for the person's future occupational prospects. We found that men in this age range who stated repeatedly that they had "already given my all for Uncle Sam [or an alma mater or while trying to make a professional sports team]" did significantly less well over the years than their peers who did not have that attitude. Not only didn't they *like* working, they didn't feel they should *have to*. It had been their intention ever since their teen years to become outstanding at a particular sport. Unlike other school athletes, who played hard while on a team but left it all behind once they graduated and got a job, these men clung to their prior picture of themselves. Their view of their situation remained relatively static from their teen years right into their thirties: they were going to be spectacular on a field, court, ski slope or track—and an enormous supply of money would magically flow their way, enabling them to live happily ever after.

A job was therefore doubly irritating to them. Although they took the same courses as many of their peers who went on to do well, they hadn't seriously prepared themselves for entry into the work world because they were quite certain, even if they modestly refrained from saying so to others, that they'd never have to hold an ordinary job. How specifically did they envision themselves spending their days once they had chosen to hang up their cleats, sneakers, or skis? This was one question they had no difficulty answering. The most common reply about what lay in store for them involved announcing and writing: "I'll probably wind up being a radio commentator or TV broadcaster, like Frank Gifford." Or, "It will be fun to write down my trials and tribulations on the way to the top, the way Billy Martin and Jim Bouton [author of *Ball Four*] did." The pedestrian jobs they were forced to take instead served as constant reminders of their failure. And a major failure it was, in their eyes, since it occurred in the only arena that had really meant anything to them all along.

Their view that they had "already given it my all" allowed such men to become involved with a high-income professional or businesswoman, take her money, offer her a host of compliments but little genuine affection, and *not* feel like a parasite. In many ways, the pairing was useful to both parties, so perhaps it should be thought of as symbiotic. The increasingly single-minded emphasis in the United States on careers had by the 1970s and 1980s turned many American women into "members of a humorless breed of new Puritans," as one described herself and her friends in 1984. The playfulness of these men (which, as we've mentioned, usually sprang from their alienation) was a needed antidote. Unfortunately, it was not as readily available from the successful woman's male peers, who generally adopted an approach that was almost—though not quite— as humorless in their own quest for career success.

It was fascinating to find that a powerful force we hadn't anticipated was in operation here, helping to make these men especially interested in women whose earnings were high and who required the kind of ego boost such men could provide. A good way to understand the force is by noting that, in high school and college, these men were attracted to the best-looking girls in their classes. But when they were in their late twenties and throughout their thirties they actually fled such women, even if they were now better looking than ever. It was an eye-opener to see that they were subconsciously avoiding such women as partners because they sensed that they were not in a position to shoulder the emotional and financial burden the women represented.

Some spelled out the reasons for their actions without our even having to ask why: "If I'd been a roaring success, a sports hero—and became a living legend—*that* is who I'd have wanted most to have at my side. Like Joe DiMaggio and Marilyn Monroe. But it didn't happen." Since they hadn't made it big they shunned the kind of woman they'd previously have sought, and instead accepted the reality of their situations. Tying up with a financially secure but emotionally insecure business or professional woman seemed like an attractive alternative.

SEX AS EXERCISE

It is tempting to dismiss these pairings as harmless; and they would be, were it not for two things. First, they take up time, in some cases years. When one such pairing is followed by another of a similar nature, and then another, as in Karen's case, they can consume an entire decade. That is an excessively long period of time for anyone to spend trying to compensate even for what they feel is their most important personal deficiency. As Karen put it, at thirty-eight, "Sex always scared me. I know that now. What kind of a partner can someone be who is still caught in the grip of that fear?" Her attempt to remedy the deficiency was admirable, particularly in light of the fact that she was flying blind, aware that something was wrong but not knowing what.

The second and more critical reason the pairings are by no means harmless is that they do not achieve the intended results. Karen's case is typical in that she had certainly become more comfortable with her erotic desires as her thirties were coming to a close, yet the goal of incorporating these desires into a satisfying long-term relationship was never reached. When all was said and done, she might as well have been learning how to ride a bike. Sex at last had a place in her life, but it had no place in an enduring intimacy—because she hasn't had one, and doesn't now.

In addition to providing pleasureable release, sex is supposed to be part of the glue that binds two people together. It was doing no such thing for Karen or her partners, as the brief duration of these pairings strongly attests. That she had developed a range of sexual skills, "and," as she proudly volunteered, "a knowledge of exactly what I like in bed and exactly what I don't," is beyond question. However, there is a world of difference between being at ease with one's own sexual impulses and allowing them to become an integral part of an affectionate and lasting relationship.

Karen had joined a gym during these years and worked out regularly there. What we are suggesting is that, although she had sexual relations at home and didn't consider them part of her workout, they might as well have been. In fact, it is illuminating to view sex as the only part of her exercise regimen that required someone else's participation. The combination of regular physical and sexual activity, two areas to which her demanding academic curriculum had forced her for years to give short shrift, made her feel healthy and outgoing.

What bothered us all along—more each year—was that this undeniably successful woman had no real personal life. She only thought she did. If the experiences of other women like her are any guide, that won't be her view either in a few years. But by then, it will be too late.

In the next chapter we will look at another large group of women who are in the same position and also don't know it: those who fall in love with a younger man. Then, in the chapter after that, we'll see what keeps them there, stuck in a frustrating situation.

10

Beth: Older Women, Younger Men

The idea of a romantic and sexual encounter between an older woman and a younger man dates back thousands of years. Oedipus' relationship with his mother, Jocasta, is the best-known classical example, even though it involves incest. The story is told from the viewpoint of Oedipus. The woman's motives and emotions in such circumstances remain unexamined.

A familiar recent example of this kind of encounter is Dustin Hoffman's portrayal in the film *The Graduate* of a young man erotically enmeshed with his parents' friend, Mrs. Robinson (now immortalized in a Simon and Garfunkel song). Once again, the story is told from the point of view of the young man, so the woman's urges, unless we think of them as purely sexual, remain unexplored. The story involving a young woman that the vast majority of people we surveyed consider most comparable, *Lolita*, has a heroine who is simply too young to be the object of the kind of detailed analysis that might help us understand the phenomenon. Mischief connected with the first budding of sexual interests is too superficial an explanation to do the subject justice in adults.

Switching from literature to life, both the men and the women in our sample think of such relationships as a "common facet of the contemporary scene." That is especially so in the 1980s, with more than three times as many members in 1984 holding that opinion as in 1959. Also, more than a third of the women in our survey over the age of thirty-five report having had such an affair by 1985, whereas only 9% of the women in this age range had had one by 1959.

This widespread acceptance of and familiarity with the phenomenon makes it all the more puzzling that answers to even the most basic questions are not available. For instance, which women are most likely to end up involved in such an affair? What happens to most such relationships over the years—and, of great importance to us, why? There is a fair amount of anecdotal material available, but no general conclusions based on a large-scale, long-term study. We were determined from the start to see what, if any, patterns existed.

One group from whom we consistently sought answers were the people currently involved in these relationships. They were usually only too happy to tell us their thoughts on the matter, and their replies became even more voluminous when the relationships finally ended. Their friends too had much to say about the subject. Nevertheless, we did not find valid the reasons given for the collapse of these relationships. The most commonly heard explanation, offered by many participants as well, was that the novelty wore off, and there wasn't enough else there to keep the relationship going. Both partners stated that they were aware of the unusual nature of the pairing but that it was precisely this atypical feature that lent a certain spark to their sex lives and conversation.

Representative remarks: "I could see that people on the street and in restaurants looked at us funny," said a woman in her early forties who lived for nearly two years with a man eleven years her junior. "It made me feel like all eyes were on us, like we were Elizabeth Taylor and Richard Burton or something." Another, who in her late thirties became involved with a twenty-nine-year-old, said, "It was a little wild in the beginning—he was passionate and a bit crazy. I liked feeling older and wiser. After a while, it just began to get stale. It wasn't exciting anymore."

The pat answers we typically received in response to our questions about why these relationships failed turned out to be mere face-saving. They sounded reasonable, and at first we accepted them as believable. Their validity was slowly undermined, however, when we began to monitor a wide variety of such relationships from start to finish. We had a guideline against which to measure them: the most conspicuous feature of one person's loss of interest in another person or thing is the quiet way in which the connection usually dissolves. If raspberry yogurt was the object of the infatuation, or classical guitar music or the boy next door, a waning of interest led to fewer yogurt purchases, other records on the turntable and a decreased number of casual visits to one's neighbor. Such associations die quietly.

That isn't what happened to these couples. Instead, they exploded, proof positive that one or, as we shall see, both parties were having serious trouble letting go. Far from being a mere fling founded on novelty, these pairings were based on a mutuality of needs as intense as any that humans have. The way in which the needs were being met was eventually resented by both parties, and in time the relationship teemed with love-hate feelings. At the end, rather than each party wandering off, tired of the exhilarating but no longer new experience he or she had tried, the relationship erupted with a force each party could still feel many years later.

One case history is sufficiently representative to display the general pattern the others followed.

HANDLING SMALL SETBACKS

Anyone who watched Beth Hannon go through her divorce would have been ready to swear she aged ten years in ten months. Her brown hair was still brown, and her picture-perfect nose was still straight (she had had it fixed at eighteen, right after graduating from high school), but those were the only features of her face that appeared unchanged. Her large brown eyes looked older and tired, the frequent puffiness offering mute testimony to the streams of tears that had flowed. Oddly, her lipstick grew progressively brighter during these months, as though she was unconsciously trying to distract the viewer from the toll her experiences were taking on the rest of her face. At times, she seemed resigned to the idea that her four-year marriage to Richard Weston was over. Other times, she was full of hope that the relationship could somehow be rejuvenated. Both possibilities made her frantic.

The peace that she had known during their best moments was based on the little things they had done together: walking down the road holding hands, while snowflakes gently brushed their cheeks, making everything around them seem part of a dream; having dinner at small, dimly lit restaurants, where their intense interest in one another reduced the raucous conversations of the other patrons to barely noticeable background sounds; listening to the radio while they drove to the beach, knowing that the music they were hearing would always be theirs, and only theirs, whether it was a Mozart piano concerto or the Top 40.

But the good times they shared radiated most of their warmth only in retrospect. When they were actually happening, Beth was too caught up in them to realize how much they meant to her. The lyric quality they possessed became most intense when they floated across her mind days and weeks later, as she was doing something totally unconnected with these events. She had shut out the world without even being aware of it.

Now, with Richard gone, it came back in with a rush, as though a vacuum had just been punctured. Suddenly everything seemed too much to her. Beth didn't have more to do; in many ways, she had less. There were fewer places to go, and fewer calls from friends, who tried their best to help at first, but finally backed away in order to let her terminally ill marriage die quietly. Beth saw the same set of faces at work, but they gave the appearance of having drawn closer now, like the sun to the earth during the summer, and they became irritating. Nothing shielded her any longer from what they said, so they sounded louder, more abrasive. They even looked uglier.

When things had been good between her and Richard, she hardly thought about him at all. Instead, she focused on the plans they had made for that evening or the following year, or the way they had spent the prior evening or the previous year. Once they drifted apart, she thought about him morning, noon, and night. She wasn't sure anymore whether she loved or hated him, yet he was always on her mind. Since she dwelt on the subject incessantly, it cropped up in her conversation with anyone who knew them, no matter how distantly, or had seen them together, no matter how briefly.

To distract herself, she tried to work harder. Beth had been able to force herself to study for finals even in courses she didn't like, and she tried the same techniques after the breakup. She liked her position as a department manager at a large retail store. It paid relatively well and, as she could see with the people around her, there were many opportunities for advancement. Becoming more deeply immersed in her work would, she thought, take less effort than coaxing herself to cram for a final exam previously did.

However, there was a difference, one that she hadn't anticipated. She was having difficulty keeping her mind from wandering. Nostalgically, she reviewed the humorous, pleasurably, and tranquil events that had highlighted the handful of years they had spent together. Their fights, which had become frequent and intense in the final weeks before Richard moved out, barely crossed her mind. As the months passed, she had less trouble disrupting her reverie. But she was still spending too much time lost in a melancholy that was often visible to her coworkers. "Hey, is anybody home?" one asked her, when she didn't reply to a question. "Should I make an appointment for you for a hearing test?"

It wasn't something she did consciously. Eventually, when she stumbled onto a method that allowed her to concentrate exclusively on her work and stop thinking about Richard altogether, she seized upon it. Scaring herself may have been the most effective way she knew to dive into her textbooks just before finals, but becoming angry was more effective where sweeping away the vestiges of her marriage was concerned. Whenever Richard's name or something even remotely connected with him came up, she would instantly get mad. She found the additional energy useful and channeled it into a number of avenues, most of them associated with work. The rest went into physical self-improvement. While never fat, her 5'4" body seemed leaner now, but there were tension lines around her mouth.

Catalogs and brochures from suppliers had arrived regularly at the store over the years, but she glanced at them briefly, if at all. Industry association breakfasts and luncheons had been held regularly during the previous four years, yet she attended only the most important ones. Manufacturers' reps visited the store like clockwork each season, but she gave most of them a polite brushoff, preferring to see their lines at her leisure with the department's buyer at her side.

All that changed in a matter of months. Beth's involvement with her work expanded dramatically as she got into the habit of arriving at the store earlier, staying later, and meeting a much larger number of people in her field. Her interest in her job had always been real, but now it took on a slightly manic quality that definitely hadn't been there before.

Distinguishing between the forest and the trees had been easy for her in the past. Beth seemed to have a built-in set of priorities that served her well over the years and allowed her to separate almost at a glance the significant from the trivial. That wasn't so any longer. She began to worry excessively about details, often at the expense of larger, more important issues that should have been staring her in the face. Coworkers and supervisors labeled her "dedicated—and hyper." What they didn't know was that she was using an abundance of anxiety and anger to help bond her to her work. The prospect of having no intimates, no one to turn to at home to rehash the day's events, generated enough nervousness to make certain that her grip on her work remained white-knuckled.

Beth was convinced that her chances for advancement had increased substantially as a result of her greater involvement with her job. And, at least at first, she wasn't disappointed. Two minor promotions occurred in the next four years, but there was nothing after that. While it would have shocked her to realize it, the people who worked with her on a daily basis considered her moody and short-tempered. They dated the change to the collapse of her marriage, and viewed the irritability as a kind of lasting bitterness that things had come to such an unhappy end.

They got the date right, but they badly misinterpreted the emotionalism and annoyance. In the final days of her marriage Beth had unwittingly hit upon the device of using chronic anger to free herself from thinking about a crumbling personal life and instead focus totally on her work. It felt good and simplified life considerably. It wasn't something she analyzed consciously, then or later, but since it served the purpose so well—eliminating her personal woes and enhancing her chances for advancement—there was nothing to think about. As far as Beth could see, she had found a cure for what ailed her, one that also increased the odds that all her career dreams would come true.

The fact that she regularly began coming to work in a huff wouldn't have troubled her even if she had noticed it. She hadn't, and no one brought it to her attention either. Days when her morning mood was cheerful and relaxed were rare. In fact, she was usually more weary than relaxed on such mornings. The two emotional states appeared quite similar to outsiders, but Beth had no trouble telling them apart. Her anger was imposing a heavy burden on top of the toll the work itself was exacting. No matter how weary she was, before her work day was even two hours old the anger was back. One of her supervisors, a woman who liked Beth, told us after transferring to a different firm, "Her frustration tolerance is low."

That it was. On any given day dozens of errors and mix-ups occur in a large store. A salesclerk pushes the wrong button on a cash register or writes an incorrect number on a sales slip, and sales figures and inventory no longer relate. Some items are mismarked altogether or parked in the wrong position on the floor. All this is par for the course and previously was handled without hysteria by Beth. She recognized that many of the store's employees were minimum-wage laborers, doing stock work and tagging, while some others were being paid a decent wage but simply didn't care. For unlike Beth, they knew that in a year or two they'd be leaving. On the whole, the store ran well enough and Beth had understood and dealt with it calmly when things went awry.

It was her fiery reaction to these little—and inevitable—annoyances that told us clearly that her inner state had changed. She was obviously carrying around all the frustration she could bear, since it took only a small setback now for Beth to reach the point of becoming visibly furious. When she saw a handful of items that were out of place, nearly two yards from where they were supposed to be, she snapped at the assistant who looked after such matters: "Even an idiot can see that that's not where they belong." As it turned out, a customer had moved them after the assistant (who brought another employee over to verify the fact) had placed them in the correct position on the shelf. "I think she drinks or something," the assistant said to his friend. That wasn't so, at least in this case, but it was clear that Beth was looking for reasons to become and stay incensed, and she was having little trouble finding them. Beth was convinced that the work itself was making her mad.

One thing was certain: the anger made her feel more determined. "I'm good at what I do, *really* good," she told us. "I've heard that my department makes more money than any other. Think of it, I'm carrying the whole store." Nothing else seemed to matter to her but her work, and since she was well aware of how often it was on her mind, she expected to be justly rewarded for her dedication. Promotions and pay raises were only half of what she expected and were things she thought about consciously. There was more, though it remained in the recesses of her mind, not far from consciousness. Somehow a satisfying personal life was also supposed to emerge.

Beth spent very little time looking for partners, and she dismissed outright everyone at the store as ineligible, thanks to their being gay, married, or unspeakably dull. Nevertheless, without ever putting it into so many words, she anticipated that a suitable lover—one who was on the same elevated plane to which she felt she'd now moved—would soon appear.

ANXIETY ABOUT ACHIEVING

During the last two years of her marriage to Richard, Beth repeatedly tried to get him to spend more time with her and less with his work. But he wouldn't. He considered every hour that he wasn't laboring a waste, and he would gladly have devoted twenty-four hours a day to his work if he could have. She got to be with him mainly when he was too tired to go on. Beth rightly told Richard that their relationship was suffering as a result. So was she, she said, at first quietly and then finally with a scream, as they neared the end: "It didn't use to be this way, and it's no good this way." The words of wisdom fell on deaf ears, even though the damage being caused by his unbalanced approach to life could no longer be denied.

Yet, ironically, here she was, five years later, in the very same position. Beth appeared to have contracted his disease, but she actually had a much worse case of it.

Enthusiasm drove Richard each day—as in the past, his parents had. He worked like a horse because, as he'd been taught, work was all that counted; if he did enough of it, it would bring him acclaim as well. Since both his father and mother had full-time jobs, he believed them when they communicated the message in a hundred subtle ways that his job should form the very core of his being. Work, not love, was all that he ever saw or heard about in his childhood home. Thanks to the blinders his parents had put on him from an early age, and to the field of computer software, which later entranced him, he poured himself into the task of developing his firm and its products with an eagerness that knew no bounds.

Beth, who came to a similar view of the world only later in life, tried hard to make up for lost time. Her parents expected her to work, since they knew they would not be in a position to leave her much of an inheritance, and they considered it absurd to assume that the man she fell in love with and married would be a millionaire. Beth found her work at the store enjoyable right from the start, yet it wasn't until she was twenty-eight that her degree of involvement in work matched Richard's in his early twenties.

However, it wasn't the seven-year head start that set these two individuals apart where their work was concerned; it was the emotions they were using to fuel their involvement with their respective fields. Anger and anxiety played a pivotal role in Beth's attachment to her work. She needed them—needed to feel them—to believe she was functioning at her best. More than Beth realized, she worried when they weren't present. It may seem insulting to say that Beth's involvement with her profession depended on anger and anxiety, since she had been interested in her job at the store when she was still happily married to Richard and these two negative emotions weren't dominant. The point is that a subtle but extremely important shift had occurred, one that was to have major consequences for both her professional life and her personal life.

We knew that Beth didn't *need* to be hostile and scared in order to feel immersed in her work because, as we mentioned, at one time these emotions were barely present and yet she thoroughly enjoyed what she was doing each day. Nor were the angry and anxious feelings generated to boost her ability to excel. Instead, she produced them naturally as her warm relationship with Richard began to fall apart; then Beth felt she needed them for self-protection and because she felt rejected.

It doesn't really matter how or why they entered the picture. The point is that once they did, they affected the way she related to people both on the job and off. Although she welcomed the presence of these powerful emotions, since they made her feel stronger and safer, in the long run they wound up doing her substantial harm.

Soon they became laced through her involvement with her work, like the fat in marbled meat. She could no longer even separate the two. When she was annoyed, she felt inspired and determined; whereas a semblance of calm, with no anger in the picture, made her think she had temporarily lost interest in her work. That thought alone was sufficient to make her panic on some subconscious level and generate enough anger and anxiety to make her once again clutch tightly to her job.

Students understand all too well how these forces operate. Some start out loving a particular course, so much so that they don't need a prod of any kind to get them to read the assigned text and others books in the subject area. Interest and enthusiasm, positive emotions, pull them happily along. Feeding their hunger for knowledge only makes them hungrier as their curiosity, rather than being satisfied and vanishing, grows. Once tests are introduced, however, the situation changes in a profound manner. Now a very real fear of failure enters the picture. For students attending full time and preparing for a profession, school is an all-or-nothing matter. Passing means they have the right, if they choose, to go on to the next step; failure means their progress comes to a halt, and it may even dash their dreams of being able to enter the field.

Unfortunately, they therefore often generate more anxiety about the prospect of failing a subject they love than one they hate but must take. One would think that if they are fond of the subject, they should have no trouble passing the course. But it is not that simple, since the tail can easily wind up wagging the dog. If they want to do more than just pass— if they want to graduate with distinction, at least in their major, their affection for their field can be transformed almost totally into anxiety. Even if they want merely to pass, and haven't given so much as a moment's thought to graduating with honors, the possibility that they might fail is ominous to them. For they would then be prevented from doing what, at the time anyway, means the most to them. In this case too, love is transformed into fear.

Notice how seemingly minor but actually radical a change has taken place in these students' involvement with their field. The key question, one whose answer shines a revealing light on what happened to Beth, is this: Once these negative emotions have entered the picture and attained a dominant position, do they leave right after final exams are finished? How nice it would be if the answer were yes. It isn't. Millions of students have instead come to the conclusion that if a subject doesn't make them nervous, they are no longer caught up in it.

Anxiety started out as a contaminant here, born of society's need to find a way to give more than sixty million students a relative ranking. Yet the contaminant ends up being the index young adults use to measure whether or not they are interested in a subject. If they don't feel anxious, they don't feel motivated. Sadly, they then mistake their calmness for indifference.

"I'VE BEEN HURT ONCE—BUT NEVER AGAIN"

Beth did, too. Her involvement with her work didn't start out dependent upon these negative emotions, these cattle prods. But once they entered the picture, as survival emotions of unparalleled strength, they took over. Their source didn't matter, nor was it relevant any longer that her reaction to the collapse of her marriage was entirely normal. What mattered greatly was that she welcomed them with open arms. As a temporary solution to her problems, these emotions—especially anger—were undeniably useful. Feeling sorry for herself, remaining depressed and viewing herself as helpless, would have been destructive responses. Getting mad instead helped her shore up her confidence and go into action. Throwing herself into her work and an exercise regimen was a healthy reaction to the emotional setback she had suffered.

But she overdid it. Without ever putting it into words, she had adopted the philosophy that "I've been hurt once, badly, and I am going to make certain that I'm never hurt this way again." Throughout her thirties, we would hear Beth repeatedly say that "Men are closed and impenetrable; you really never know what they're thinking." For some of the men she was describing, that certainly seemed to be true. Yet it had become an accurate description of herself as well. The abundance of emotion she displayed made her feel that she was revealing herself much more than they were, and that she was more open and accessible than the men she criticized.

Anger and anxiety may be fiery emotions, capable of filling the air with electricity, but used day after day by anyone, male or female, they usually serve the purposes of camouflage, not revelation. They are a smokescreen behind which troubled people often attempt to hide. Nor are they particularly revealing emotions. People who are chronically mad or nervous point a finger at many things that have no connection to the real source of their discomfort. A threatening situation may provoke these emotions in anyone, and in that case the person will have no trouble identifying the stimulus. However, if the threat is internal—a need that has gone unmet or a desire that one has classified as forbidden—it persists. So too must the defense against it persist.

Although Beth claimed over and over again that men don't let themselves be vulnerable, she was as determined as any man we have ever studied to make certain that *she* wasn't either. The emotions that Beth openly displayed were evidence of past pain, not the sign of a willingness to risk suffering more of it in a future relationship.

In fact, chronic anger and anxiety were telltale indications that she had taken out an internal insurance policy to guarantee against a repetition of her agony. The wall that she erected served two crucial purposes simultaneously: it held in many of the tears that she hadn't allowed herself to shed, and it would also, she hoped, prevent any more tears from being added to the heavy load of them that she was already carrying.

Beth wanted to feel safe and secure on her own, and anger and, to a lesser extent, anxiety rushed to the fore to help ensure that state. It may have been an effective method, but it was very expensive. Moreover, this was one insurance policy she might as well have bought from the Mafia. Through no fault of her own, no inherent weakness that she possessed—remember, millions of highly motivated students, male and female, have suffered a similar fate on both the undergraduate and, especially, the graduate level—she became addicted. As anyone who watched her on the job and off could attest, Beth no longer could live comfortably without daily doses of hostility and fear. Why did that have a profound effect on her professional and personal life? Because from then on, she mistook her own anger for ambition and her job-related anxieties for interest. As far as she could tell, she had no other interests but her work.

UPLIFTED BY LOVE

Between the ages of thirty-two and thirty-five Beth went out with a variety of men. Two were old friends, a third was a neighbor; a fourth, also a neighbor, had less income than she. Their three-month relationship resembled the one Karen Sherman was having at the time with Paul Heller. However, it wasn't until Beth was thirty-five that she had the kind of affair that Mrs. Robinson, in *The Graduate*, would have recognized. The fact that the relationship occurred when it did in Beth's life was no accident. A woman has to reach a certain level of income before it becomes likely that she will become involved with a man who earns less than she. To some extent, it is merely a matter of arithmetic. Thanks to inflation, the amount the woman must earn each year for relationships such as those described in the prior chapter to occur also keeps rising. Not so with age; after thirty-five, pairings involving an older woman and a younger man become more common, and they do so regardless of the woman's income.

Although it didn't usually happen with such predictable timing, seven months into her thirty-fifth year Beth met Alan Cooke. At the time she was fed up with her job ("fed up with *everything*," is what she actually said), and she decided to take a vacation. On the way to work she regularly passed a travel agency. In its window she had recently seen pictures of a beautiful island scene, and it was this scene that suddenly sprang to mind as she found herself dwelling on what seemed to her to be the monotonous nature of her activities at the store. Beth left work a few minutes early that day to get to the agency before it closed, and there she met the man who was to be her first younger lover.

Although thirty, Alan Cooke was often mistaken for someone in his mid-twenties. His straight, sandy brown hair flopped naturally to the side, with a few strands always covering his forehead no matter how often he brushed them back. A crisp, conscientious manner accompanied the casual look of his hair and clothes, and it seemed incongruous at first. Customers welcomed it, however, because their initial impression of Alan might have led them to think of him as indifferent and his information as unreliable. Quite the reverse turned out to be the case; this was a diligent and ambitious young man who was convinced that one day his love of work would throw off a handsome annual income. The fringe benefits, free travel and hotels, also appealed to him.

The two spent nearly an hour and a half discussing the $499, seven-day package that was advertised in the window. Each played it very straight, focusing only on the subject at hand, while making it appear that everything else they talked about was related to the topic in some way. "I think I told him my whole life story," said Beth with an uncomfortable laugh. "My job, my boss, my income—everything. I guess I was letting him know why I wanted to get away for a week." As Alan later commented, "There were other things on our minds, but we talked about the trip—sort of."

Beth returned from her vacation tanned but not relaxed. She was eager to call Alan to let him know how it had been, but she didn't want to call him too soon. What "too soon" was she wasn't sure, so she waited for two days. As it turned out, he also wanted to call her, and did so a few hours before she was about to place her call. "Just checking up on you," is how he began the conversation. When Beth started to give a lengthy description of the hotel and the setting, Alan interrupted after a few minutes with, "A customer just came in. Could we have dinner—maybe Saturday—and talk about it?" Beth was thrilled at the unexpected invitation and quickly agreed. When she started to give him her address, he said, "Thanks, but I think I already have it, don't I?" Beth found herself pleased at the realization that he did.

From the time he arrived that Saturday evening until the time they parted company at 1 a.m., the two talked nonstop. The trip had actually been uneventful, which was as it was supposed to be. But between Alan's extensive knowledge of the travel field and Beth's varied observations of what she had seen not only on this trip, but also on others, the two were never at a loss for words. Beth had gone on the trip with Sharon, "a so-so friend," as Beth described her, and when Beth got tired of discussing what she thought about the sights, she repeated the comments she had heard from Sharon.

It has often been observed that the essence of a really good business transaction is that both parties walk away afterwards thinking they got the better part of the deal. What was occurring here certainly wasn't business, but because each steadfastly maintained the fiction that evening that it *might* be, both wound up feeling that they were getting the best part of the bargain. Alan's actions could have been interpreted by a cynical outsider as basically those of an aggressive salesman who hoped to do more business in the future, if not with Beth, then with her coworkers and friends. In that case, Beth's warm replies to his questions were a victory for Alan, since another customer in her position might have brushed him and his inquiries off. Beth too viewed their evening together as a victory—for her—on this score, since she reminded herself at least three times during the conversation that not every travel agent would have been interested in hearing a six-hour description of her trip. As she remarked later to us, "It took me as long to tell him about it as it took me and Sharon to fly there and back." As long as Alan made it seem that business was somewhat on his mind, Beth was flattered. By the time the evening was over, there was no doubt in the mind of either that they were going to end up in bed—next time, when both dispensed with the excuse that had served so naturally to let them get to know one another a little better. Offhandedly, they made plans to see one another again the following weekend.

Beth was on edge all week, this time with a positive instead of a negative kind of energy, since she felt less angry than she had in months. "It must be the vacation," she told a coworker, and let the matter drop. When Alan showed up the following Saturday evening, he kissed her. It was a friendly peck that was supposed to land on her cheek, she later realized, but she turned her head accidentally and it landed on her lips. She reached up and touched his face as they kissed, and as she later commented, "I was sure at that moment that I could fly. It was tender, and wonderful." Although the kiss probably lasted only three seconds or so, she said, "for all I know it could have been *years*." They had dinner at a nearby restaurant and then went back to her apartment. During the following week, Beth described to us what happened a few hours later: "The lovemaking was exquisite. I've never experienced anything like it before."

Unlike Karen, Beth had been relatively comfortable with sex ever since her teen years. Yet neither she nor anyone else she knew thought of her as sensuous or openly erotic. "That's not me," Beth said more than once. It would have been more accurate to say that "That wasn't *me*," for she changed in a matter of days. Now she spoke freely about how good it felt to be in bed with Alan, talking, laughing, and making passionate love. Nor did it take long for her appetite to return after each session. No sooner did he leave than she began looking forward to his return, at most a week later.

For eleven months, they saw one another regularly, and even took a trip together. The thick cloud of romantic and erotic feelings that surrounded them gave Beth a different way of seeing things and protected her from life's little thorns—there each day, but not as painful now. It was a way of living that Beth hadn't experienced since the early days of her marriage to Richard. What she had with Alan seemed even better to her than what she had previously known, for this time she allowed herself, as she put it, "to wallow in it," and consciously acknowledged how good it felt.

WHO'S BOSS?

Things rarely go wrong overnight in a relationship. That was especially so in this case, for the problems that finally surfaced were there from the start. After Beth and Alan had been seeing one another for just over a month, Beth heard him say for the first time, "Stop bossing me around, will you?" It was said with gentle good humor, the way all their remarks to one another were voiced during these early days. The aura of warmth that surrounded the pair made even the darts they threw at one another seem like Q-Tips. The comments were often pointed, yet they didn't sting when they landed.

Nevertheless, the topic of bossiness cropped up again in their seventh and eighth month together, this time in a markedly less friendly manner. The incident during their eighth month involved the best route to use while driving to a large discount appliance store at which Beth wanted to buy a color TV. She was convinced that she knew the fastest way there; Alan was equally convinced that *he* did. However, before he even had a chance to tell Beth which way seemed the most appropriate, she started giving him directions. "Go there," she said, pointing to a road that Alan viewed as wrong. His reply was, "That's not going to take us anywhere near where we want to go." Beth repeated irritably that she had taken it before, some time back, and "got there quicker than if I'd flown."

Twenty minutes later they were lost. As Beth put it, "He was as mad as if a bee had stung him." Replying to our question, she added, "Yes, that's the angriest I've ever seen Alan." He pointed out at the time that he wasn't angry about their being lost but rather that she had insisted she knew the best way to get there. "You always act this bullheaded," he said, glaring at her. "You know everything. Well, I'm not so sure you know anything." They managed to get back on track by asking directions and got to the TV store at last, but the relationship never got fully back on track after that. Discussing it on the phone that week, trying to patch things up, Alan commented quietly, "There's no real back and forth— you tell me what to do. It's annoying sometimes, it really is."

Beth felt chastened by the fight and thought about it more than any other they'd had. There was no doubt in her mind, even after the conflict, that she was older and wiser than Alan. The five-year difference in their ages made her feel that there were many things she already knew that Alan didn't. Yet she clearly recognized for the first time that he had been reacting badly to her "bossiness" all along and holding in his irritation.

That is, until he could hold it in no longer and it came pouring out at the next provocation, no matter how slight. Wanting to keep the relationship intact, not viewing this as a major issue, Beth resolved to say the same things in the future that she would ordinarily have said, but in a more civil and less peremptory tone.

Although that was her expressed intention, it suffered the same fate as most New Year's resolutions come February. And it did so for a good reason. "At times, Alan is boyish," Beth said affectionately, one day when she was in a good mood. "He makes me feel like he needs me to look after him and all that." The nurturing attitude she was evidencing was strong, though it was emerging in Beth for the first time at thirty-six. It certainly was nowhere in evidence when Beth was married to Richard.

Why not? Because at the time she didn't have the confidence required to let the feelings, much less the actions, surface naturally. It takes a certain amount of self-assurance to care for someone calmly. Lacking the confidence in her early twenties, Beth repressed the nurturing feelings she had. "Repression" is the right description of what had happened, for she erased them from her conscious mind every bit as diligently as Karen continually erased sexual thoughts from hers while she was married to Bill.

There is an important parallel between these two pivotal aspects of an intimacy. When Beth's nurturing feelings were finally allowed freer expression—first, because she was now in her mid-to-late thirties, and second, because she had chosen a younger partner with whom they seemed more appropriate—they emerged clumsily. The same thing happened to Karen's long-repressed erotic impulses. When she unleashed them at last in her thirties, they too surfaced in a clumsy manner. For instance, initially Karen's bedmates found her intense interest arousing, yet they soon found her gestures—her touching them first too hard, then too soft, then too hard—a turnoff. She was intently trying to do what she hoped was stimulating, as she'd seen it in movies or imagined it, but the lack of practice during the prior two decades made almost everything she did at her age seem forced or brittle. As one ex-bedmate of hers put it, "It's kind of spastic—misses in lots of little ways that really add up. I'm not sure she's ever going to get it right."

Beth found herself in the same boat where a different set of feelings were concerned. Now that she was finally allowing herself to express the desire to look after someone, it came out in a manner that was comparable in its awkwardness to Karen's sexual behavior. However, while there are similarities between the results of repressed sexual and nurturing feelings, an important difference exists as well. There is an illuminating way to see what the difference is, and why it causes such harm to the personal lives of women who are successful in so many other spheres.

INSECURE MANAGERS

The behavior of executives isn't our main subject, but it can be used to shed an important light on what happened to Beth. People who have had no experience managing, and who suddenly find themselves in a managerial role, act in an interesting manner. Without an internal picture to guide them, one that they have assembled slowly over the years that is uniquely theirs, they often become a caricature of the person they are supposed to be on the job. The instructions they give, they give too forcefully. They are convinced, subconsciously, that if they speak in a normal tone of voice, they won't be heard. In fact, they are so convinced that this will happen, they act as if it already had. Since they haven't been heard, their instructions aren't being followed. So they feel perfectly justified in becoming openly annoyed at a subordinate—even though they are in the process, only then, of issuing the instruction in the first place. Call it anticipatory punishment; they are dishing it out beforehand because they are certain it will be well-earned later, when the subordinate doesn't do as he or she was told.

Nevertheless, the basic problem is theirs, not their subordinate's, and it springs from insecurity. What is of great interest about this situation is that the words and attitudes come out as the reverse of what they were originally intended to be. Paradoxically, insecure managers end up mistreating the very person they started out liking and wanting to work with most. Thanks to their low level of confidence, they frequently scold instead of complimenting or quietly addressing a valued subordinate.

The same thing typically happened to the women we studied in their thirties who had always wanted to love and look after someone but had never allowed themselves to. What prevented them from acting in the supportive manner that, one assumes, society strongly encourages? Two things, one private, the other public. As we've said, the psychological impediment was a lack of security; it takes a goodly measure of self-confidence to care *calmly* for someone one loves. However, there was a social impediment as well, one that had great power during the 1960s and, especially, the 1970s and 1980s. The prevailing attitude during these decades was that, in essence, anyone who wasn't continually being selfish was a fool. People would have recoiled if they'd been asked whether that was an apt description of their approach to life. But words aside, the behavior of the majority made it clear that their chief operating guideline was, "Selflessness doesn't get you anywhere. Besides, it makes you look too soft, a pushover." The most widely held view was that it was essential to be hard and determined, and fearless at times, if need be. Sometimes the attitude sounded like the code of ethics of a spy about to go undercover. Here too a cloak of casualness would be needed to mask the determination to succeed, perhaps without help from or even communication with anyone who could legitimately be labeled a friend.

The combination of forces, this one-two punch of psychological and sociological pressures, nearly guaranteed that the marriages of millions of women who were in their twenties and early thirties during these decades would collapse. A certain amount of self-centeredness is normal, but the exaggerated egocentric attitude of "looking out for Number One" had become dominant. In fact, it was readily visible during these years in the behavior of many individuals who claimed to be rejecting the attitude. That was easier said than done.

Condemning the attitude on moral grounds doesn't offer us any great insights, and neither does viewing it as a revolutionary step forward for women, now allegedly free of having to think about anyone but themselves. What *is* highly illuminating is a careful examination of how a large number of individual women actually responded to the intense and continuing pressure to go it alone and concentrate exclusively on success in business. Each day's actions by these women may seem insignificant and unrevealing, yet recorded patiently and looked at as a whole they form a mosaic with a message that is difficult to ignore.

Women who wanted to act in a nurturing manner with a man but were prevented from doing so in their twenties by the conjunction of their own lack of confidence and the prevailing attitudes that were hostile toward such behavior typically wound up divorced. They weren't genuinely "supportive," and neither were their husbands, which is precisely why both used the word so often. The topic was a frequent part of their conversations with one another because any supportiveness they did dispense, they noticed—and expected back. Taking so pivotal a part of a relationship and turning it into a mere bargaining chip destroyed its ability to serve as glue. Each might as well have been saying to the other, on a regular basis, "I'll tell you I love you, but only if you'll tell it to me as soon as I'm finished saying it."

Far from being the end of the story, the divorces that occurred as a result of such petty dealings (that eventually inspired great animosity) were only the beginning. After a few years of dating, what usually happened was that these women concentrated on their careers, complained about their paltry personal lives, and reached their mid-thirties. That is when many found a younger lover. Was it for energetic sex, as they themselves often suggested? In part, yes. In much larger part, it was because at last they wanted someone to look after. The prospect had scared them before, since it seemed to represent too large a drain on their time and emotions. Now, a decade later, it appealed to them far more than they were aware. A key question is: If they were searching subconsciously for a man they could nurture, why did they so often end up acting in a scolding rather than a supportive manner once they found him? The behavior of novice executives and sexually repressed women such as Karen points to the answer.

That they were willing to give a substantial part of themselves to a lover didn't mean they knew how. The process is more complicated than it seems at first glance. Without the experience of having done this for years with an intimate, so that one becomes accustomed neither to underdoing nor overdoing it, both extremes tend to surface in rapid alternation. Finally, only the negative side is seen. Beth sensed that her words often sounded more harsh than she meant them to be. "There's something wrong with me," she said, as her relationship with Alan visibly started to sink. "I keep putting my ice cream cone in the middle of my forehead instead of into my mouth."

Beth wasn't psychologically disturbed, and in fact her behavior under the circumstances (and during this era) was par for the course. She simply hadn't had the decades of practice required to interact smoothly and affectionately as part of an enduring intimacy. For some peculiar reason, people almost always assume that if they are willing at last to shower someone with warmth, they will do it well. Their view is that this is an inborn ability we all possess and can put into effect any time we please. As Beth once remarked, "You shouldn't have to *rehearse* how to love someone."

Her comment cleverly misses the point. We aren't talking about loving someone, we are talking about living with them. More accurately, what is at issue here is loving and living with them at the same time, two tasks people apparently often find at cross purposes. Beth found herself unable to feel great affection and to be close, day after day, to Alan. The reason was that, thanks to her lack of practice at it (remember, she had *not* done this with her first husband, Richard), she wound up being enormously clumsier in this area than she anticipated.

When she chided Alan, she leaped to the conclusion that she must have had good reason for acting this way. Even when her words seemed to her more critical than she actually felt, which was often the case, she would say to herself, "I know what I'm doing." Perhaps, but what was occurring here wasn't so much rational as rationalization. First came the behavior, springing from sources unknown, then came the explanation for the behavior. Unfortunately, it wasn't even close to being accurate.

The upshot was that the critical words led to more of the same, as Alan reacted irritably to the brusque treatment he was receiving. That put Beth on the defensive. She had said something, was challenged, and now had to justify her comments, something she did vigorously and well. This intelligent and articulate woman was good at thinking on her feet and had no trouble coming up with a variety of explanations for why she had said what she did—*and* for the way she'd said it. The one explanation she never offered, the one that didn't even occur to her, was that she wanted very much to please and to help him and didn't know how. Not once did she openly explore the possibility with Alan that it was this inability, born of a lack of practice, that was causing her words to come out cold and harsh instead of warm and helpful.

Her adult thoughts and behavior in this area had been shaped during an era of militancy, in which women unwittingly became soldiers in an unending battle against men for business success. The mentality of the time made the very idea of trying to make a man happy seem ludicrous. He was—they all were—the enemy, and only a traitor aids the enemy. As a result, Beth had had no experience at what she now wanted to do. Although in her mid-thirties, she was still a novice in this area. So she interpreted her own brusque remarks as having a valid basis. That compelled her to continue defending whatever she said or did, even when she sensed that her words and actions did not reflect her real feelings. Each rationalization, like any lie, only produced the need for more of the same, and the pit she was digging for herself rapidly grew deeper.

"I DON'T WANT IT TO END THIS WAY"

Soon there was no peace to be found. When Beth tried to express the affectionate feelings she had for Alan, he recoiled. Any way he looked at it, the tidal wave of positive emotions that came his way at what seemed the oddest moments struck him as excessive. He feared being inundated by the wave of warmth and couldn't understand where it came from. At no point did it occur to him that he was witnessing a lifetime of loving feelings, finally let loose and emerging in an awkward manner. He was sure that she always acted this way in any intimate situation—"It's her style," he told us—but the reverse was true. Beth had long kept a tight rein on her affectionate feelings, viewing herself as a realist.

Alan was puzzled by his own reactions to Beth's mood swings, which were visibly increasing. Near the end he told us, "I love her—still—but I don't *like* her anymore." As far as he could see, she was a menace to him now in good times and bad. Alan would gladly have tolerated the spasms of excessive warmth had it not been for the "needles," as he called them, that she also kept aiming his way. "Who needs that crap from her?" he asked rhetorically, two weeks before their final fight.

It came when the two were at dinner in a neighborhood restaurant. Beth mentioned that his shirt looked a little old. Fed up, Alan said, "Yeah, and so do you." He had never said anything like that to her before, and treated her more courteously—except in bed—than any other partner she'd had. Beth instantly realized that they, in her words, "were about to have a fight that could spell disaster," so she hastened to explain that she hadn't meant anything by the remark. "It's time for us to go buy you some new ones, that's all," she said, too late. Something had apparently snapped in Alan, because the barbed comments flowed fast and furious, this time in her direction. "You're a dried up old prune," he told her, putting two twenty-dollar bills on the table for the check, even though they were still in the middle of their meal. "I don't ever want to see you again." She raced after him, arguing as they walked down the street. "I was making a fool of myself," she later told us, "but I didn't care. I just wanted to talk some sense into him." Then, her eyes starting to fill with tears, she added, "I didn't want it to end this way."

Phone calls followed, more than a half-dozen from each to the other, but there was no going back. Although they met accidentally on the sidewalk in subsequent weeks, they didn't spend so much as an hour together after that. The love-hate feelings that filled their final moments as a pair are there to this day, six years later.

Beth may not have wanted things to end the way they did between her and Alan, but the fact remains that that is what happened to the vast majority of such relationships we monitored. Sometimes the older woman had already married the younger man; in other cases, she was living with him (or more accurately, he was living with her); in still others, they were simply seeing one another steadily and exclusively, like Beth and Alan. The legal and living arrangements turned out to have surprisingly little influence on the relationship's final outcome. Nor, surprisingly, did it matter whether the woman had had children with her former husband.

We say "surprisingly" because we initially assumed, when our study began, that a woman who had raised at least one child, or was in the process of doing so, would be able to manage a relationship with a younger lover more successfully than women like Beth, who had no children. We were wrong. A mother may learn something quite valuable about young boys by bringing up a few of her own, but it clearly doesn't carry over and improve the chances that she will have a more satisfying intimate relationship with a man who is younger than she.

The fate of these relationships instead depends on the forces that bring them into existence in the first place. Different internal forces produce different kinds of personal relationships.

Let us summarize briefly our findings in this area:

A woman who is more sexually repressed than her peers during her teens and twenties is significantly more likely than they to become divorced and, in her thirties, to have a least one low-income lover.

A woman who represses her desire to play a nurturing role with her husband during her twenties, and does this more than her peers typically do, is significantly more likely than they to become divorced and, in her mid-thirties or later, to have a younger lover.

In short, sexual repression in a young woman tends eventually to produce relationships with men who earn less than she, and repression of nurturing instincts tends eventually to produce relationships with men who are younger than she.

A few comments are needed here, since so many different kinds of relationships exist. Nurturance repression turned out to be more destructive than sexual repression to the personal—and later, professional—lives of the women we studied. That is, women who repeatedly erased from their minds in their twenties any thought of nurturing their healthy husbands (and did so in the name of realism) were even more likely to end up divorced than women who repeatedly scrubbed their minds of sexual thoughts (in the name of morality).

For convenience, let's call these two groups, respectively, "toughies" and "prudes." While an enormous amount has been written about toughness in men and prudery in women, almost nothing has been written about women who are trying to be tough. This is a nearly unexplored subject. What is important about such research and writing is that it be objective and useful rather than anecdotal and insulting. Our study indicates that most women who are trying to act tough as adults had a quite difficult time during both their childhood and adolescence. What they wanted most to receive—and didn't—was the very nurturing they become so niggardly about dispensing to their husbands during their twenties (if they marry at all). By their mid-thirties they typically find themselves divorced and, much to everyone's surprise, including their own, caught up in a tense relationship with a younger man. These feelings force their way to the surface and lock onto another person after all.

However, the relationship is usually of short duration even if it leads to marriage, which, unfortunately for both parties involved, often happens. The source of the trouble can be traced to the lifelong philosophy of such a woman, which is that being tough is a paramount goal. That may make her a source of inspiration to friends who are feeling temporarily depressed or defeated. And in the beginning, it even helps encourage her young lover to strive. But it doesn't take long for her to start becoming annoyed about having to give what she herself never got. In a flash, and typically without realizing it, the supportive behavior she brags about providing her friends and lovers turns into criticism and scoldings—which her truly depressed friends may tolerate, but which causes her young lover to flee. Once again, she is alone.

What is interesting is that the outcome of these relationships was the same whether or not the woman thought of herself as a feminist. If any-thing, the ideological baggage merely caused the relationships in which she became involved to collapse more quickly, since it gave her a ready-made sermon to deliver to her partners in a hostile manner. However, the psychological pressures were obviously of much greater strength than any political beliefs the woman held, since the same pattern was seen no matter what her beliefs on this subject were.

The women in our sample who were spending their lives trying to be tough generally came from homes in which there was substantial and continuing friction between husband and wife. Typically, the then-young girl's mother, whose own personal problems were causing her unwittingly to harm her daughter in the first place, blamed her husband for any un-happiness the child experienced, not to mention herself. "It's all your father's fault," the young girl heard her say repeatedly. That made it easier for the hardier daughters stuck in such a situation to adopt a stoical stance, lick their own wounds, and leave the house at the earliest opportunity.

Years later, when the marriages of these now-grown women failed because they refused to give what they'd never gotten, they moved on to younger lovers, and low-income ones as well (there was a sizable overlap between the two groups, and we'll see in the next chapter how it affected the sexual responses of the women who became involved). Then, almost automatically, they began to sing the songs they had learned at their mothers' knees. Instead of nursery rhymes, these tunes involved the same scapegoating each woman had seen her mother do. This time, the daughter's own husband was the chosen target.

It is easy to see why even career women who came from less dis-turbed families than this found such an emotionally constipated and chronically hostile woman useful. They wanted her to exhort them to be good soldiers, a regular reminder they felt they needed in their quest for business success on their own. What they never realized was how chaotic the personal life of almost every "tough" woman was, a chaos she could avoid only by deliberately having no personal life. Especially if she was in the public eye this seemed the preferable route to her, since she wasn't about to have her status compromised by having the truth about her em-bittered relationships become widely known. A few calamitous affairs in her past actually boosted her credibility, allowing her to claim that she had tried and found it impossible to sustain a relationship with a man. The obvious implication was that if she couldn't succeed, other women shouldn't even bother trying.

In spite of her posturing for public-relations purposes, the friends and coworkers, as well as current and ex-partners of each of the "tough" women we studied, proved the most reliable source of information about why she was so destructive, both to herself and to them. Thanks to her troubled childhood, she had made a virtue of a necessity—if she couldn't get any real affection, she would declare it irrelevant and unnecessary. The problem was that in making it a virtue, she allowed it to displace all the others. Her partners soon realized that warmth, spontaneity, and intimacy mattered more, things of which they eventually found her incapable. Only when there was a common enemy could she cooperate with anyone. One sentence was heard more often than all the others combined when we asked ex-spouses, friends, and lovers to pinpoint what they saw as her primary problem with personal relationships. Their reply was, "She stunts your growth."

This walking embodiment of self-suppression couldn't help but suppress others as well, in spite of her self-serving and frequent comments to the contrary. Why, then, did people put up with her? Men, particularly younger men, thought they were receiving encouragement. They quickly learned better, and left. Women, on the other hand, looked to her to stoke their furnaces so they could be more persistently ambitious. She offered them outrage and they gladly accepted it. However, they also became infected by the rest of her troubles. Most learned too late that they too had lost their ability to sustain an intimate relationship.

11

The High Cost of Climaxing— Without Losing Control

This is a book about women, not men—the men we studied need, and will have, a separate work, since their perceptions, thoughts, actions, and reactions differ in so many ways from those experienced by women. Nevertheless, one thing men have long done where women are concerned is important, since it helps us to understand something women now do that substantially diminishes their chances of having a personal life.

Virtually every boy who grows up in the United States will hear at least one male classmate or friend brag about his sexual exploits with women. Women who hear such boasts are offended at being thought of as mere sex objects. Although their annoyance is understandable, in a surprisingly large number of cases it misses the point. There are indeed many men who view women solely as sex objects, and aren't interested in them otherwise, but we had very few such men in our original sample (56 out of 3,011; less than 2%). Almost without exception, the men we studied were white-collar professionals or businessmen who looked forward to sharing their lives with a woman, and more than 90% of these men eventually married. It is the 1,600 blue-collar men we also studied who made derogatory remarks of all kinds about women not only as adolescents and young adults, but continue doing so to this day as well, when most are in their thirties and forties.

Knowing that white-collar men wanted women as companions every bit as much as they wanted them as bedmates, we paid particular attention whenever one of them started to sound like a blue-collar worker. We were especially interested in seeing *when* such negative feelings surfaced. Every effort was made to determine what, if any, connection the critical remarks had to events that were occurring, or had recently occurred, in the lives of these men.

To summarize our results briefly, what we found is that intelligent and educated men usually used biting comments about women—especially, hostile sexual references—as a way of imposing distance between themselves and specific women from whom they wanted to dissociate themselves. A great deal has been written about lack of commitment in men—their alleged tendency to avoid committing themselves to any of the women in whom they seem interested. We found the reverse to be closer to the truth: they generally used an antipathy or a coolness to women as a way of helping themselves sever a bond that had previously held them close to a particular woman. Defamatory remarks about women, far from being evidence of a pattern of noncommitment, were part of an ongoing attempt by the men in this group to dissolve a connection that had developed. Although the typical man involved in such an internal (and, later, external) struggle may not have realized why he was marshaling the feelings of aloofness in the first place, the fact remains that he had already become committed and now was seeking to get out.

This pair of scissors was used in a wide variety of settings, everything from one-night stands to marriages. While a blue-collar man who spent a night with a woman he had just met might engage in sexual bragging, a white-collar man who ridiculed to his friends a woman with whom he had just spent the night was usually seeking to accomplish a different goal. The put-downs were intended to erase any warm feelings for her that accidentally surfaced as a result of the sexual experience they had together. (Interestingly, when he really thought their sex together was unsatisfying, he had little to say about her to his coworkers or friends.)

We found that the key to understanding such remarks was this: *during a sexual climax, people ordinarily hand over a piece of themselves. More accurately, merely having sex with someone, even if no orgasms occur, accomplishes the same thing, if high levels of arousal are reached during the act.* An alternative way to look at this phenomenon is that during intercourse each incorporates some part of the other. Mental barriers are lowered as the level of arousal increases.

That may come as a surprise to people who have used intercourse with someone as a way of ridding themselves of a sexual or even romantic obsession with that person. Their view in essence is that sex, perhaps repeated a few times, killed the relationship. It may have indeed, since any affectionate feelings they developed for the person (as a result of sleeping with him or her) were more than offset in this instance by negative feelings that developed toward the other person (as a result of getting to know him or her better, in part through sex).

Be that as it may, the mechanism of handing a bit of oneself over to a sex partner with whom one has an orgasm, or at least becomes highly aroused, appears to proceed automatically *unless* one deliberately interferes, either consciously or subconsciously, with it. Such disruptions of this fundamental mechanism provide a far better explanation for why the white-collar men we studied were inclined to mock certain ex-partners and not others, and did so at certain times (usually soon after the sex act had taken place) and not others.

Anyone who has ever been in love knows how inadequate words can be to express feelings so intense. Uttering a phrase such as "I love you" or "I'm crazy about you" does little justice to the thoughts and emotions involved. The same applies to gratitude. People who have been on the receiving end of an unexpected helping hand when they badly needed it are often at a loss for words at that moment. They may spontaneously say "I'm grateful to you" or "I don't know how to thank you enough," yet they are the first to realize that only a small part of what they felt was actually embodied in the words they used. The problem here—and it has major consequences, as we'll soon see—is that making such intense private feelings public *trivializes* them.

Anyone who has had a personal experience that he or she wants to trivialize needs only to drag it into the bright light of day to have that happen. Telling friends about it, making it the butt of jokes, discussing it almost as if the event happened to someone else, achieves the goal. An experience that had previously seemed meaningful and huge can, in this way, be rendered pint-sized and stripped of significance. Or so one hopes. In short, men who talk openly about what happened between themselves and a woman with whom they had a climax may well be seeking to boost their own social status in the group. However, a more private purpose is served as well by such comments: the psychological goal is to sever any ties that automatically sprang up during moments of sexual intimacy the two experienced.

HOW HOLLYWOOD DEPICTS TOP EXECUTIVES

Do women act this way too? When our study first began in the 1950s, it was common for women to discuss the emotional dimensions of their personal lives but not the erotic aspects. If a relationship they were having was sufficiently troubled to warrant their bringing its details into the open in the first place, usually as part of a discussion with a friend or relative, sex was underplayed. The woman's own personality, that of her partner, and the specific areas of personality conflict were given prominence. "Going public" with such a description in these cases did not result in a trivialization of the emotions and events under discussion, for the speaker's involvement with what she was saying made it clear that the feelings were still very much alive. Her agony allowed the emotions to retain their substance.

Slowly at first, then more rapidly, that changed. During the 1960s women in their twenties and thirties became less inhibited about discussing their troubled relationships, with sex no longer excluded automatically. To many observers (psychologists and journalists, for instance, who could hear the changes explicitly) that seemed a step forward, part of a new and refreshing candor. However, during the 1970s and 1980s, the trend acquired a different tone altogether. Now the physical dimensions of the relationship were given prominence and personality underplayed. The progression, if that is the appropriate word for what happened as the decades passed, went as follows: women's descriptions in the 1950s of their personal involvements highlighted the emotional and nearly eliminated the sexual aspects of the pairing. In the 1960s, there was a better balance, with both aspects receiving attention. In the 1970s and 1980s, a growing number of women in their twenties and thirties discussed men as though they were sides of beef.

Some readers will say, "That's only fair, since that is how men have always looked at and talked about women behind their backs." Nevertheless, a closer examination of the comments men make, to see *which* men make them, and when, reveals that that definitely isn't so. Far from attaining "a sweet kind of revenge" or "poetic justice," as some of the women we studied characterized their new attitude toward publicly discussing the details of each intimate encounter with a man, these comments were actually harming those who made them.

To see how these women were doing themselves serious harm, both personally and professionally, one simple fact must be noted: white-collar women who were in their twenties and thirties during the 1970s and, even more so, the 1980s were copying the personality characteristics and public behavior of *blue-collar* men. Most of these women wanted to copy a man, at least to some extent. That much was deliberate, for each hoped that doing so would improve her chances of competing effectively against men in the business world. To her, the old cliche, "If you can't beat 'em, join 'em," seemed a recipe for success that simply couldn't fail. The mistake she made, and it was a monumental one, was to copy the wrong ones. She was unwittingly patterning her behavior after what, by any measure, are usually the *least* successful men in business. As an added bonus, she destroyed the possibility that she would ever have a satisfying personal life.

Why did that happen? What made women copy the wrong kind of men? Two factors were especially important. First, the men they should have been imitating struck them as dull. "The man in the gray flannel suit" had been a standard description during the 1950s for the type of man thought to be responsible for managing major corporations in the United States. Emphasis was usually placed on the word "gray," since, in the view of many women we interviewed while this phrase was popular, it characterized not only the suit, but also its wearer. At the time, women weren't interested in modeling themselves after businessmen, much less ones who fit this description, so they didn't hesitate to point out how bland such men seemed to them. After 1960, men too shared the desire to look a little less drab in dressing for the office, and with a youthful new president in the White House, everything from bell-bottom trousers and wide ties to more colorful suits and no tie at all was soon to be seen.

The improvements were the cause of much comment among the members of our sample, but young working women in particular viewed men as falling into two distinct groups, blue-collar and white-collar, though few used these specific labels. The color of a man's collar while he worked, not to mention that of the rest of his clothes, mattered to them far less than his general demeanor. What they noticed above all was the amount of excitement he radiated. Even after 1970, when it became common for women in their twenties and thirties to put all their eggs in the business basket, they still told us repeatedly that they found the personalities of male executives dull by comparison with those of blue-collar men.

How were they able to make this comparison? By using movies and television. Each year we carefully assessed the degree to which women who were in their twenties and thirties during the 1970s and 1980s actually got to know the senior executives in the firm for which they worked. If the company for which the women worked had fewer than a dozen employees, that happened almost automatically. For the vast majority who worked in firms larger than this, less than 4% of these women came to know well even *one* top corporate officer. More than 35% of the women saw senior executives at the firm regularly, usually in the hallway or elevator, and could identify some by name. But most had little direct contact with such men and certainly hadn't gotten to know them as well as they had their own immediate superiors, for example.

The distance we have from someone we don't know usually causes our image of the person to flatten. Under the circumstances, it is understandable that we may see him as relatively lifeless and uninteresting. However, we need a picture of what executives in the business world are like even if we don't know any personally, since our lives are directly affected by what they do. Enter Hollywood. If we don't have the opportunity to watch top executives in action, and few of us do, we don't come to appreciate the complexity of their positions and personalities. Films fill the gap. All we need do is turn on our TV sets or go to the movies.

Accuracy isn't the main goal of the people who make such films; by their own admission, entertainment is. That is convenient, since they themselves have little real experience in the business world and have generally watched no corporate officers in everyday actions on the job. Of the more than three hundred writers and directors we surveyed during the fifteen-year period 1970–1985 who had helped turn out TV or Hollywood movies in which business executives were portrayed, only six had previously attained what could reasonably be considered a middle managerial position before turning to their current profession—and all six had been only too happy to leave. "Business is boring," the majority told us. "*This* is exciting." Their lack of interest in and experience with senior management as it actually functions daily in business firms throughout the United States make them remarkably similar in attitude to the audience for whom they are making films. It also relieves filmmakers of the obligation to go beyond what they already know. Instead of attempting to give the audience the truth, they give it what they claim it wants: confirmation of its prejudices.

Perhaps to some extent that is what the public seeks. People who aren't at the top of the business world, but wish they were, often believe that those who *are* got there by being wicked and deceitful. It is a face-saving rationalization for what they see as their own failure to achieve a comparably high level of income and social status. However, film depictions of the kind we are discussing do more, without consciously intending to. They instruct young adults—especially ambitious young women—in how to behave in their quest for success in business. The men we studied also drew dangerously incorrect conclusions at times from what they saw in a movie, but women during the 1970s and 1980s particularly wanted to believe in the validity of what was presented on TV and movie screens. Like their male peers, they were not seeing an alternative version at the office from which they could have drawn some reality-based lessons, and they were almost excessively hungry for an "inside view" of what it takes to get to the top.

The people making films couldn't provide such inside information because they didn't have it. Nor did they see it as their responsibility to discover and disseminate these valuable insights. Instead, as they repeatedly made clear to us, the guidelines they use to shape their product from start to finish involve simplicity and looks. Specifically, each person's personality and appearance on screen have to be kept simple enough to be "instantly recognizable." Also, the central characters have to be handsome or pretty so that the viewing audience will quickly identify with them. As one director of a number of popular TV series told us, "I sometimes wonder if viewers realize how uncommonly attractive the people they see on TV are—everyone from newscasters to the stars in sitcoms and soaps—and that that's why the public finds it so easy to 'get into' these shows. They'd be the best-looking people at a typical party given anywhere in the United States." He and the others we interviewed mentioned two important exceptions to the rule about good looks. Someone who is being held up to ridicule (Archie Bunker, for instance, or Mel, the owner of the diner on "Alice") doesn't have to be physically attractive. "It helps if they *aren't*," a casting professional told us. "It's easier to laugh at someone who's at least a little bit funny looking." Second, supporting players can and should be plain or even unattractive, since that makes the stars of the show seem more visually—and hence emotionally—appealing by comparison.

The relevance of all this to the business and personal lives of the women we studied is that year after year they were seeing convincing portrayals of the most two-dimensional stereotypes imaginable of people who were allegedly "at the top." They were absorbing a message while they watched, being instructed as well as entertained, and not only by shows that presented business executives, no matter how flat and distorted the depiction.

THE REAL MESSAGE OF "DALLAS" AND "DYNASTY"

Ambitious women in our sample were the first to point out to us that the businessmen they saw on TV and in movies, or read about in popular novels, made less of an impact on them than such characters as Sylvester Stallone in *Rocky* and Marlon Brando in *The Godfather*. Other films and film stars that moved them included Burt Reynolds, in his Smokey and the Bandit series; Robert de Niro, in *Taxi*; John Travolta, in *Saturday Night Fever* and *Urban Cowboy*; and such movies as *Fame* and *Flashdance*. What is important about the impressions gained by young women from their many hours of movie and TV viewing is this: all these men were clearly blue-collar. The implication they couldn't help but draw, if only subconsciously, was that they too would have to behave the way the lead characters they had seen did—if they themselves hoped one day to become famous.

It struck us as bizarre that so many educated and intelligent young women from middle- and upper-middle-class families were unwittingly modeling their business behavior after that displayed by blue-collar men. It was happening by osmosis during their viewing hours, not as a result of conscious copying; but since they weren't seeing examples on the screen of bright, attractive, well-mannered, and thoughtful white-collar men who went on to become successes in business, by default they were forced to imitate what they *did* see. According to everything shown them on TV and in movies, white-collar men were merely wimps, whereas blue-collar men were exciting and were also the ones who were attaining fame. The choice of which group to mimic was obvious.

Some readers may say that this steady stream of subtle (and not-so-subtle) messages communicated by the mass media was finally contradicted by the two most popular TV series of all, "Dallas" and "Dynasty." Watched on a regular basis by the majority of young women in our sample, these shows at last seemed to concentrate on what allegedly was happening in the executive suites of most major corporations. The sky-high incomes and lavish lifestyles of the people involved clearly indicated that viewers were getting a rare chance to see how top businessmen and women behave.

Yet the fact remains that the real achievement of shows such as "Dallas" and "Dynasty" is to take undeniably blue-collar behavior, put it in a white-collar setting, and make it seem believable. The hostile confrontation-seeking of the most important characters is appropriately set in Texas and Denver, but in movies made a few decades ago, the same roles would have been played by conniving cattle ranchers, upstart gunslingers, and women who ran saloons. The final showdowns would have occurred in muddy streets, not plush offices in a high-rise.

The trappings of wealth, which "Dallas" and "Dynasty" use to convince their viewers that they are watching upper-class behavior, do indeed work. The old saw, "Nothing succeeds like success," is exemplified here, where the mansions, limos, expensive offices, and even more expensive clothes overshadow and recolor the pugnacious attitudes and actions of the main characters. That the wealth of these families is based on oil helps convey a clean-hands image that cattle ranchers, constantly brushing dust off their ten-gallon hats, could not have portrayed as convincingly. In short, if the women we studied had any doubts about it before, these two shows gave many the go-ahead to behave the way they thought successful men and women did. That allowed them to go to the office and, verbally at least, act like thugs.

When these women were subsequently passed over for promotions or were fired for their chronically abrasive and antagonistic stance, they immediately assumed they were being singled out because they were women. And they insisted on that interpretation even if a woman turned out to have been the one responsible for firing them. What they couldn't see, but any large-scale study such as ours would have confirmed, was that *men who acted in this way were brushed aside or fired even more quickly and more often.* Less tolerance was shown them for what the firm considered the stance of a juvenile delinquent. Had the men and women who un-wittingly modeled their office behavior after some mixture of Reynolds, Eastwood, Bronson, Travolta, Stallone, and J. R. Ewing been seeking to make their way to the top of a company full of manual laborers, it might have been effective. But the modern business world in which they were striving for success was concentrating more each year on services instead of manufacturing, and that called for an even more radical increase in civility than did the switch from cattle to oil. Being considerate and soft-spoken were no longer ornamental qualities in a rough-and-tumble open-air marketplace; they had become essential ingredients in anyone's rise—especially *within* the firm. Salespeople and those directly involved in the production of goods might be forgiven for raising their voices on occasion, since it may have been necessary for them to be heard to get their work done. But a far larger number of people were involved in quiet interper-sonal transactions in which brains, not brawn, were emphasized—or sup-posed to be. Accidentally restaging at the office the showdown from "High Noon" cost many a young man and woman their jobs and, finally, their careers.

This proved to be a more serious problem for the women in our sample than the men because a working woman in her twenties or thirties during the 1970s and 1980s was much more likely to believe that such behavior was appropriate and even commendable. "I'm standing up for my rights," many claimed. Others stated, "I'm speaking my mind." How-ever, given the nature of the office setting in which each was spending her day, the actions backfired. *Basically, she was aspiring to a senior position in a white-collar firm using what she didn't realize were dated and unacceptable blue-collar techniques.*

LEARNING TO ACT TOUGH

Nevertheless, the internal picture she had assembled over the years as a guide had come to have a life of its own, especially since it was being reaffirmed by everything she saw in movies and on television or read in women's magazines. Her view of her own business behavior was therefore no longer open to discussion. On this subject she was closed. She knew what she had to do, knew how she had to act, and now was fully prepared. It is small wonder that so many of the women we studied spent what was by any measure an excessive amount of time trying to find the right clothes to wear to the office. The nearly obsessive search for a dress-for-success formula led them to buy many books and read dozens of articles that were useless. Given the apparel choices of the large number of women in our sample who have done well in business, it is clear that no formula even comes close to being "right" for a substantial minority, much less the majority.

Why, then, the intense concentration on how to dress in order to get to the top? Because nothing else about these women—except their clothes—was open to discussion. Their behavior wasn't about to change, since each was convinced that she finally knew precisely how to act on the job in order to move ahead. The only thing left that she was willing to modify was what she wore to the office.

Look at it from her point of view for the moment: there was no question in her mind that she wanted to be a success in business, though in few cases did she fully understand why. Since she wasn't doing nearly as well as she had hoped and expected, she looked for easy answers. (In such circumstances, we all do.) But the one place she wasn't about to look for answers, either simple or complex, was in the area of her own everyday attitudes and behavior. These were off limits. By default, that made her dwell excessively on how she looked. Here was a visible and external dimension about which she could do something by merely visiting a few shops and salons. An anxious air surrounded the search, for if she couldn't find a mode of dress and makeup—a look that brought her success—she sensed that nothing else would. The key point is that without realizing it she arrived at this conclusion because she wasn't willing to consider changing anything else about herself.

In fact, she was afraid to. The picture of "appropriate business behavior "for the ambitious" that she had assembled over the years, and which she thought of as her own personal possession, was actually the same one that the overwhelming majority of other ambitious women in business had. It was no woman's personal possession, in spite of each having come to see it as uniquely, and even originally, hers.

The fear that seized her during the rare moments when she thought about changing her attitudes and behavior was therefore rational. Such modifications would indeed have pulled her from the mainstream and increased her sense of social isolation. The desire to be part of the crowd doesn't disappear after high school, it merely decreases. Humans are social beings and want to be noticed by others, even if they have to concoct some differences to flaunt in order to call attention to themselves.

What *was* the mainstream in which these women were unwittingly trying so hard to remain? There is one thread that runs through the comments and actions of the vast majority of women we studied during the 1970s and 1980s, regardless of their field, religion, background, or location. We can highlight it best by seeing what preceded it. During the 1950s, the primary goal of women in their twenties and thirties was to appear morally and ethically virtuous, good partners and parents. Sexual repression was viewed as right and even necessary in a civilized society.

Sounding educated and intelligent was deemed worth the bother. The 1960s was primarily a decade of rebellious transition. To what? To a new set of standards in the 1970s and 1980s in which attaining success at any cost became the name of the game. Ambition was in, sexual repression was out. Ethics and morality struck people as dated topics, since most were well aware that the new guideline implied that the ends justified the means. The goal of success was too important now to worry much about how one attained it.

Summarizing so major a shift, one that involved many millions of lives, is never easy. But thanks to the remarkable similarity during these years in the words and behavior of the women we studied, it can be done without oversimplifying what happened. It is important to keep in mind, though, that each saw the stand she was taking as solely hers and only sensed subconsciously, if at all, that she would be separating herself from the mainstream if she adopted a different position.

In short, *between the 1950s and the 1980s, (the most important trend affecting women in the United States was that all the prudes became toughies.* That is, in the 1950s, women were expected to imitate the eternal virginity of a Doris Day or Debbie Reynolds. (As one movie critic commented at the time, "I knew Doris *before* she was a virgin.") By the late 1970s and early 1980s they were expected to imitate blue-collar men who were TV and movie idols. As one recent Radcliffe graduate put it in 1984, accidentally speaking for the rest, "I ain't no lady, so please don't call me one."

AN ON-THE-GO IMAGE

People who think they are tough always feel compelled to show it. Being tough means acting tough. Flaunting it is imperative. As mentioned earlier, the majority of women we studied did decide unwittingly to flaunt it regularly, in varying degrees, at the office. It got them fired or, more typically, passed over for pay raises and promotions. That they thought this was evidence of sex discrimination is unfortunate, since they were unable to take the steps necessary to remedy the situation. In fact, their interpretation of what had transpired and was troubling them usually made the situation worse by inclining them to become still more belligerent.

It was in bed, however, that they were really determined to show how tough they were. As they knew from many years of watching how blue-collar men approached women, anything connected with sex presented a golden opportunity to "strut my stuff," as one manual laborer put it. The overt and crude behavior to which the women in our sample had been subject over the years, especially during their teens and twenties, had made a real dent in their thinking. They found the noises, obscene remarks, and clawing paws of passersby—most of them minority men or blue-collar workers—infuriating. Now, without realizing it, they were in the process of mimicking what they had seen. In their case, it was more words than action. After all, they were still relatively civilized white-collar women with college educations. Nevertheless, there was no question in their minds that the new, more verbally aggressive posture they had adopted was right. It felt good and, most important of all, it gave them a satisfying sense of something for which they had long yearned: revenge.

The trouble is that they were about to take revenge on *white-collar* men, ones they hadn't even met yet, for insults and abuse the women had received over the years from *blue-collar* men. It was hardly a recipe for romance.

Although they talked much about their personal lives, and the many problems they were encountering in this sphere, these women were actually much more interested in getting even. As every Clint Eastwood or Charles Bronson fan knows, seeking to avenge an insult or right a wrong gives people all the excuses they need to be brutal and even sadistic, an opportunity to show how undeniably tough and aggressive they are.

Educated women in the 1970s and, particularly, the 1980s thus began to view men as stud animals. The same kind of catcalling and estimation of each man's sexual "delivery power," comments that women had been hearing for decades when they passed a site full of construction workers or a street corner full of minority men, now became all the rage among mainstream women. "I'll bet he's really well hung," said a twenty-seven-year-old to her best friend, age twenty-nine, after a stocky coworker passed them in the hall. "The bigger the better," was the friend's reply. That weekend, both women went to a club that featured male strippers, where the two bellowed and laughed as loudly as any pair of blue-collar men would have in days of yore at a burlesque house.

Key question: What kinds of love lives did these two women have, and why? By now, the answer shouldn't be hard to guess. When the twenty-nine-year-old, Carolyn, met a man named Steve in the Hamptons (on Long Island) to whom she was very attracted, we thought she might drop her toughie stance and act in a more relaxed and open manner, especially after the two had dated and slept together a number of times. Coming to know one another better would, we anticipated, induce a switch in her behavior. That, after all, is what blue-collar men usually did with the women *they* eventually married.

It was startling and revealing to see that that was not what white-collar women intent on proving their toughness did. On the contrary, since they had someone at last to whom they were drawing near, and whose presence might have caused them to feel secure and fulfilled, they tried even harder to stay lean and mean. More than ever, they were determined to be closed and inaccessible, so as to remain candidates for the brass ring—the public recognition—they wanted above all.

A centuries-old French maxim is *Plus ca change, plus c'est la meme chose*—"the more things change, the more they stay the same." Perhaps that is so about certain things, but not exercise in the 1980s. Carolyn and Steve, a lawyer three years older than she, dated for nearly two years and then got married. Soon afterward she began a strenuous exercise regimen. While she and Steve had gone skiing and swimming together frequently during their courtship, by the tenth month of their marriage Carolyn felt it was essential to start exercising regularly and hard.

Her comments about what she was doing made it seem as though nothing had changed: "This is what women who want to look attractive for their husbands have always done." The remark was a smokescreen, intended to distract both her listeners and herself from a much more important, though unspoken, goal. Only to a small extent was this activity undertaken with her husband in mind. As we'll soon see, to an enormously larger extent it was motivated by two forces that were merging and pushing her in the same direction. Like most of her peers, Carolyn, now thirty-two, wanted to stay hypervigilant, lithe, and limber, ready for any opportunity or setback that might come her way at work. Second, she wanted to be thought appealing by everybody. Being physically fit was going to make her more radiant and photogenic. Her chief goal was an audience of many, not the inherently inadequate audience of one she had at home.

Everyone who dreams of success has an image of what that success looks like to others. Carolyn's mental picture was so vivid when she was thirty-two that she had little difficulty imagining it in print. At one time, during the early years of our study, women dreamed of being in the movies; now, most hope one day to be on the cover of one of the better-known women's magazines, each with her story told in loving detail in that issue's pages. Carolyn, by then the associate producer of a TV show in New York, was certain that it was only a matter of time before that happened to her.

"I don't want to look like a cover model," she said at thirty-three. "They are pretty, all right, but dumb." The picture she had in mind called for her to be striding briskly toward the camera, and hence right out of the magazine's cover, with her wavy brown hair flowing behind her, held down on the top of the head by her glasses. Unlike most of the women we studied, Carolyn was aware that this affectation was the equivalent for a woman of a man who loosened his tie just the right amount to convey the message, "Wow, have I been busy." Carolyn felt that positioning her glasses in this way projected the appropriate "on-the-go" image.

Her smiling face, clear skin, sparkling brown eyes, and a sweater draped over her shoulders with its sleeves tied ever-so-casually in front of her completed the picture. "Oh, yes," she quickly added, "I'm carrying an attache case. I want people to know that I'm a successful *business*woman, and not just another attractive face."

The time she spent alone with Steve was therefore more of a letdown than she was willing to acknowledge either to herself or anyone else. Rather than a fulfillment of something for which she longed, being with Steve was, in her mind, at worst a detour from the road on which she wanted to be traveling, and at best preparation for her coming renown. However, she knew that it could hardly be viewed as a step toward bigger and better things for herself in the public eye if she and Steve became too close. It was, as she put it repeatedly, "absolutely essential to maintain my own separate identity."

As many other ambitious women were saying the same thing in the 1970s and 1980s, Carolyn saw no reason to analyze what her words actually meant. Yet she would have been stunned to realize why she felt compelled to say them so often: there was only *one* person on the magazine's cover.

BEATING MEN AT THEIR OWN GAME

In bed, where an important tie between two people steadily grows, Carolyn had to be especially careful. In her view, sex involved bondage, not bonding. That forced her to deliberately distort sexual relations, making them seem like pornography, a subject about which she had many hostile things to say. Yet the pornography against which she regularly railed was in *her* mind, not her husband's. (He found the whole subject adolescent.) Casting intercourse in such a mechanically genital and oral-genital light served a crucial purpose of Carolyn's. On many an occasion she said, "I don't want to be used; I'm not a mere sex object." From a single woman without any partners who is afraid of being sexually exploited and abandoned, the remarks would have made sense. No one wants to be subject to this kind of manipulative and indifferent treatment by another.

However, it is noteworthy that married women in their twenties and thirties, or those who were living with or seeing a boyfriend regularly, were the ones most likely to be voicing such remarks in the 1970s and especially the 1980s. The main reason was that they were looking for an excuse to maintain a strong sense of separateness from the spouses or partners with whom they were involved. Thinking of men as users, sexual exploiters, served the purpose perfectly. It allowed each woman to assume the preliminary stance, "Don't fence me in." Since she badly wanted to take a solo bow in the near future, there was actually no room in her life for a real partner.

Previous generations of American women used the "all men are beasts" theme as a way of maintaining their own prudishness. Each woman piously proclaimed herself spiritual, while perceiving each man as an animal. Oddly enough, the same theme is used by the current generation of young career women, with a fascinating twist. Viewing men as beasts this time allows each woman to become not a prude but a toughie. In a previous era, women reacted to the alleged brutishness of men, even their own husbands, by becoming ever more civilized and refined. Now women react to the alleged brutishness of men by becoming every bit as hard-hearted and aggressive as they think men are, and then some.

What is the underlying goal in both cases, past and present? Above all, competing effectively. Previously, women were intent upon beating men in a *different* arena, one of their own making, since they weren't permitted to play in the same one as men. An appropriate label for the women's strategy was, "If you can't beat them, start a new contest." Currently, with men and women openly competing in the same arena, women have decided that the best way to beat them is to play the same game men are playing, only to do it even better. As we've seen, the tragedy is that they are copying a game played by men who are largely losers.

The key point, one to keep in mind when assessing why some women have successful professional and personal lives and others don't, is that prudes in the past and toughies now are intensely competitive people. Regardless of what they say, they aren't interested in intimacy nearly as much as they are in a victory—and a public one, at that.

The prospect of truly being open to a man, inviting him into her being as well as her body, scared rather than exhilarated Carolyn. She had a healthy interest in the physical aspects of sex, and said candidly, both before and after she met Steve, "A good orgasm, like a good workout at the health club, makes me feel fabulous." The problem she faced was a simple but pivotal one: how to climax without handing over control.

When Carolyn felt herself drawing near an orgasm, she quickly substituted another partner in her mind for Steve. This is what the majority of women we studied who were seeking to escape—without being detected—did. "In the beginning, when he's just doing foreplay, I know it's him," she said at thirty-two and again at thirty-three. "But once I'm aroused, he kind of disappears and someone else is there." What the comment omits, which became clear only during later interviews, is that after a while Carolyn couldn't reach the stage of being "very aroused" unless she *first* switched lovers mentally soon after each lovemaking session began. In essence, Steve had become an impediment to the heights of sexual exitement she was trying to attain in order to climax. The range of lovers she fantasized while having intercourse with Steve was wide and managed during the first three years of her marriage to include more than three dozen men Carolyn had met or seen. Actually, it didn't matter whom she imagined herself having sex with at that moment, just as long as it wasn't her husband.

Many women seeking to achieve the same goal used a different route. Instead of conjuring up another partner while the one to whom they were married made love to them, they focused on something else altogether, something nonsexual. The most common thoughts on these women's minds at such moments were about the day's events at the office, or those that would take the place the next day. How did they view what they were doing when they were supposed to be aroused and enjoying the lovemaking? The most frequently encountered reply (though it was one few husbands heard) was, "I guess I just can't get my mind off my work."

That sounds logical, and from time to time it could happen to anyone. But after it happened enough times to these women, it became clear which was the chicken and which the egg. In cases such as Carolyn's best friend, Marilyn, cause and effect proceeded from her deliberate lack of interest in her lover to her dwelling upon something—anything—other than that lover. Avoiding sexual thoughts, and thereby interfering with the natural bonding processes that would otherwise have taken place during sex, was the real goal.

There is an interesting way to look at the events we've been discussing, and it has to do with erotic imagery even more than erotic reality. From the start of our study in the late 1950s, we were interested in seeing whether the sexual fantasies of working and non-working women changed over the years, and if so, in what way. Specifically, we wanted to know whether the images (if any) to which twenty-seven or thirty-seven-year-old women usually climaxed in the 1950s and 1960s would be the same ones to which twenty-seven or thirty-seven-year-old women climaxed in the 1970s and 1980s.

Important shifts did indeed occur as the decades passed. In the 1950s, the virginal self-image that many single and married women tried to project publicly was typically accompanied, during foreplay and intercourse, by seduction fantasies—dashing men, usually resembling leading actors the women had recently seen in the movies, were overwhelming them romantically and, finally, sexually, until both climaxed simultaneously.

Why did these women, who fell into the category we've labeled "prude," even need such an image? Couldn't they have openly enjoyed the sexual reality they and their husbands were living each day? The answer is no, and the reason is that they didn't think they were supposed to. More to the point, it was revealing to discover over the years that the more any particular woman disliked her husband, the more likely she was to engage regularly in these nightly flights of sexual fancy.

By the late 1970s and 1980s, the majority of ambitious women we studied had made the switch decisively from prude to toughie. That is, a success-oriented twenty-seven or thirty-seven-year-old woman was likely to be sexually prim and proper in the 1950s, whereas a similarly success-oriented twenty-seven or thirty-seven-year-old in the 1980s was now just as likely to be open and (verbally) aggressive about sex. Seduction fantasies, right down to being carried in a faint to the nearby canopied bed where the explosive embrace at last takes place, seem a bit dated and tame to the latter group, unless they themselves are doing the seducing.

One of the women in our sample, Cathy, age thirty-six, a veteran in the apparel sales field, characterized the shift very well in the spring of 1984. To describe her briefly, Cathy tried so hard day in and day out to be a toughie, we worried that she might sprain herself through excessive posturing. Her comment was, "The only women who fall for that kind of soppy junk now are the ones who still keel over when they see a mouse and drop a hanky behind them to catch a man's eye." The expletives with which she deliberately peppered her phrases, to convey the appropriately hardboiled impression, have been deleted.

A new set of fantasies had to be created by the members of this group; the images used in beds across the nation made sex suddenly seem like an Olympic athletic event. "The bigger the better" was a comment certain men had long made about women's breasts, and the men's response to nude photos made it clear that they meant what they said. Now the same comment was being applied by women to men's genitalia, as was clear from the fantasies to which women frequently climaxed.

Once again, the more militant reader may ask, "Well, that's only fair, isn't it? Women are merely doing today what men used to do yesterday." The sentence ducks an important question: namely, *which* men were doing this in days gone by? Even more important, which men are doing it now? The answer would shock the women we're discussing, since it brings us to the same conclusion we arrived at previously from a different direction: blue-collar men were—and are—the ones most likely to be enamored of Jayne Mansfield types then and Dolly Parton types now.

In short, for every woman in the 1980s who was marching against pornography in the seedier downtown parts of the city, there were tens of thousands of her sisters entertaining pornographic images at home, especially as each approached orgasm. The main reason the women were secretly doing so is that it represented a good way to mentally dispose of their partners while still managing to climax.

ANXIETY AFTER INTERCOURSE

One of the most surprising findings that emerged during our study concerned the way women behaved once each sex session was finished. There was much to be learned from analyzing their actions and images before and during intercourse. However, the most pivotal reactions usually didn't surface until each session was over.

Best of all, while people often forget the images and fantasies that helped them attain a climax, their behavior after intercourse is visible to their partners. In this instance, two stories are better than one, and much that would otherwise have remained hidden to us as researchers, mainly because it was forgotten by the people involved, came to light.

Before we see *why* the behavior of these women immediately after intercourse is so revealing, let's look at *what* typically happens. When a large enough number of cases is examined for a sufficiently long period of time, it becomes clear that they fall primarily into two groups. In the first group are women who usually become anxious when each episode is through. That might be expected to happen if a woman has just had sex with someone she doesn't know very well. However, the cases we're considering are different. The men in question are either the women's husbands, roommates or steady boyfriends. One-night stands and short-term flings have been excluded.

The woman's post-coital anxiety in such circumstances is puzzling, since one would have anticipated a period of peace, a moment of calm, after a number of powerful and primitive physical and emotional needs have been met with someone for whom she presumably cares. How does the anxiety evidence itself? Most often, as fussing—a tense and restless concern about one thing or another, anything from the prospect of the sheets becoming soiled to nervous phrases, such as, "I just remembered something I *have* to do tomorrow." Similar thoughts might occur to anyone from time to time, particularly during the moments of lucidity that are normally present after a climax. What is under discussion here is another matter altogether, since it recurs with great regularity and is there with a variety of partners. Even with a second husband this is often one of the few constants in the sex lives of women in this group.

The second group of women consists of those who are inclined to become irritable rather than anxious after intercourse. They are looking for an argument and, not surprisingly, they can always find one. Criticizing a peaceful partner is easy; all that is needed is to start criticizing him for being so peaceful. If he is falling asleep, that makes him even more of a sitting duck, for then his drowsiness can be condemned as a sign of indifference. (Oddly, few of the men we studied who repeatedly found themselves in this situation asked why their partner was so riled up when they were so relaxed. Instead, they usually rushed to defend themselves, a fatal error that only caused the situation to deteriorate further.)

There is a sizable number of women who become angry on a regular basis after intercourse. And precisely because each blowup is seen in isolation, and taken at face value, the underlying pattern is overlooked. In some cases, the hostility is aimed directly at the woman's partner, while in others it attaches itself to someone with whom the woman had business or social contact during the day. Again, it is important to emphasize that "getting annoyed only in retrospect" is a common occurrence, one that is closely related to the idea that "I should have told that S.O.B. where to go while I still had the chance."

People also find themselves annoyed after the fact if they manage to think of a wonderful comeback to an insulting sentence that was aimed at them. They may say with a smile, "Why didn't I think of that at the time," but the interchange about which they are thinking is more aggressive than the smile indicates. The sentence alone reveals that they have been mentally fashioning a spear all along. The fact that they now want to throw it, or wish they had, is only to be expected. The point here is that the peaceful moments people experience after a climax may be just the right setting for them to find the spear they were seeking, so a momentary display of open hostility may well be seen. The key question is: How often is it there?

If it is present after even a quarter of the woman's sexual relations, and with one partner after the next, one is entitled to wonder whether the anger is merely serving a self-protective purpose that has nothing to do with the countless number of issues to which it attaches itself night after night. Maybe the woman who is angry—or anxious—after a climax is afraid that something terrible will happen to her, or worse, that it already has.

What is she afraid of? *Losing control.* It is only after one monitors a large group of women over a period of decades that one comes to realize just how central the idea of control is to those who are bent on becoming successful. Of all the means they will use to the end they are seeking, this is the one they deem the most essential. But it gives rise to a considerable and, in many cases, crippling quantity of obsessive thoughts and compulsive behaviors. Rather than springing from an unknown source, as the majority of these women would have us believe ("It's just the way I am," "I was born this tense"), these harmful side effects are direct consequences of the self-imposed pressure the women are under to attain wealth, position and renown.

Their inability to function at their best, except for brief but intense spurts, eventually costs them dearly. Yet we now know this to be an inevitable result of the excessively controlled approach they are using. How does it radically reduce their chances of success? What, specifically, is the pitfall in their approach?

The damage begins at home. Women who have unwittingly based their quest for success primarily on self-control cannot leave this approach at the door as they enter their apartment or house. For one thing, they don't realize how much of each day they spend being guarded and hyper-vigilant, trying hard to look and sound tough. Nor do they realize how many years they have been doing this. Since the stance was adopted sub-consciously, and each lives it without giving the matter much thought, the perspective needed to see it for what it is—and change it—is missing.

Second—and this is one of the most bizarre findings in our entire study—the majority of women who are using self-control above all to get ahead at the office become even more control-oriented toward themselves and the people around them at home. Precisely at the moment when they might be expected to lower their guard and relax, they raise it still higher. Why in the world do they do this? Because here, at home, they can more successfully exert control.

On the job, they may want, robot-like, to be fully in command of their own words and emotions, actions and attitudes, but most recognize they aren't. Coworkers and superiors often make comments or decisions that leave the women rattled or surprised. That is par for the course in the business world, where unpredictability is one of the few things that is predictable from one day to the next. (There *is* more predictability over the long term, but we're discussing day-to-day events here.) The jolts are especially jarring to the ambitious women we studied, given what is in most cases their excessively high degree of self-control.

While the office setting may leave them frazzled and frustrated, home is the place where they can finally wield the kind of controlling influence they don't feel they have at work. Not only does that make them often act in an irritable and demanding manner with their husbands and children, but they are also no less harsh with themselves. When they make minor mistakes in the kitchen or bathroom in the evening, knock-ing something over, for instance, they are very critical of themselves, and they have the same response toward any other slip-ups they or those around them make. When they are asked about their own reactions, they claim that they act this way because they have been under stress all day and it is spilling over now and affecting their evening mood.

No doubt there is some truth to this explanation, but not much. What the evidence indicates is that they treat themselves even more harshly at home than they do at the office because at home it is reasonable for them to anticipate that they will be more in control of their own be-havior. Their self-expectations are higher, even though the stakes, presumably, are lower. When a mistake occurs their expectations are disappointed and they are even *more* self-critical than they are on the job, where they are well aware that slip-ups take place regularly that involve them but are none of their doing.

"IF I LOST CONTROL, I'D GO INSANE"

Something crucial is lost in the abundance of internal tension generated both on the job and off by women who are determined to succeed at any cost: a chance to unwind. There is an important paradox here. Since the women we are discussing never really permit themselves this luxury, they are continually talking about it. Typical comments are, "I should go to a spa," "Maybe a massage would loosen up these tight shoulders of mine," "It would be nice to work for a month, then vacation for one, and so on," and, "I need a change of pace." The point is that someone who has a good night's sleep doesn't go through the next day longing for one. However, those who don't allow themselves to get the rest they need (when they are supposed to) spend their days consumed by the subject (when they are supposed to be concentrating on other tasks).

As things now stand, there is little chance that these highly motivated and intelligent women will find their lives changing for the better unless they start immediately to attack the basics instead of the superficial aspects upon which most women's magazines endlessly dwell ("Instant Makeover: A New You in 15 Minutes!"). The articles might as well be about rearranging the deck chairs on the Titanic. The causes, not the consequences, of the problem should be each woman's main focus.

Specifically, what is at issue here is that, first, her control expectations—too high to begin with—rise even higher when her work day is done. Second, she is afraid of her husband—emotionally, not physically. Having looked at the first, let's consider the second. She knows very well that it is hard for either a man or a woman to climax and not lose control. A loss of control is an inherent and pivotal part of this sexual experience, if it is to be satisfying. But something primitive (acting on behalf of her career goals) stops her—a fear that once she loses control, she may not be able to regain it. Worse still, she fears that she may not *want* to regain it. If the grass really is greener on the other side, and one can live there just as easily, why come back? Worst of all, and this is what scares her most, she senses that when she loses control sexually, her husband acquires it. And that is indeed true: *each* partner ends up handing over a great deal of control to the other. However, she isn't interested in what he loses, perhaps happily; she worries only about what she stands to lose—to him—and perhaps be permanently unhappy about later.

The fear affects their entire sex and love lives as a pair. Remember, even though we are talking primarily about orgasms, and how an ambitious woman distorts them, she subconsciously considers every aspect of sex as representing one more step toward an ultimate, and therefore catastrophic, absence of self-control. As Carolyn put it once, and only once, "If I really lost control, I think I might go insane. They'd have to lock me up and throw the key away."

Why, then, does she (and millions of women like her) even bother to have sex? Isn't something this troubling simply better avoided altogether? Turning off her conscious mind, reducing the act to its most obvious dimensions ("I have physical needs, you know"), she proceeds. However, once the passion that got her going in the first place abates, sanity returns—and anxiety or hostility surfaces. Now that she is no longer on automatic pilot to guide herself through the act, and get from it whatever she can, her views on this subject are even stronger than they were before: sex itself with someone for whom she truly cares represents an unacceptable loss of control, of which a climax is merely a small but important part.

Becoming anxious or irritable afterward allows her once again to seize control of herself, while expelling her partner, cancelling any inroads he made. Without ever saying so, she is able to resurrect her guard, usually to heights that far exceed the level they were at before the act began. All is well now. She has managed to take back everything she accidentally handed over not only while aroused and during her climax, but also during the whole sexual episode. Reverting to her toughie stance makes her feel secure again.

The ambitious women we studied are more than four times as likely to act this way than are their peers whose aspirations are more moderate. The highly motivated make a glib and convincing case for how their careers are wrecking their love lives, and they clearly believe what they are saying. But the facts tell a different story. The approach they are using in the hope of attaining success rules out a satisfying personal life.

The big question is: Does it, in fact, help them achieve the success they are seeking? Or is the toughie approach, so fatal to intimacy, even more destructive on the job? To find out the answer, we need to look at what the relatively small number of women who are doing well both professionally and personally have in common. They have some monumentally important lessons to teach us all.

FINDING THE SOURCE OF THE TROUBLE

The most important finding that emerged from our study of the connection between the personal and professional lives of women can best be understood by thinking for a moment about environmental pollution. Air and water pollution are linked. Many correlations exist between the two, and for good scientific reasons. For instance, air pollution becomes water pollution during a rainstorm. It therefore makes sense to talk about "directionality": how A affects B or, conversely, B affects A. But unless one examines the *source* of the pollution, the study remains superficial at best, cut off from the real core of the subject.

That is even more the case where people's personal and professional lives are concerned. Once again, there are many correlations between the two areas, and a tidal wave of books and articles discussing directionality has appeared in recent years. Each purports to explain how people's work affects their love lives, and vice versa. The material makes interesting reading, even though most of it is demonstrably false—about as valid as the connection between a full moon and lunacy. However, the real problem is that this approach omits the core of the subject altogether.

What we found is that the most critical problems women have in their personal and professional lives spring from a common source. Some women long more for a satisfying personal than professional life and therefore complain more about its absence. For others, the reverse is the case. A third large group is dissatisfied on both fronts. It is now clear that they will remain so unless the conditions that simultaneously determine the outcome in both areas are changed.

A key consequence of this approach is that solving a problem in one area by finally getting to its source often solves it in the other area. The toughie stance that has subconsciously been adopted by millions of women for what they feel are good and even necessary reasons is having an undeniably detrimental effect on their careers, and in fact is doing so at companies where no men are employed.

Since few women who have adopted the stance even realize they have done so, it is hardly surprising that they are unable to identify the source of their troubles. What they notice most is the reactions of others, not their own actions. Nevertheless, being a toughie means that one is, unwittingly, searching continually for an adversary, someone with whom to do battle. (What good is an army without an enemy?) The vast majority find one, daily, for reasons that escape them totally—and then they watch their careers go slowly down the drain.

The toughie stance also causes massive harm to their personal lives, and it does so even before they have tied up with (one is tempted to say "locked horns with") a particular partner. *The stance severely limits the range of men available to a woman using this approach to life.* To be specific, our study indicates that a woman with a chip on her shoulder is shunned by the vast majority of successful men. Taming their own aggressions—a key ingredient in their success—makes them recoil when they see someone, male or female, who has failed to do the same.

That leaves her largely the "losers" from which to choose, as she herself will later label them. At least initially, these men find her toughie stance believable and think it springs from an inner strength rather than fear. Eventually, they realize that they were mistaken. They have a scared and hostile partner on their hands, and, as they openly tell us (though not her), they no longer like her. That makes it easy for them, from then on, to do anything—lie to her, steal from her, cheat on her. Now that they see her for what she is, they have the green light to do as they please.

The question perhaps occurring to the reader is one we asked ourselves repeatedly throughout our study: Why didn't these disillusioned men simply get up and leave? The answer goes right to the heart of what makes the men unsuccessful in both love and life. When a situation isn't to their liking, they take little action to remedy it. They complain more, but they *do* less about it than most.

Another reason they stay is that they actually like the idea of being part of a relationship but not having to worry about their partners anymore. They feel freed. Very few of these men wanted to be permanently intimate to begin with. That involves a two-way flow of affection and concern, and they are interested only in a one-way flow, with themselves as its object. Now that their partners have disappointed them, they feel justified in giving as little to (while grabbing as much as they can from) the pairing.

The women eventually sense that something is wrong but come to the erroneous conclusion that "this is the way men—all men—are." This self-serving remark, often heard when two unhappy toughies talk, prevents them from realizing how major a contribution they are making to their own distress. Not only have they tied up with the least successful men, they have radically reduced the chances that the men will in time do well. These men need a helping hand, and a large part of what attracted them to toughies in the first place was that they thought these women were in a position to provide it. As each man finds out that his partner can't help him—in fact, can't even help herself—revenge soon surfaces. He now holds her responsible for having sold him a bill of goods. Instead of blaming himself for being foolish enough to accept her toughie act at face value, he points a finger at her and accurately characterizes her behavior as an ongoing fraud.

What is lost in the (mostly guerrilla but at times open) warfare that develops between the two is the fact that she needs help every bit as much as he does. Unfortunately, he can't give it to her. He never could. In the final chapters we'll meet women who met and married men who could indeed have helped them, but the women rejected all such assistance because they too were caught up—though not nearly to the same extent—in the toughie mentality which gripped career women in the 1970s and 1980s in the United States. At least these women had the right partners; the ones we've been discussing did not. Even with professional assistance, few of these relationships are salvageable, though, sadly, many last a lifetime.

Avoiding such relationships to begin with is best, but that is likely to happen only to women who attack this problem at its source. As we'll soon see, that also significantly improves the chances that they will be successful in their careers.

PART
FOUR

12

Characteristics of Successful Women

Happy people don't make headlines. In the beginning, it made our research team worry that we would accidentally place too much emphasis over the years on troubled individuals. Their complaints seemed likely to take up the lion's share of our time and attention. And that was justified, to some extent, since it was the unhappy who needed help, not those who were doing wonderfully.

Still, we were determined from the start to see what we could learn from women whose lives were satisfying, both professionally and personally. The problem is that this group tends to be relatively silent. Its members don't brag about the success they are having, at home and on the job. In fact, they are of the opinion that it doesn't even warrant discussion. It was interesting to find that people who are unhappy as adults think everyone else is too, and those who are content have somehow managed to convince themselves that everyone else is similarly pleased.

We weren't about to challenge either group's view, especially since the gap between the two groups has steadily widened during the past fifteen years. Economists often categorize the nations of the world in terms of "haves" and "have-nots." The words are synonymous with "rich" and "poor," but it turns out that they more aptly describe college-educated women in the United States with each passing year. Some are "haves" (and usually don't realize it), while most are "have-nots" (and are painfully aware of it).

The key question we wanted to answer was: Where is the fork in the road? That is, what sends one woman traveling down a path that becomes littered with divorces and abrupt dismissals, frustrating jobs and unsatisfying personal relationships, while another with the same background and personality profile finds satisfaction on both fronts?

The most worthwhile aspect of doing a large-scale, long-term study such as ours is that one gets to see people *before* they succeed or fail making the decisions that ultimately produce these outcomes. It is important to stress that only in retrospect did we recognize how pivotal some of the events we recorded were. At the time, they certainly didn't seem all that earthshaking, though we noted them diligently. The power of these decisions, however, was not only in what lay behind them (and we hadn't yet seen), but also in their recurrence as the years passed, until eventually they could indeed be seen shaping the person's destiny.

Having carefully and repeatedly analyzed the mountain of material we collected, we now know that there are certain characteristics that distinguish women who will have successful careers *and* personal lives from those who will have only one of the two—or, more likely, neither.

IDOLIZING SUCCESSFUL DOPE PEDDLERS

The first characteristic that separates the two groups has to do with anger—in particular, outrage, as we discussed in Part Two. *Women who went on to become successful at work and at home never became addicted to outrage.* And that's what it is, an addiction. Earlier we discussed why anger and outrage became such prevalent emotions among educated and ambitious women in the 1970s and 1980s. Basically, these fiery emotions are fuel-boosters, and the women definitely felt, subconsciously, that they needed more energy just to compete respectably. (That is the reason books like *Eat to Win* and other diet books in disguise became bestsellers. Instead of eating and growing fat and sluggish—an outcome that more than 70% feared—they could now stuff their faces and emerge victorious *at work*. If that isn't a fantasy-come-true for many modern women, what is?) However, as they soon realized, neither food nor exercise, cigarettes nor coffee, gave them the extra daily thrust they needed, so they unwittingly latched onto a different energizer, one they could generate internally (once a cheerleader gave them a suitable rationalization).

Why didn't they recognize the extent to which their chronic use of outrage was hurting them, both on the job and off? Because they were like slum children, deceived by the successful appearance of the dope peddler. Most middle-class men and women are of the opinion that they have nothing to learn from what goes on in the run-down sections of major American cities. "Animals live there," is the typical remark heard in suburban surveys we have conducted. Whatever truth the comment contains, it overlooks the fact that many youngsters raised in slums come to idolize the local pusher, especially if he is a big-time dope peddler, because he is one of the few visibly successful men they actually get to see. (Celebrities from the worlds of sports and entertainment are also looked up to, but they are too remote.) The neighborhood pusher is of the same race or ethnic group as they, which facilitates the process of identifying with him; and he is vastly wealthier and better known than, say, their own fathers.

Women in the 1970s and 1980s who began to aspire to success in the business world looked for models, but at this early stage they could find few of the same sex. Well-known women in the worlds of sports and entertainment were not only too remote, they were in the wrong fields. The aspirants we're talking about wanted to follow in the footsteps of someone who had done well in the business world. Enter: *women in public life who had only outrage to peddle, not strategies for—or a record of—success in business*.

From lecture podiums, on television and radio programs, and in the pages of books and magazines, they gave ambitious working women the "fix" they thought they needed in order to keep striving harder. Since these were bright, well-educated addicts from relatively affluent families, we kept expecting them to realize what was happening to them. In particular, we thought they would soon grasp the fact the the addiction they had developed was hampering rather than furthering their careers.

Slum teenagers with drug habits could have told us why the flash of illumination never occurred. The pusher markets his wares initially under the guise that "it helps you get through the day" and "makes good things happen to you." As we know, what it really does is radically reduce the chance that a promising youngster will ever achieve his or her potential— or worse, even bother to try to develop it. Once they become addicted, those young adults who still want to better themselves have only one thing left to which they can realistically aspire. They may no longer be able to attain a prominent position in the mainstream of modern life, but they can indeed strive to become well-known pushers themselves. That allows them to feed not only their own habit, but also to become prosperous and popular by creating and then feeding everyone else's.

Women who become outrage addicts radically reduce the chances that they will ever be successful in the mainstream of modern life. As a result they too shift gears, without even being aware of it. Instead of feeling defeated, they give themselves a new target to shoot for. If they can't be a success in business or in a profession, they too, by default, will become "pushers." The renown of the more popular outrage pushers makes women who are actually falling by the wayside think that this is an acceptable substitute profession. After all, it involves writing and public speaking. That blinds them to the fact that these women generate only the illusion of being successful in business, just as the neighborhood dope peddler generates his own illusion of success. Nevertheless, each aspirant can calmly say, just as slum children do, "Well, she must be doing *something* right, she's certainly more famous than my mother."

Traveling this alternative route allows such women to provide themselves and others like them with the fix they allegedly need in order to function well day after day. But each additional dose of indignation only takes them that much farther afield. This is one detour from which many women never return. For as addicts who become peddlers well know, time passes, doors quietly close, and being a pusher becomes the only way of life possible for them. In the final chapter we will see that breaking this destructive habit means first realizing that one has it.

In short, far from being insulting to women, the evidence we've accumulated indicates clearly that peddlers of outrage are damaging women who aspire to success in business or a profession every bit as much as children who are turned into heroin addicts are harmed by the neighborhood pusher. In many ways, the position of working women is worse, because dope addicts at least know that that is what they are; few of the women we studied who are outrage addicts realize it. Failure on both the home and office fronts is typically the first sign they will receive that they have long been dependent on this daily fix.

FRANTIC IN THE OFFICE

To say that women who go on to become successful both professionally and personally never became addicted to indignation may seem like a negative way of characterizing this group. "They never did so-and-so, and therefore they went on to do well." Yet the sentence describes what actually happened, since it does indeed explain why so many talented and intelligent women who should have done well did poorly. In essence, they took themselves out of the race without ever knowing when or why.

A more positive way of looking at this crucial issue is to say that successful women have been using their daily supply of energy efficiently. The statement may seem bland at first, but anyone who has watched working women during the past twenty-six years try to adjust the amount of energy they need to the task at hand knows how difficult "using energy efficiently" can be. Running all out in a sprint is easy, where this kind of judgment is concerned, since one merely opens the throttle for a brief period. At the other end of the spectrum, sitting around waiting for something or someone is also relatively easy, since any extra energy one pumps into the situation comes out as tension and fidgeting. It is the in-between situations—calling for just the right amount of energy to do the job well—that are the most difficult. Overdoing it (and becoming tense and fidgety) or underdoing it (and not feeling sufficiently motivated to do the job) is common.

The point is that the women we studied were significantly more likely to tinker with their metabolism or thermostat or furnace (all the analogies are appropriate) than were their male peers. Extraordinary binges accompany such tinkering—and, in fact, motivates most of them. Some observers take a dim view of these practices. "Women are more reactive than men; this is really little more than hysteria," a psychologist at a large state university told us. "When the pressure is on, they quickly become more frantic."

From our study a different explanation emerged for the wasteful way in which many women go about this energy-matching process. It has to do with the contrasts between blue- and white-collar work. Regardless of one's ideological sympathies, an undeniable fact about housework is that it is largely manual, while office work is largely mental. Assembly-line labor in a factory may require continuous physical effort; but we found in monitoring the day's activities of a wide variety of homemakers each decade from the late 1950s through the mid–1980s that the work is quite *episodic*. There are periods of physical effort (for instance, cooking or cleaning), alternating with sitting and reading a magazine (waiting for the kids to come home). The steadily increasing number of labor-saving appliances and products introduced in the last three decades (for example, microwave ovens, nonstick frying pans, and disposable diapers) have made housework even more physically episodic.

Office work may be more mental, but it is also more continuous, less subject to the extreme swings seen in physical activity at home. In every office there are peak periods and slack ones. But precisely because it is an office, not one's home, variations in intensity are decreased. The high level of vigilance and readiness—the "office personality" one necessarily adopts—coupled with the lack of real privacy for most workers (they are on call throughout the workday for their bosses and often for customers as well); the need to look one's professional best on short notice—these all add up to a level of chronic strain that sets work in an office in the 1980s worlds apart from that experienced by college-educated women who were homemakers in the 1950s.

In brief, women who switched en masse from home to office and aspired to business careers instead of working as homemakers made a more radical switch than has commonly been recognized. Episodic physical labor was replaced by *continuous* mental effort, connected with becoming outstanding in one's profession. Unlike domestic chores, which frequently could be finished in minutes, the new professional tasks and projects tend to be large in scope; may extend for weeks or even months; and usually overlap one another. Also, in contrast to housework, there is a significant audience watching the day's activity (as opposed to a few snoopy neighbors)—even if it is merely an anticipated and imaginary audience of appreciative admirers who will show up somewhere in the not-too-distant future. This continual "on stage" character of most careers adds an electricity that may be exciting, wearying, or both, but it is always present. For it is part of every profession, and every professional's secret dreams.

The shift from the blue-collar world of housework to the white-collar office world by millions of women had an effect even on those who never took time off from their careers to raise a family. That may sound odd at first, since we found that in high school and, to a lesser extent, in college, women tended to use their energies more efficiently than men, at least where homework was concerned. Why then should a switch slowly take place after graduation? Once school is through, what happens to the self-disciplined woman with good grades that causes her to become steadily more frantic and unproductive in her career?

A large part of the answer can be traced to the deteriorating quality of the personal lives of such women. If there is "directionality" here, it is from their unhappy relationships *to* their troubled careers. The first has a marked effect on the second. To summarize our findings in this area: *Women with satisfying personal lives are significantly better at using their energy efficiently in the office.* Over the years, that had a substantial effect on the rate of promotions and pay raises they received.

It should be emphasized that these are all the makings of a downward—or upward—spiral. Women who managed to find a personal life that was just right for them subsequently saw their business lives improve. That, in turn, helped their personal lives, since it relieved the strain that setbacks at work might otherwise have caused at home.

Unfortunately, downward spirals occur too, and in fact, they have been seen far more frequently than upward ones in recent years. Much of the reason for this can be traced to the attitude of the times. No fight between two people takes place in a vacuum. Without realizing it, the pair always act to some extent in accordance with large-scale social forces that shape the attitudes each has at the moment. It is important to be continually mindful of the influence of what is "in the air," for the background pressures can give a fight one outcome during a specific decade and an opposite one during a later decade.

It is illuminating to look at an example to see precisely how these background forces affect the personal lives of working women.

"KEEP YOUR GODDAM LAWN MOWER"

Lori and Annette didn't come from the same upper-middle class family, but they could have. Both were raised in the suburbs of New York City. Among the many things they had in common were high intelligence, good health, trim figures, grades that were well above average, lots of exuberance and plenty of friends. Neither girl was as popular as she wanted to be in high school, and yet each was rated by classmates (behind her back) as attractive and "a member of the in-crowd." That would have surprised them, since their own view of themselves was more modest. "I kind of take my face for granted," Annette told a friend at the time. "It's OK, but it's not going to launch any ships." Then she added, with a gentle, quick wit that is there to this day, twenty-four years later, "I guess it won't sink any either."

The reason for examining what happened to these two when both were twenty-seven is that the fights they had with their respective husbands had very different endings. Before seeing why, we should mention that for all the similarities between the two women, and their husbands as well, Annette is ten years older than Lori.

From the beginning of our study, we have been examining what happens as the years pass to groups of women who were initially the same in most important respects. However, it has also been intriguing to see how pairs of women who were similar but lived in different decades responded to identical situations. Some readers may protest that "if they lived in different decades, the two can't possibly have been the same. The mentality of the time, its customs and history, would make them as distinct as apples and oranges." That is certainly true about many of the developments in their lives. Embedded as they were—as we *all* are—in a particular cultural context, their reactions to most situations couldn't help but differ.

Nevertheless, on a number of occasions events cropped up in the lives of these two women, each in her respective time frame, that were nearly identical. Then, we got to see the effect of the cultural environment of each on her behavior. We can be more confident that that is what we're witnessing if almost every other such pair we have isolated reacts in similarly opposite ways. That is indeed what happened. The fight about money that Annette had with her husband when she was twenty-seven (in 1961) led to a reconciliation a few days later. The marriage grew stronger as a result. The nearly identical fight that Lori had with her husband when she was twenty-seven (in 1971) led eventually to divorce at the age of twenty-nine (in 1973).

Monitoring what happened to hundreds of such pairings across time produced an important conclusion: *The attitude toward marriage in the 1950s and early 1960s was so positive, many couples remained together who would otherwise have split up. Conversely, the attitude toward marriage in the 1970s and 1980s had grown so negative, many couples split up who would otherwise have remained together.* Too much of an effort was made during the earlier period to keep the pairing intact, and both parties suffered needlessly; too little of an effort was made in more recent years, and both parties again suffered needlessly.

The prevailing attitude in the 1970s and 1980s affected not only the personal lives of working women. It also had a destructive impact on their careers. Had they realized that there was even a connection, fully 74% of the women we studied would have been surprised by it. For, revealingly, they were of the opinion that the dissolution of marriages represented a *positive* development in the quest by women for career success. As Lori put it at twenty-nine, "My priorities have changed. What I really care most about at this juncture is coming into my own and becoming an executive at [my firm]. I'm free now. I want people to appreciate me for *me*, not because I'm Mrs. So-and-so, and have a husband and 2.3 children, like everybody else."

During these decades a growing number of women in our sample took their work seriously precisely because they became convinced that their marriages, while stable at the time, would ultimately fall apart. Not surprisingly, that made them want to be prepared for the inevitable. "I *have* to learn about money and finance, and have a career of my own," one told us. "That's all I really have to fall back on." The argument is perfectly rational; there aren't any logical flaws in it. A modern consumer society eventually becomes comfortable with the warning, "Let the buyer beware." We are all supposed to protect ourselves against the schemes and negligence of others. The point, and it is a critically important one, is that an abiding belief in the process became a self-fulfilling prophecy.

In hundreds of cases we studied, women accidentally precipitated the very disaster they feared most. First they got mad at and then they walked out on the partner they were afraid would soon walk out on them. If this kind of behavior seems silly and self-destructive, keep in mind that we all do it from time to time, especially when we feel we are being slighted by someone from whom we expect better treatment. An appropriate name for what we do under these circumstances is the You-can't-fire-me-I-quit syndrome. A good way to see how it works is to spend a few minutes watching Harold.

Harold's lawn mower broke, and he decided to go up the street to his friend, Fred, to borrow his for a few hours. As he passed the first house on his way to Fred's, Harold said to himself, "I recently lent Fred my lawn mower when *his* broke, so there's no reason why he shouldn't lend me his now." As Harold passed the second house, he said to himself,

"But what happens if he *won't* lend me his?" Passing the third house, Harold began to fume, "Why, that no-good S.O.B. I lent him mine, when *he* needed it, and now he won't lend me his." Finally, after arriving at Fred's house and ringing the doorbell, he shouted as Fred opened the door, "Keep your goddam lawn mower!" and stormed off.

This behavior is less deranged than it may seem at first glance, once you accept the premise that Harold truly believed his request might be denied. As we discussed in Part One we all want to be ready for any setbacks that are about to hit us, and not ever to be caught off guard. It is human nature, and for many hundreds of thousands of years in the past it undoubtedly served us well, helping us to survive as individuals and as a species. However, in modern times, if anything is responsible for the extinction of the human race, this will probably be it. Nuclear war may well be the immediate physical cause of our deaths, but the psychological tendency that precipitates the calamity in the first place will be this ever-so-natural desire to act like good Boy Scouts and Be Prepared—so prepared, in fact, that we indirectly trigger the very catastrophe we wanted most to avoid.

On a more everyday plane, we do this constantly. Some of the men we studied were so afraid of being victims of street crimes, burglaries, or financial setbacks that they walked around chronically anxious and tense, which contributed significantly to the heart attacks that actually did them in. Similarly, the women we studied were so frightened in the 1970s and 1980s by the growing number of headlines they were seeing and stories they were hearing about men abandoning their wives that the wives decided to make preparations for this injury well before it might be inflicted. The result was a self-inflicted injury. They came to believe that their careers would save them, acting as life preservers in case their personal lives vanished. However, once they had developed their career interests sufficiently, they began using this defensive shield as an offensive weapon. Now it was You-can't-fire-me-I-quit time. That certainly did surprise an enormous number of husbands who, like Fred, had no such intention in the first place.

There is no doubt whatever that many of these women sincerely liked their work, but the question that needs to be asked is: How well were they protecting themselves by using their work as a weapon, a shield, so that no man could ever hurt them again. (We need the word "again" here because, like Harold, they had felt rejected just thinking about the possibility that they might soon be rejected. So even if they'd never been hurt in reality, through divorce or abandonment, they had been hurt before merely by thinking about the prospect.) The question about how well they were protecting themselves should be followed by an even more important one: Did using their work as a weapon or as a safe harbor to hide in decrease the chances that they would excel in their chosen field?

Remember, many women in the 1970s and 1980s were willing to tell us outright, though in confidence, that they were far more interested in career success than they were in trying to find a satisfying personal life. Besides, they were convinced that the former would lead to the latter. Like Lori, after her divorce, they had realigned their priorities to reflect the world as they felt it really was. They were being realists, they insisted, in placing work first and love second, if they could find love at all. For that reason, it is imperative to ask whether using their work as a cocoon into which to crawl—to keep them immune from personal injury—was actually harming the quality of their work.

RISING EXPECTATIONS

Our study indicates that it did exactly that. Women who decided to make their careers their primary interest in life should have experienced a fair amount of peace while they were working, either alone or with others. That, at least, is what we expected to find, since they were actively involved in the area that, by their own admission, meant the most to them. They were doing what they wanted to do.

What we found instead is that women who told us that career success was their number one priority were significantly more likely to seem to us—and, more important, to seem to their coworkers, superiors, and subordinates—to have a chip on their shoulders. This chronically hostile stance, always based on fear and rejection (real or, far more often, imaginary), eventually cost them dearly. For it brought them still more rejection, this time unquestionably real. Here was one downward spiral whose effects we could measure financially.

Lori provides a good example of what typically happens. Approximately fourteen months after her divorce she met a man named Geoffrey, whom she came to like very much. "He's tall and nice-looking," Lori told us, "and has a terrific position with his [multinational shoe manufacturing] company." A little over a year after they met, the two began living together. However, Lori had no intention of marrying him—"or anyone else," she usually interjected. "I don't want anyone telling me what to do. I come and go as I please." With a personal life that was exactly what Lori claimed she wanted it to be ("This *suits* me"), we anticipated that her professional life would flower. As she put it proudly, "I have everything in place."

The people in her office had a strikingly different view of Lori's daily behavior. Not only did they see her as irritable and quick to criticize others, they noticed that she was also too tense. Lori was convinced, as many in her position were, that she was simply not using her energy well. As we mentioned earlier, this was—and is—a more common cause of concern among college-educated women than has previously been recognized—a problem whose roots lie in the absence of a truly fulfilling personal relationship at home. However, the straw that broke the camel's back and finally caused both Lori's relationship with Geoffrey and her job to end abruptly was her steadily rising expectations at work.

One of the most important characteristics of women who go on to have satisfying professional *and* personal lives is that their expectations are moderate, not high. That deceived us mightily at first, for we had assumed initially that unless people wanted something bad enough they would never get it. In a highly competitive world, we considered it a safe hypothesis that desire—a great deal of it—would of necessity precede attainment. That turned out not to be so. A certain amount of hunger for something does indeed have to be present merely to make someone wander down a particular path. But if the hunger is too great, the person doesn't stay on the path long enough, or explore it with sufficient thoroughness, for it to produce the anticipated rewards.

Rita Danziger, for instance, did not seem to us at first glance a woman who would go places. In high school, Rita was a serious girl with only a few friends, and she gravitated toward other girls who were as serious as she was. Only once, during her junior year in high school, did she even attempt to befriend the in-crowd. In fact, in what she felt was a real brainstorm, she decided to invite the entire group to a party she was giving. There were 850 boys and girls in her suburban high school, approximately 200 in her class. All sixteen people whom she and her classmates agreed constituted the real stars in her year (nine boys and seven girls) were invited, and they came. Rita's parents had consented reluctantly to the idea, and went out for the evening with friends. "We'll be back at midnight," they told her.

As Rita described it to us the next day, "It was a disaster. They couldn't have cared less that I was there. They wrecked the place—beer cans under the bed, cigarette burns in the carpeting and furniture, things broken." That wasn't the worst of it. "The best-looking boy in the class asked me to dance," Rita said glumly. "Yes?" we prompted, since that sounded like something about which she'd have been pleased. "I was thrilled," she went on. "The lights were low—I had dimmed them in the living room—and then he put his hand on one of my breasts. I quietly said, 'Don't do that.' We'd never even *talked* before, and I was also afraid that the lights would come back on. He just said, 'Okay,' and walked away. After that, I didn't exist. He spent the rest of the evening with his crowd. I felt like a real fool." Then, crying, she said, "It was a big mistake. I'm not like them. I'm never going to be one of them." Even though she viewed the experience as embarrassing at the time, it allowed her to see herself in a realistic light sooner than most of her peers.

Rita was even more serious in college (where she majored in fine arts) than she was in high school, but she no longer envied the members of the loud, footloose and socially hyperactive groups she so frequently saw on campus. She had her own circle of friends and, although she seemed unaware of it, a growing number of her classmates rated her as attractive. As a twenty-two-year-old college senior, Rita wore her shiny brown hair chin length and frequently tied it back with a ribbon. People usually noticed the warmth in her brown eyes and commented on the long lashes fringing them. She was of a frail build and delicately boned at 5'2", but was flexible and very good at gymnastics.

Always unpretentious, Rita had less difficulty than her classmates coming to terms with the fact that school was through and work was beginning. During the early years on the job at a small ad agency she displayed none of the bluster and bluffing that consumed many of her peers as they tried to sound as though they knew far more than they actually did. The result was that, while they postured and posed, she listened and learned. Their antics were more frequently discussed around the office than her steadily growing competence, but it was revealing to discover that, when her bosses wanted something important done, they almost automatically sought her assistance, not that of the poseurs.

Between the ages of twenty-two and twenty-five Rita dated a number of men and slept with several. Nothing serious developed with any of them. One month before her twenty-sixth birthday she went to talk to an officer at her bank in connection with her application for a credit card. Charles Lewis, who was two years older than Rita, spent nearly ninety minutes helping her fill out the forms. By that time, both were certain they wanted to see one another again, and soon. "I thought she was gorgeous," he later told us. Rita's view of Charles: "I could have talked to him forever." The relationship was slow to gel, mainly because both bided their time, wanting to be sure that they were right for one another. Slowly, the doubts evaporated. Sixteen months after they met, they were married.

"I'M GIVING IT MY ALL NOW"

Rita and Lori are the same age, and are similar in many other respects. Nevertheless, one important way in which they have differed over the years since they began working has been in the expectations each has had of *what* her work would bring her (as measured by pay raises, promotions and renown) and *when* these rewards will arrive. Job-related expectations are so pivotal, we have monitored them throughout our study. What we have learned by doing so is that *women whose expectations are high—and who work hard—usually do poorly, while those whose expectations are more moderate—and who work just as hard—usually do well.* In the previous section we explained why that happens. Impatience prevents those with high expectations from going far enough down a particular path, calmly, for them to still be there when it finally yields its prizes. The overnight success for which they are eagerly waiting causes them to quit—or be fired—long before it realistically could have been expected.

Elevated expectations can clearly cause serious trouble, but what causes expectations to become elevated in the first place? Comparisons involving thousands of working women over a period of more than a quarter of a century indicate that one factor is more central than all the rest combined: their personal lives. Expectations aren't fixed, they vary. We are all aware of the daily variations that occur, in connection with the little victories and defeats, steps forward and back, that we experience from hour to hour. But larger events in our lives have a lingering effect that we are far less likely to notice. For instance, the end of Lori's marriage made her expectations soar. In fact, they more than doubled during this period. We never asked her, "How come?" We didn't have to. She repeatedly volunteered the answer, without being aware that she was even giving us one: "I'm giving it my *all* now." Since the level of effort she was expending at work had increased, there was every reason for Lori to anticipate that the rewards she was seeking would come her way sooner and also in larger measure.

It doesn't work that way. In Lori's case and in the thousands of others we monitored, once women scrapped their personal lives the extra determination they brought to their work caused its quality to deteriorate, not improve. Unfortunately, they were among the last to notice the change. A good way to see why the deterioration took place is to think about a car driving on a slippery, wet road. Stepping hard on the accelerator doesn't make the car go faster, it sends it into a spin. There is an optimum level of energy to expend, and it is no easy matter in real-life situations to find what that level is.

Apparently, a large part of what deceives working women is the experience they had in high school and college with homework assignments and tests. Virtually all the women in our sample told us, both at the time and later, that if they hadn't pushed themselves hard on occasion to do their schoolwork it would not have gotten done. This is admirable self-discipline and nothing we say is intended to be critical of it. Yet it was plain even to many of the students we followed that it is possible to be *too* motivated—to want so much to do well that one can't settle in and do the work at all.

This paradoxical state is at the core of the difficulties most talented and dedicated women encounter at work. The problem is compounded by the presence of other workers. Students, in isolation, can prevent themselves from working well merely by wanting badly to do well. In a business setting, with other people nearby, the need to coordinate one's efforts with those of others adds a complicating dimension of its own. This is the equivalent of the slippery road upon which the car is driving.

In short, not only do women with sky-high expectations use their energy inefficiently, they also dangerously undermine their own situation by creating conflict with coworkers, who always seem to be moving at "too slow" a pace or "in the wrong direction." The women we are talking about have the ability to do good work; that much we know from having spent so many years monitoring their lives. They also have the ability to work well with others, as we've seen them do any number of times in the past. However, once they "move into high gear" and "really give it my all," as Lori usually described it, they are capable of failing simultaneously on both fronts.

Keep in mind that these are *not* two separate problems. The women we studied were more than forty times as likely to notice that they were having trouble with coworkers than they were to notice the difficulties they themselves were having working well in isolation. If they were aware of the latter problem at all, they generally blamed it on the troubles they were having at the time with coworkers and customers. It was merely a spillover, affecting each woman when she was alone. "How can anyone expect me to get my work done when I'm surrounded by chowderheads?" Lori nearly screamed into the phone one Sunday, while talking to a friend. What the remark neatly omitted is that both her private and public business-related activities were suffering from the same excess of energy and determination that she was pumping into each situation. Unbeknown to its driver, this car was careening wildly on the slippery road upon which anyone who expects to get somewhere in the business world must somehow find a way to safely travel.

Rita, by contrast, went about her work so quietly that her coworkers often forgot she was even present. The word that best describes her business *and* personal life is "uneventful." As we mentioned earlier, that is what made us mistakenly conclude that she would fare less well than her peers. We were aware that troubled people have more problems, both on the job and off, but assumed that their coworkers and superiors would make allowances for that, recognize the talents these troubled people possessed, and promote them anyway. If nothing else, they were certainly adding color and spice to the office gossip and to the firm itself. Our assumption, to put it mildly, was to prove naive.

Business firms did tolerate women like Lori for a certain length of time, and then an abrupt switch took place. Suddenly, their patience exhausted, the superiors of such women, whether they were male or female, got rid of them. As Lori's boss described her, less than a week after she had been fired, "Lori is like sand in a machine. She causes *friction* wherever she goes." Examining hundreds of similar instances made us realize that we would have to revise our preliminary conclusion, which was that the Ritas of the world were doing well only because able women such as Lori kept shooting themselves in the foot, which took them out of the race. Our initial assessment was that we were watching yet another instance of the meek inheriting the earth.

It took us a number of years to discover what the superiors of these women were also discovering: the Ritas of the world were coming into their own not because of anyone else's self-destructive behavior, but because they themselves were the ones actually doing the lion's share of the work. That they did it year in and year out with a bare minimum of fuss and fury masked the sheer quantity they were producing *and* the relative ease with which they got along with others. (To be fair, some were tempted to cause a little chaos, just to call attention to themselves, because, like us, they had mistakenly concluded that this was a worthwhile kind of attention to get. Fortunately, most resisted the temptation.) The one-two punch they regularly delivered—quality work together with no self-imposed impediments to working well with others—made them formidable competitors, though they rarely thought of themselves as such. In the long run, that made dark horses such as Rita the real winners.

THE RIGHT LEVEL OF SERIOUSNESS

What is interesting about hard workers such as Rita is that while most people's incorrect self-perceptions eventually get them into trouble either at work or at home, hers helped both her personal and professional life flourish. For instance, as we mentioned, she was a serious girl in high school and was even more so as a college student. That wasn't just our opinion; it was also that of the more than fifteen people we interviewed during those eight years who knew her well. "She likes to laugh, and has a good sense of humor," Rita's college roommate told us, "but she *thinks* about things a lot."

Because Rita thought of herself as *less* serious than others saw her, she usually tried to lighten things up when she was with friends. They appreciated it, for that meant she was attempting to make them laugh rather than merely bragging about herself to them.

The reason this inclination was so useful to her personally and professionally is that it was the reverse of what most people do. Intent upon making a good impression, determined to look and sound like heavyweights instead of lightweights, they unwittingly try hard to present themselves as being *more* serious than they are. It doesn't work. The audience usually finds them stiff and phony. Worse, they have to sit there while the person blows his or her own horn to bolster the impression of substance. The listeners may not know why, but they typically end up feeling annoyed rather than impressed. Once Lori's professional expectations went through the roof, as a result of her disappearing personal life, she fit this category quite well. She wanted everyone to feel that she was, in her words, "on my way" and "just one or two steps from the top." With much bluster, she delivered this sermon to anyone who would listen to it. Rita, by contrast, simply tried to make people laugh and feel at ease, for that was genuinely the picture of herself that she felt was—and still is—most valid.

The same thing applies to her work-related expectations, an even more important topic if we are truly to understand why women like her are the ones most likely to have both a successful professional and satisfying personal life. As we stated earlier, Rita's expectations were more modest than Lori's. It is critical to point out, however, that *she* didn't think they were modest. Rita demanded much of herself and was quite disappointed if she failed to live up to her own high standards. Having worked that hard, she couldn't help but anticipate that, ultimately, a good measure of success would be hers. There was certainly little question in her mind that she deserved it. Still, it was striking to see that her expectations were indeed modest.

That was particularly apparent when a reward of some kind came her way. Thanks to Lori's higher expectations, any raise or praise was deemed inadequate—if not immediately, then soon afterward. She expected more. Rita, on the other hand, reacted to similar pay raises or compliments with a surprised smile. She expected less. In fact, if the reward was sizable, she expressed disbelief. In spite of her allegedly high expectations, she was often genuinely moved by the magnitude of what she received. That helped her both personally and professionally because she usually said little or nothing about the promotions, pay raises, or applause she got. Her good mood spoke volumes. When she did discuss her accomplishments, she did so quietly and without making her listeners feel a notch below her if they had nothing comparable to which to point. Lori, by contrast, did substantial and permanent harm to both her work and her love life by complaining continually about the recognition she felt she deserved but hadn't received. As she put it repeatedly, "I'm *worth* much more than I'm getting." In fact, all she seemed to notice was what hadn't yet been bestowed upon her.

As the years passed, it became clear that the reason Rita was able to handle the steady stream of rewards so well was that they weren't her first priority. She liked the creative work she as doing at the ad agency enough so that she felt somewhat removed from the earnings increases and compliments it brought her. Nevertheless, more than once she chided herself for not paying sufficient attention to just how well she was doing, as viewed from an external perspective. "I guess I'm not much of a businesswoman," she commented, after she heard a coworker say that for the second year in a row he had gone to his boss, asked for a 15% raise, and been granted it.

Rita's self-critical remark didn't fit the facts. Working now for a larger ad agency, she was earning twice as much as Lori, and the fellow mentioned above—the one with a well-defined "career plan"—was eventually fired. Apparently he got openly miffed once too often when the company wouldn't keep step with his widely broadcast plans for himself.

Odd as it may sound, the fact that Rita did not have a similar plan was one of her secret strengths. (It was a secret to her as well, since she thought of it as representing a deficiency of some kind.) We found that the vast majority of men and women who succeed do so in a way that few of them forecast. The road always turns out to be more complicated and tortuous than they thought it would be. At times, it didn't even look like a road, because they are actually doing something different and unique. People with a map drawn beforehand dismiss as detours the most worthwhile routes for them to take. In Rita's case, the quality of her work was taking her there more surely than her minds's eye, surveying the terrain before the journey began, ever could have.

THE BEST LAID PLANS

It is one thing to discover that moderate, not high, expectations are a key to success, and quite another to discover what the right level is for any given individual. Can women tinker with their level of expectations and finally find the one that is just right for them? We've watched thousands try—and few succeed. What typically happens is that the person wants badly to do better than she is doing, and hence convinces herself that, as one put it, "the problem is that I haven't been setting my sights high enough." By raising them she hopes to motivate herself to do better. That is rarely the end of the story. Since she also needs someone to blame for what in her eyes is the unacceptably low level of her achievements thus far, she points a finger at her partner. Scrapping her personal life or, more often, rendering it totally secondary will help her do well, or so she firmly believes.

We found that it accomplishes exactly the reverse, and after many years of studying the process in detail, we finally know why. *Expectations are basically daydreams—once people have attained something, it is no longer an expectation, it is a reality.* Expectations make up for whatever is lacking in their lives. Lori's expectations soared as her personal life sank because she was trying to compensate (in one area) for what she was missing but still yearned for (in another).

If women who raised their career expectations could actually achieve the success they seek, all would be well, at least as far as they are concerned. For they would then be in a position to say (and many intended to once the time was right), "I may not have much of a personal life, but I'm well on my way to becoming a star." That is not what happens. Instead they begin to fail at an even more rapid rate. Their response is simple, and appalling: they attempt to raise their sights still higher. Knowing what we now know, that shouldn't come as a surprise. These women have neither a satisfying personal nor professional life, so expectations rush in to fill the gap. These Band-Aids that promise, "All will be well in the future" nearly guarantee that the women will have no worthwhile future. Rather, each grows ever more likely to be left stridently proclaiming, "You have to *plan* what you want—and then really go after it—if you're going to be a success." Then she will have to hope that no one wonders why she herself is such a failure in business.

Finding the right level of work-related expectations is critical for any woman who wants to have a productive career and a fulfilling personal life. What complicates the search is that a level suitable for one woman might be too high or too low for another. Each needs a level that is tailored to her own unique mix of interests, abilities, and needs. That is what makes it all the more remarkable that, in more than a quarter of a century of studying this topic, we have found that there is only one way for her to find the level that allows her automatically to function at her best on the job: find a satisfying and enduring intimacy with someone for whom she truly cares. To flower at work she needs the right partner to be with when each day is done.

Some readers will probably not like the following explanation of why this is so effective a solution. However, we have intensively examined the stages involved, and it is indeed the way the process works. Falling in love is viewed in so positive a light by society that something important has been overlooked in all the beautiful songs, lyric novels, and dreamlike films the experience has inspired: love has a profoundly asocial dimension. Not for the individuals involved, since they are clearly ending their isolation and merging their two beings, as best they can, into one. Instead, it is the pair of lovers who become asocial, though it is a coincidental state, since the two aren't *against* anyone so much as they simply don't *need* anyone else anymore. Like lovers throughout history, they have become a self-contained unit.

People who had previously been close to either member of the pair are usually the first to notice how radical a change took place once love entered the picture. Songs about wedding bells "breaking up that old gang of mine" are only a small part of the story. For, in many ways, the person who falls in love might just as well have vanished altogether. When Lori and Rita were with the men they each eventually married, they might as well have not been present at all, as far as passersby were concerned. Each was involved with her partner first and her profession second, if indeed the latter even existed in her mind any longer. Perhaps that is the reason falling in love is so often a stage of only brief duration; it allows two people to become a pair and then, as its intensity lessens, they are able to return to the world as they had previously lived in it.

It was no coincidence that Lori returned to it long before Rita did. As Lori put it, "I felt like I was on another planet—and that made me uncomfortable after the first few weeks." She went back to her prior quest every bit as determined as she had been before meeting the man she married. That, as we now know, was a tell-tale sign. In fact, the courtship and marriage might as well have been a brief romantic and erotic fling for all the difference it made to the approach she was using at work. Rita, on the other hand, never really came back. She valued her marriage sufficiently, and felt that it merited enough attention in its own right, to not shove the man she loved from her mind and emotions in order to concentrate single-mindedly on her work.

A decrease in career expectations is an inherent part of falling in love. Rather than being a cause for rejoicing, that scared many of the women we studied. They were afraid that with their interest in their careers ebbing, the odds of attaining success were rapidly approaching zero. Some panicked. In an attempt to revive what they felt was their one hope of attaining glory they subconsciously began severing the ties that bound them to their partners. As Lori put it once when she was angry, "I'm not going to be denied—because of him—my big opportunity." Such a bald comment was unusual; yet most women did the same thing subconsciously. If they said anything at all, they claimed to be doing something *for* their careers, not *to* their marriages. But unmistakable evidence of an underlying shift was difficult to overlook. Here, as in the majority of similar cases, Lori's work-related expectations slowly but steadily climbed.

The feeling of being one step removed from the world made Rita giddy rather than fretful. The difference between the two women was becoming more striking each day. "Being in love is like having a warm, protective cloak around you that you can feel but no one else can see," Rita said a few weeks after her marriage, just at the time that Lori was starting to get jumpy. The distance that Rita felt, and has continued to feel, did not make her seem estranged from her coworkers and indifferent to her work, as Lori feared. Instead, it made Rita appear peaceful—and, importantly, it allowed her more easily to persist. Her interest in her work was real (so real she was often able to think of the applause it brought her as being for someone else), and she labored away happily, year after year, with what can best be described as quiet determination.

In short, any woman who is looking for the ideal level of expectations and energy to make the time she devotes to her work most productive—*and* her relations with her coworkers as free of friction as possible—should first fall in love, then take her personal life every bit as seriously as she does her career. Maybe more. Far from being a detour or an interference, a satisfying and enduring intimacy heightens significantly—in fact, maximizes—the chances that she will ultimately be a success.

THE BEST FALLBACK POSITION

It is worth noting that women who deliberately married, or decided to live with, a man who loved them but whom they in turn did not love, did not do well at work in the long run. That surprised not only them, but us. The women kept insisting, correctly, that they had all the "supportiveness I need at home," and that "there really *is* someone in my corner." That was true, but the men each of these women chose to pair up with lacked the ability to yank her out of her workaday mentality and into a different frame of mind for a while when she sorely needed it.

Because, in most cases, she selected a basically meek man who would let her do pretty much as she pleased, she had no way to escape her own increasingly overheated quest for success. The irony here is that she had chosen him precisely because he wouldn't—indeed, couldn't—interfere, and then found herself needing him to do so.

Any woman who wants to derive not only the personal but also the career benefits that come from an enduring intimacy must choose a man she loves, not merely one who loves her. Otherwise she will soon find that she is unable to take a break from her work, even when she is at home and recognizes how necessary a rest is. A good test of whether the relationship is doing what it is supposed to do for her personally and professionally is this: She must be able to answer yes to the question of whether she feels that she and her partner could always go elsewhere, if need be, start over again, and become successful.

As long as she truly feels that, as a pair, they could do so, she will have an invaluable fallback position that she will in all likelihood never have to use. That should prevent her from ever feeling deeply threatened and cornered at work, a situation that quickly feeds on itself and is surprisingly visible to coworkers and superiors. The security she gains from having a real partner pays a steady stream of dividends over the years that can make or break her career.

Conversely, not having a real partner she loves always generates enough anxiety to make any position she holds, particularly after the age of thirty-five, tenuous. In fact, we found that the anxiety, which steadily grows, is the single greatest underlying cause of firing for women in the age range of thirty-five to fifty-five. It turns out that the asocial aspects of love have a number of very constructive consequences.

"TAKE ME AWAY FROM ALL THIS"

With so many women afraid of having their energy level and career expectations lowered as a result of falling in love, it is hardly surprising that they secretly fled in droves from the experience during the 1970s and 1980s. However, their desire for intimacy didn't disappear. They publicly pined away, or complained bitterly about its absence. Anything people want this much—but prevent themselves from having—always crops up again in a different form, one that is more acceptable to contemporary attitudes.

That is certainly what happened here. What did women who were secretly fleeing from men do? They unwittingly made the switch from men to mentors. Instead of looking for a man with whom to structure a satisfying personal life, each began searching for a mentor who would help her further her professional life.

Although she was unaware of it, the line that separated these two categories in her mind was extremely thin and usually missing altogether. The comments ambitious women made about one category often sounded suspiciously as though they were talking about the other: "I want someone who will look after me and give me the individual attention I need," and "My mentor should be thinking about me—and what's best for me—constantly." The old romantic fantasy of a knight in shining armor, riding on a white horse, who would "take me away from all this" had been replaced by a new, no less romantic fantasy of an executive in a three-piece suit, riding in a chauffeur-driven Rolls, who would "take me away from all this."

These weren't mere rescue fantasies. Something had indeed changed; the women wanted to be promoted, not just rescued. The romantic encounter was supposed to lead them to the executive suite, rather than the altar. What they really wanted, in the crowded, competitive career world, was to be rescued from oblivion.

If that was going to happen, it would have to do so in accordance with the prevailing mentality, which called for everyone to be able to say "I did it *my* way," and "I made it *on my own*." These women could no longer simply be handed their good fortune, and they knew it. One way or another, it would be crucial for them to appear to achieve their success on their own, without so much as an ounce of help from anyone.

The United States has always held the individual, his or her rights, and, even more, his or her attainments in high regard. As the 1960s arrived, and the leading edge of the seventy-six million-member baby-boom generation began pouring into the work force, the demand for individual achievement intensified. It was becoming harder than ever to stand out in the rapidly growing crowd, yet it was more strongly demanded than ever before. The United States had become sufficiently affluent to finally move on: Fame was the name of the game now, not money, and remaining anonymous throughout one's career was the equivalent of remaining dirt-poor for life.

Teenagers were the first to sense and react to the new demands. Since their lives were still fluid, they could more easily mold their dreams and themselves in a contemporary vein. They hadn't yet been saddled with the responsibilities that would later hold them back. Without ever putting it into words, they knew exactly what they had to do. First and foremost, it was necessary to leave home. As long as they were living under their parents' roof they would never be able to convincingly claim that they were on their way to making it on their own.

Even when they moved to another state on the other side of the country, and were trying to establish themselves there, they remained uneasy about taking money from home. Their marked ambivalence told the whole story. They needed the money; of that there was no doubt. But it compromised their public position—or, more accurately, the position they *wanted* to have. Fortunately, cash moves quietly, and they felt primarily guilt (about compromising their own standards), not shame (about violating those of their social group). Besides, as each insisted, "It is only for now," and "I need this check from my folks just to tide me over."

At home, their mothers missed them. The phrase the women used most often, in every region of the United States in which we interviewed them, was, "This house has become an empty nest." The children were aware of it but, as the vast majority of young adults put it, "I have to do what I have to do." Many couldn't bear to come home even for a visit. The reason they gave us was, "I don't like my parents, they drive me crazy," but the real reason they stayed away was one they couldn't admit: they hadn't yet succeeded on their own. In that case, going home was tantamount to an admission of failure. What made it worse was that they knew their parents would openly offer them assistance, which only made the absence of the success for which they were striving more painfully obvious. Paradoxically, their parents' well-intentioned offers of help came out sounding cruel, at least to the younger generation's ears.

What applied to their parents' place of residence applied even more to their family business. If they couldn't live near, much less with, their parents, they certainly couldn't stomach the idea of entering the same line of work as their fathers. School made that easy during their teen years and early twenties, since the youngsters were studying liberal arts or one of the professions (everything from pharmacy to business administration), whereas the majority of their parents weren't even college graduates. The sense of occupational distance kept this issue relatively quiet, while the topic of location—one's physical distance from one's parents—took precedence.

However, once school was through, the problem of earning a decent living caused the issue of occupational distance to move to the fore and flare up. Now that took precedence, particularly for children who had been away at college for many years and had come to view living on their own as a fact of life, a given about which there was nothing to discuss, much less argue. Although most youngsters growing up in the 1950s and 1960s had an image of the businessman as a man in a gray flannel suit reporting for work at some large, equally gray corporation, most fathers of the children in our sample worked in small- to medium-sized firms. Since this was primarily a middle and upper-middle class group, in many cases the men actually owned the companies at which they worked. They had started the businesses from scratch and continued to work there side by side with the other employees. Long before the word "entrepreneur" was draped with the glamour it would have in the late 1970s and 1980s, these men had successfully founded their own firms.

Did the children want such firms? They scoffed at the very thought. "I'm insulted," one young woman, a senior English major, replied to our question about her father's expanding insurance business, which he was urging her to join. "Do you think I'm incapable of doing anything better on my own?" If going home and living with her parents when she was in her twenties was proof that she was unable to make it on her own *financially*, joining her father's business would have been proof that she was unable to make it on her own *professionally*, which was much worse. That would have meant that she had failed at her chosen career. As Lori, whose father was a prosperous lumberyard owner, put it, "Everyone knows that you go into your father's business only if you can't *do* anything else well enough to make a living at it."

There was nothing new about any of this. For generations, a certain proportion of Americans had turned their backs on their parents' hometown and the family business and headed west, intent on starting anew. What *was* new was the record number of young men and, now, women who felt they had no choice but to strike out on their own if they were ever to avoid the stigma of having been handed their success. As they well knew, there couldn't be even a *hint* that someone else assisted them. In the public's mind, all such aid had to be subtracted first in calculating the amount of applause someone truly deserved. If the person had gotten too much help from others, perhaps she deserved no applause at all.

With thoughts such as these firmly planted in their minds, young men and women in our sample shunned their fathers' successful businesses. By the mid–1980s less than one father in twenty-six could ever count on seeing his sons or daughters join the profitable firm of which he was sole or majority owner. This is the corporate version of the empty-nest syndrome.

It was amusing to see the lengths to which most of the young adults in our sample unwittingly went to avoid being in the same field as their fathers. Two young men, both the same age, whose fathers were, respectively, in real estate and in the stock market, recoiled at the thought of entering these fields. But the two young men worked hard and finally succeeded, respectively, in other fields. The real estate broker now has a son doing well in the stock market, while the stockbroker has a son doing well in real estate.

THE STAMP OF APPROVAL

Women who weren't about to let their parents help them certainly weren't about to let their own partners do so. Laying claim to something that could be thought of as solely theirs eventually cost many their marriages. They never noticed the connection. They were merely acting in accordance with the relentless demand that we all do something strictly on our own if we are to be considered worthy by the nation of any renown that comes our way.

That is where mentors come in. The number one goal of every good American, especially those in their twenties and thirties, had become the attainment of fame in his or her field. Of course, statistically speaking, that was impossible. Well under one percent can do that in any field, even if, as Andy Warhol has jested, they each were to become famous for only fifteen minutes. What are the rest supposed to do in order to be able to hold their heads high? The next best thing to public recognition is private recognition, and that is what having a mentor is supposed to give those who claim to have had one.

They have to be careful about stating that they have one, since it would be relatively easy to verify whether or not they are fibbing. However, if they casually claim to have had one in the past, that isn't so easily checked by the ordinary listener. (Thanks to our practice of interviewing the members of our sample at least twice a year starting from the time most began working, we knew that almost all the people who tell a friend that they have had a mentor are lying. Our records show that typically less than 3% of those making the claim are telling the truth.) This is a clever lie, since the people most likely to have had a mentor are those with talent. Presumably, mentors don't squander their own precious hours, tutorial skills, protective efforts, and promotional assistance on just anybody. They save them for younger workers with above-average abilities.

In short, mentors are the talent scouts of the business world, senior executives who allegedly sift through the junior staff, ferret out the gifted, and help these select few develop their gifts. That the mentor is largely a myth, a subject about which most young workers kid themselves as well as others, is irrelevant. For this is a very revealing lie, one that says, "Even if *you* can't see it, I'm special. I must be. I've had a mentor. A veteran professional in my field has looked me over, checked me out, and given me the needed stamp of approval." Or, as some might have said, if they had put the matter honestly to themselves, "If I can't get public recognition—and for now, anyway, I clearly can't—I'll have to make do with private recognition. That, at least, I can hope to find by telling people I've had a mentor. It's not a bad substitute for the moment, since it is a lot more than most working stiffs will ever have."

Women in the 1970s and 1980s who began searching en masse for mentors weren't doing so merely because they were taken in by such tall tales. They wanted proof of their own worth and, most important, to feel that they were succeeding on their own. Some readers may say, "Wait a minute, how could they claim to have made it on their own once they actually found a mentor? Wouldn't a woman who proudly aspires to being self-made be better off to avoid mentors altogether, male or female, even if they come her way?"

What makes this such an interesting question is that it shines a light on one of the key hidden aspects of mentors which made them so appealing in the first place. Schoolteachers deal with children, while mentors deal with adults. Youngsters are still in their formative years, a period of rapid physical and intellectual growth. With enough of the right kind of training they can be moved very far in one direction or another. Their abilities can be shaped. That is definitely not so with adults. By the time they enter the work force, they are already much of what they will be, physically and intellectually. No one could easily reshape them at this point. By their late twenties and early thirties, the time when the majority are hoping most earnestly to find a mentor, that is even more true.

Far from being unfortunate, that is very good news. Because anyone who declares them talented now must be discovering something that is already present, not an ability implanted by the mentor doing the discovering. That is what's so wonderful about mentors: they can only *recognize* gifts possessed by others, and help refine those abilities. Mentors can never lay claim (though some try) to having given someone such enviable abilities in the first place. By default, then, the talents belong to the owner.

In that sense, saying that one has, or had, a mentor is a highly self-congratulatory statement, one of the few that people can make publicly and not be greeted by jeers. It should be clear now why so many women could actively seek a mentor and not feel they had compromised themselves—though it is fair to say that most merely hoped, rather than searched, for one: *The basic service a mentor is supposed to provide is to recognize abilities that already exist and, having done so, proceed to speed the rise of the person who possesses them.* That women who are trying so hard to be tough competitors could believe that this degree of saintly selflessness exists in any real-life professional or businessperson is simply astonishing.

Regardless of what such people so cautiously say about the subject, they actually view mentors as magic carpets that carry the ambitious to overnight success. Think of them as a gimmick that frustrated underachievers are hoping to use as a way of attaining instant acclaim.

One question that kept recurring over the years while we were analyzing what was fact and what was myth about mentors was this: Why didn't at least some of these women think of their husbands as mentors? Less than a quarter of a percent did. Now that we better understand what women wanted from a mentor to begin with, it is obvious why that is so. After all, mentors, as the alleged talent scouts of corporate America, would never say that a woman possessed an ability she really didn't. Preserving their own reputations as astute scouts would prevent them from lying. Self-interest could be counted upon to keep their judgments honest.

The same self-interest might cause a loving husband to tell his wife she possessed talents that she didn't. Or, more commonly, *he* might believe she had them, even if no one else can see them. To someone who says, "Beauty is in the eye of the beholder," he can rightly retort, "I *know* her better than you do." What it boils down to is that if she must find public proof of her own worth in order to meet the demands of the times, her spouse can't provide it. He suffers from the permanent defect of being only one person, and nothing less than a large, cheering throng can give her the confirmation she needs.

The second and even more important reason husbands aren't seen by their wives as mentors has to do with the demand being made upon everyone, male and female, to achieve something solely on his or her own. It is the achievement of the individual, not of companies or countries, that people most often talk about admiringly with friends. In such an atmosphere each woman's husband, as a party of one, is not only incapable by himself of proclaiming her a star, he can even be seen as a menace. Her very association with him could jeopardize in her own eyes—and, she fears, in the eyes of others—the all-important public position for which she is secretly striving. For it is entirely possible that any audience that comes to know them both will assume that he helped her.

Reacting as the teenagers we discussed earlier do, she therefore shuns real intimacy with her husband, or avoids marriage altogether, until she has become an unequivocal success. Then, like young adults who finally feel secure enough with their attainments in their chosen field to go home, she plans to find a husband. Small wonder that so many women are subconsciously convinced that becoming renowned in their field will automatically produce a personal life as a bonus. However, as we now know, without a satisfying personal life her chances of attaining the success for which she yearns are radically reduced.

Summing up, the main reason the women we studied needed a mentor was that they couldn't allow their husbands to help them. In fact, each had to be certain she pushed him off the stage whenever the curtain was about to go up. Instead of finding the imaginary partner for whom she hoped, she wound up throwing away the only real partner she had. Then she needed a mentor, this fictional saintly soul, even more. Soon her personal and professional life began to sink in an endless sea of frustration. In the meantime, without any fanfare, the Ritas of the world kept quietly making headway.

13

Where Successful Women Go Wrong

In this chapter we want to focus on two groups of women: those who found love and lost it, and those who haven't been able to find a satisfactory partner at all—who, in fact, are beginning to doubt that they'll ever have one.

The most important mistakes that career women make in their personal lives rarely seem serious at first. Unlike banging one's thumb with a hammer, no pain is felt immediately to signal an error. Only as the years pass does it become apparent that something is wrong, perhaps drastically so. Even then it usually isn't clear where the source of the problem lies. The enormous emphasis in the United States on individual freedom increases the number of opportunities each person has to succeed or fail. However, what we found striking during our study was how far afield a woman typically had to wander before someone said anything eye-opening to her about what she had been doing to cause herself grief. The great freedom women now have to chart their own courses, personally and professionally, is a real plus, but it shouldn't blind us to the fact that there is a dangerous negative in the picture; namely, there is no one close enough to most working women—and sufficiently knowledgeable too—to prevent each from doing herself major and, in many cases, permanent harm.

Some readers will reply, as did many of the people with whom we discussed the subject, "That's the way it *has* to be. If we're not going to supervise adults—if we're truly to allow them to do as they please with their personal lives—then we have to be prepared for the possibility that many will end up creating a real bed of nails for themselves."

The argument seems callous, especially since the women we're talking about are well-meaning and hard-working, trying as best they can to meet the many conflicting demands being made upon them. Anything we can learn from a careful study of the mistakes made by a wide variety of career women may turn out to be of significant use to others on the same road.

It has become so difficult for two people to find each other initially, much less start living together or decide to marry, that one would imagine they would go to great lengths to preserve the relationship they have. Some do, but approximately 80% of the couples we studied who paired up in the 1970s and 1980s do not. Well over 40% of these marriages have already ended in divorce, or soon will. What is surprising is that all 80% don't. There is indeed a strong argument to be made for that outcome. Instead of calling it quits, the two needle one another, and will typically continue to do so for decades. Apparently, this is one process that feeds on itself. But what got them started on this road in the first place?

When couples split up, it is always possible that they weren't right for one another to begin with. That is what they and their friends almost automatically conclude. However, this kind of reasoning quickly becomes circular, since there is no sure-fire way of knowing whether any two people are "right" as a pair. Only they can decide. Obviously, then, if the two stay together they are right—or if they split up, wrong—for each other.

The topic is too important to allow the couple to obscure the underlying experience with self-serving descriptions, slogans and labels. For as the two know better than any outsider, they will switch labels in their minds hundreds of times as the relationship begins to deteriorate. Optimism may alternate with pessimism dozens of times in a single day. The explanations and justifications each continually concocts to have ready for the public keep chasing the quickly shifting facts. No researcher can learn much from this dazzling display of quick-change artistry, except perhaps how far people are prepared to go to save face.

It took us nearly ten years to realize that the same intense devotion to face-saving was present before, not just after, the relationship began to collapse. People don't wait for a calamity to befall them, one in which their own actions may have played a major role, before coming up with a publicly acceptable story about why it happened. ("I was just standing there, minding my own business, when . . .") Well in advance of the setback, they spin their tale and put it on the shelf, just in case company drops in and wants to satisfy its curiosity. That may seem quite wasteful and anxiety-producing, but it is indeed what people do. They interview themselves many times before the actual interview takes place, if it ever does. As we've said repeatedly throughout the book, they want to Be Prepared.

In short, any woman who has had a satisfying personal life and lost it—or, more important, wants to prevent its loss—must assess the *amount* of face saving she does and the areas of her life in which she does it. No one but she need know the results of the assessment, and the potential payoff is well worth the effort involved. It provides a degree of self-acceptance and peace with one's partner that is not available from any other source.

REPACKAGING THE PAST

The aspects of people's lives about which they most strongly feel the need to save face are precisely the areas in which they perceive others around them are doing well. It sounds as though an unacknowledged competition of some kind is going on, and it is. That is how the people who are trying to save face always feel. They are losing, at least in their own view, and they don't want anyone else to notice it.

In school their classmates couldn't help but notice. From elementary school right through college and graduate school, students are continually being compared to others. Whether it is looks, brains, sex appeal, or athletic ability, each is measured repeatedly—often daily—against the best in each category, and found wanting. Falling short in some or even all the categories isn't the end of the story; it is merely the beginning. We found that not one student in a thousand can say, "So what?" and walk away, indifferent to the idea of having been classified as second-rate. Instead, a face-saving machine almost audibly clicks on and starts to generate defensive explanations and postures intended to ward off any embarrassment at being found lacking by an audience of one's peers.

Anyone who has studied this self-shielding process carefully can't escape the conclusion that it is fruitless from its inception. For it is designed to protect youngsters against a critical view of themselves that, unfortunately, they have in most cases *already* adopted. Although they clearly are unaware of it, the fact that the insult has become internalized, and is an integral part of their self-image, means that all the defensive posturing will be in vain. In fact, it further interferes with their ability to accept themselves and, equally important, to interact comfortably with others. Decades later it will still be doing the same thing.

Even after we realized the amount of energy that was being wasted by adolescents in rearguard thought and behavior, we still assumed that the defensiveness would decrease as they became more established members of their fields and had families of their own. That isn't what happened in the 1970s and 1980s; the women in our sample became more defensive, not less, as they passed through their twenties and thirties. What we hadn't foreseen was that a switch in emphasis from looks and sex appeal to less tangible criteria was taking place. Specifically, the audience was less concerned now about *attributes* and interested instead in *achievements*.

Young adults couldn't do a great deal about how they looked, though they tried, and many even considered plastic surgery. Since, as one put it glumly, "This is my face and I guess I'll have to live with it," they would have to defend what they had. But as they grew older, and the emphasis shifted from attributes to achievements, they saw far more room to maneuver. Their attainments were by no means as plain as the nose on their face, and while the right light might do little for a nose, it could do wonders for what they had accomplished in life.

Given the size of major United States cities and the frequency with which Americans move, it is easy for people to rewrite their own histories for conversational presentation to others. We saw this in the previous chapter, where the majority who claimed to have had a mentor had not, in fact, had one. They viewed it as a worthwhile relationship, so they readily convinced themselves that they had had one. The point is that they came to believe what they were saying even though it was flatly contradicted by the facts. This wasn't the only area in which the rewriting of one's personal history occurred. It is important for us to look at another example of the same phenomenon, since it is one of the best indicators that a successful woman, with what would seem to be little to worry about either personally or professionally, is well on her way to causing her personal—and, ultimately, her professional—life to collapse.

Lois Tanner's life is representative of an enormous number of others and shows how easy it is for serious trouble to develop in a relationship before it is acknowledged by either partner. By then, it is often too late to salvage the situation.

When Lois finished high school in Georgia she breathed a sigh of relief. Not that she had any doubts about graduating, since her grades each semester usually averaged B. What made her suddenly feel more at ease was the fact that she was no longer an object of the intense daily scrutiny to which teenagers subject one another. "I hate it," she said at seventeen, as her senior year began. "Somebody is always making remarks about you—your clothes, your home, who your friends are—there's always something." Despite all that, Lois knew she would miss some of the friends she had made, especially during her junior and senior years, and she was a little anxious about going away to the college in New England to which she'd been admitted. All in all, Lois was glad to be leaving. "High school was great," she said, two weeks after it was through, "but I've had my fill of it."

When she went to college that fall she wanted to fit in, not just get an education. It was a natural desire, one that virtually all of her college classmates felt as well; otherwise they would not have chosen the school in the first place. There was a variety of ways to fit in, with the mainstream up-and-comers and the campus rebels the two most conspicuous groups to join. Lois knew that if she fit anywhere, it was with the former. But being accepted by her peers subjected her in many ways to even more pressure than she had felt in high school. "Here, people can tell what part of the country you're from just by the way you look and talk," she said in the spring term of her freshman year. The realization amazed her and made her visibly uncomfortable. By the end of high school she had had enough of feeling like an outsider, and hoped that in college things would be different.

That makes it sound as though Lois was more socially and less academically oriented than most. The reverse was closer to the truth. But the fact that she went through high school unable to find even the moderate level of popularity she had badly wanted left her with a sizable appetite for it. Paradoxically, if she had experienced more social acceptance in high school, she would have been less hungry for it in college.

It was available, that much she knew, but it could be hers only with effort. Like many people in her position, that made her unwittingly try to be rid of what she labeled "the dead giveaway" regional characteristics that allowed others to pigeonhole her so readily. By incorporating a little of everyone else's dialect into her own from suburban Atlanta, she wound up producing a kind of synthetic speech pattern that couldn't be readily identified as coming from any particular place. Her subconscious goal had been to sound like a cross between a telephone operator and a TV network newscaster, and she eventually succeeded. "What happened to your voice?" an old friend from high school, the boy who had been her first bedmate and who had stayed in Atlanta, asked her casually when she returned home during Christmas vacation her senior year. The question surprised Lois, and she mechanically answered, "I must be getting older; soon I'll be really gravel-throated." Her reply neatly ducked the issue, since it wasn't how high or low her voice had become that had prompted the question in the first place. It was, instead, the disappearance of her familiar Georgia accent.

Lois was a twenty-one-year-old sociology and business administration major whose career goals were as distant and vague in her mind as her own death from old age. "I don't really know what I want to do," she said, shrugging her shoulders, in the spring term of her senior year. "I'll see what job offers I can get. I might want to open a restaurant. That always looked like fun. Maybe a gourmet shop, with lots of neat little things to buy." At 5'6", with brown hair and blue eyes and a lanky body that wouldn't stay still whether she was seated or standing, Lois radiated a restlessness that would still be there decades later. She reminded some of her college classmates of Faye Dunaway, particularly when Lois was attempting to make a point and no one responded. If there was one thing that could be counted upon to throw this intelligent and verbal young woman, it was this. Once she got started in a conversation, she automatically assumed that it would pick up speed and turn into a high-tension interchange. But when it didn't, it was interesting to see that her need for momentum would often cause Lois to reply to her own comments.

IS LOVE EVERYTHING?

She had a number of boyfriends and lovers in college, but nothing serious grew out of any of the relationships. After graduation she was able to chart the first stage of her career course without a partner influencing her. First Lois chose the city she wanted to live in: "New York, because that's where everything is happening." Then she chose employment where her chances for rising rapidly on the corporate ladder seemed best. The entry-level position she landed was with a medium-sized mail-order gift company. She spent four years there in the promotion department, trying to find new ways to get the public to respond to her company's product line. By that time she had become good at what she was doing, and she had made many useful suggestions, but the work didn't excite her. "I still don't know what I'll be doing for a living when I grow up," she commented, with feigned fatigue, at twenty-five.

Lois may not have known what she wanted to be yet, but she knew that she wanted to be a success at it, whatever it was. "I intend to be outstanding—at *something*," she had said at twenty-two. However, even at this early stage, it was clear that the fame and fortune her work was eventually supposed to bring her was more important than the work itself. That could easily change, and she might subsequently develop a passionate interest in one area of professional activity or another. Hundreds of young men and women we studied followed this route. First came their desire to excel (usually instilled in them by their parents). Only later did they hit upon something at which they could indeed excel.

For Lois and the majority of her peers, that hadn't happened yet. They were good at their work, and it earned them a living, so they kept at it. That made them still better at it, even outstanding. But it might as well have been a card trick they had perfected to please an audience. In and of itself, the trick meant little to them as performers, since they knew they could repeat it at the drop of a hat. It was when no audience gathered to see the show that the time spent perfecting the trick suddenly stood revealed to them as having been wasted.

Many talented people never experience the crisis that was looming on Lois's horizon because, as in her case, there is enough of an audience present to make the show seem worthwhile—that is, they are getting paid to do the work and others are involved in it. It looks real enough for them to forget even their own doubts. After a while, though, the whole performance feels empty to them, no matter how skillfully they keep presenting it in public. What the majority of people we studied do in this situation is to start pressuring their friends and, even more so, their intimates to make up for what is missing. They unwittingly expect their private lives to magically compensate for the prolonged periods of absorption that they want but are lacking in their professional lives.

Unfortunately, that isn't what happens. Being part of an enduring intimacy offers the participants a permanent sense of protection (each partner feels more secure thanks to the ongoing presence of the other), but it cannot offer a permanent feeling of being absorbed (people in love experience this feeling for only brief, not prolonged, periods). Instead of being as caught up in their love lives as they had hoped, they soon find it every bit as empty and mechanical as their work has become. It is interesting that few people realize they are looking to their personal lives to make up for what their professional lives aren't providing. Still fewer are aware that an intimacy cannot give them, year after year, what they are looking for. Apparently, it can do this only in conjunction with a satisfying work-related activity that fills most of each person's day. We found that anyone who tries to obtain from his or her partner everything he or she needs emotionally ends up heaping an extra burden on the personal relationship that eventually causes it to crumble.

At the time, Lois was aware of how alienated she felt from her employer: "Would I miss this company tomorrow if it burned tonight? Not a bit, except for my paycheck." When she got an offer from a large cosmetics company through a business associate, she seized it. This position too was in the promotion department, but everything at the new location seemed to her so much more polished and professional. "The offices are modern, and decorated really nicely," she said proudly, two months after joining the firm. "I like coming to work here. It's so elegant."

Lois's love life was another matter entirely. The succession of men she met, some of whom pursued her avidly, struck her as disappointing. "Where are all the quality men?" she asked, genuinely puzzled. From many women who were single in the 1970s and 1980s such a question could be interpreted as a sign of laziness or hostility. Not from Lois. She wanted very much to be married, and there was no doubt in our minds that she eventually would be. What took us by surprise was the series of events that occurred after she met the man who became her husband.

When Lois had her first encounter with Jack Walters, she was twenty-eight and doing well at the major cosmetics company to which she had moved two years earlier. He, on the other hand, was a twenty-nine-year-old writer and college English teacher who seemed little interested in doing well financially. In fact, the world of business might as well have been taking place on another planet. "I don't have anything against commerce," he told us at thirty. "It's just not for me." We've discussed in Part Three pairings between successful businesswomen and aspiring "artists"—parasites, really, using their commitment to art as a fashionable excuse for their current poverty. Jack didn't fit this category at all. As later events were to prove, he was dedicated to his craft: turning out short stories and novels. One of each had been published by the time he and Lois met. In the meantime, he obtained a bread-and-butter income by teaching college, a position he took seriously. Lois's steadily rising earnings hadn't turned him into a sexual opportunist. He loved her for herself. Jack may have felt estranged from the commercial world, but he looked as though he spent his days in a corporation rather than on campus. Unlike many academics, whose rumpled clothes and appearance made it seem as though they had jumped into a washer/dryer fully dressed and then gone straight to the office or to class, Jack's appearance was always neat. At 5′11″, with his dark brown hair kept short and parted on the left, he sometimes looked like an overgrown teenager. Shunning jeans even on weekends, Jack usually wore khaki slacks and a dress shirt with a woven cloth tie. His evenly trimmed mustache helped a clear-skinned face that at times looked almost too boyish and bright-eyed to appear older and more reserved. Health-minded, though not a jogger, he regularly tried to get Lois to stop smoking.

They met on an uptown bus while he was on the way to his publisher and she was going to get a haircut. They dated for two years, then got married, having virtually lived together (sometimes at his apartment, usually at hers) during the prior six months. Two and a half years after their wedding they had a daughter, Stacey, and moved to a larger apartment. Lois went back to work soon after Stacey's birth. They were clearly happy together and were both doing well professionally. By the time Lois was thirty-four she was earning $67,000 and had been promoted twice. Jack, at thirty-five, had just had his second novel published, though he insisted on reminding us that it sold only 3,800 copies and wasn't issued as a paperback once it went out of print as a hardcover book.

People who got to know Lois well during these years often described her as "driven." She talked about her work constantly, analyzing for hours even minor incidents that displeased her. The typical conversation the couple had on evenings and weekends consisted of Lois complaining about her coworkers, with Jack listening attentively but saying little. The same pattern was seen when the pair got together with friends.

"I'M A WRITER, NOT A MOVIE STAR"

During her thirty-sixth year an event occurred that shocked Lois. As she tells it, "At 7:30 Thursday evening Jack and I were heading for the front door, saying goodbye to the baby-sitter, on our way to meet friends at a nearby restaurant for dinner. The phone rang. Roberta [a friend in the marketing department] was calling to tell me that my boss had been fired. She didn't know why." The reason turned out to be that while sales were up, profits were down for the third quarter in a row. Nearly three dozen other middle managers were also dismissed. "Lois was very tense during dinner," Jack later said. "I was awake most of the night," Lois quickly added. "I was scared stiff, sure they were going to fire me too."

They promoted her instead, giving her her old boss's position. Lois was now a vice president, earning $110,000 a year. "For the first three weeks," she said, opening her eyes wide, "I just couldn't believe it. It was a dream come true." A little over a year later, Jack received some good news as well. His third novel was published, this time by one of the nation's largest publishers, and while Jack had predicted that "it will put book reviewers across the country to sleep, just as the other two have," the reverse happened. A number of reviewers at newspapers and magazines in major cities raved about the work. Word of mouth did the rest, with satisfied readers strongly recommending the book to their friends. It never made the bestseller list, but it sold more than 27,000 copies in hardcover and, thus far, more than 100,000 in paperback.

His fourth novel, for which he received a $40,000 advance, was published three years later and was an even bigger success, although it too never made the bestseller list. However, it did make Jack, at 42, an established author. Two incidents brought that fact home to him in an unmistakable manner. When he was leaving his office at 5:30, a tall student, clearly nervous, stopped him. Haltingly the youngster said, "I hate to bother you, Professor Walters. I can see you're leaving." Silence followed. Jack asked, "What can I do for you?" The student didn't reply. Reaching into his backpack, he pulled out a tattered copy of Jack's latest book and asked, "Could you please autograph this?"

It wasn't the first time that Jack had signed one of his novels. He had autographed dozens of copies at a reception the publisher of his second book had held in his honor, which was attended by about thirty people, most of them connected with the firm. In Jack's view, however, that was business. This was different. "I'm hard pressed to find an ulterior motive," Jack said, still digesting the experience. "He wasn't even one of my students." After pausing for a moment, he commented, "I always thought I'd be dead long before people started liking my books." What amazed him was that it was not only happening while he was alive, but that his audience was also leapfrogging the barrier he had unwittingly imposed between himself and the world—namely, books—and wanted some contact, no matter how slight, directly with him. That made him uneasy. Shaking his head, he said, "I'm a writer, not a movie star."

The gap between the two categories narrowed considerably six weeks later when Lois got a call from Roberta, the same coworker who had told her that her boss had been fired. This time, "The company blabbermouth," as Lois had labeled her, was nearly shrieking, "Your husband is on the cover!" A magazine had done a feature article about Jack and his work and made it the cover story, including a photo of a smiling Jack in his office. For weeks afterward the phone didn't stop ringing. Jack's novel was selling well, aided by stories such as the one that had run in the magazine. Jack started to get offers to appraise, in print, new books from other novelists. He liked doing it; he wrote more thoughtful reviews than most, and it kept his name before the public between the appearances of one novel and the next.

TO PICK A WINNER

Instead of being pleased by the obvious success both were experiencing, Lois was becoming visibly more anxious and irritable. Her own achievements weren't troubling her; Jack's were. She had been concerned ever since adolescence with making an appealing presentation of herself to the public. It might as well have been a short story entitled "My Heroic Accomplishments." In the 1970s young adults often called these thumbnail sketches of one's attainments a "rap," as in, "He was laying his rap on her, and she was giving him *her* rap." In a country characterized by frequent relocation, one in which people spend most of their time with men and women they haven't grown up with, the brief presentation of a verbal resume is a normal practice.

However, we found that these resumes were subject to more falsification by far than the ones prospective employees send to an employer. Americans want very much to be liked; hence it is hardly surprising that they try hard to put their best face forward. The problem is that the facade, this two-dimensional picture of themselves, can do real harm to the three-dimensional reality they are supposed to be living. Like many political figures, they flatten their personal lives to make their public image simpler and more appealing.

Lois wasn't a politician, but she might as well have been. Now forty-one, she was still doing the same thing adolescents do to impress their audiences. The difference was that she had a chance to rewrite the story more times than they. Also, her parents weren't on hand any longer to contradict her tale by their presence or comments (a prospect feared by many of the status-conscious strivers we studied). Leaving the South and going to school in the North provided the first opportunity for her to repackage her past. Entering the business world gave her a second such chance. Changing to a more prestigious firm offered her a third opportunity, which she put to immediate use. That there were only three major revisions mustn't be allowed to obscure the fact that Lois was continually updating the verbal resume with which she was determined to impress anyone she met. Far more than she realized, this was one of her central and continuing concerns.

Suddenly, all the years of repackaging into which she had pumped so much effort seemed on the verge of going down the drain. Ever since she had met him, Jack had always been a marginal character in the story about herself that she was constantly composing in her mind. Even after they got married his role remained minimal. She didn't want anyone else in the spotlight with her, and there wasn't.

Yet the success of Jack's novels was rapidly undermining Lois's long-time efforts to create a fiction of her own. Not that he had any such intention, or that he even welcomed the increasing amount of public attention he was receiving. More than once, Jack complained bitterly to us that the acclaim was interfering with his ability to get his work done. From a man who complained as rarely as Jack did, the remarks were striking.

Ten weeks after Jack's face appeared on the magazine cover, Lois said to us, incensed, "I'm not going to live in *his* shadow." As she continued talking, a note of panic entered her voice. There was no question that she was worried most about what her imaginary audience—the one she had been carrying in her head since her teen years—would think of her. Until now, *she* had been the only person in whom her audience was allegedly interested, endlessly and adoringly. A sentence, uttered by a friend two days before, had really hit a nerve and was motivating Lois's current outburst. The friend, whose name was Wendy, had casually mentioned, "You must be a real asset to Jack." Lois unthinkingly replied, "Thank you," and let the matter drop. But with each passing hour, it was causing her to become increasingly annoyed. "I never realized what a roaring bitch Wendy is," Lois loudly stated. "The comment is so vicious. Is that *all* she thinks I am?"

Lois was not only anxious about what her audience would think, but was also fearful about her husband's thoughts. She had been attracted to him in part because, soon after they started dating, she became convinced that he was likely to become outstanding in his field. Her comments, ten months after they met, were, "He's really on the ball," and, "Jack has a lot going for him." To a friend, a few months later, she remarked that "Jack is a winner, that much I can tell." Since she was convinced that he was going places, she immediately jumped to the conclusion that he felt the same way about her. In fact, she believed that he in turn had chosen her because her career prospects were so good.

That contributed substantially to the image Lois held up to us as an ideal, year after year. Like most highly motivated working women in our sample when discussing other couples, she considered it best if husband and wife moved up with equal speed. As she remarked more than once, "Both should be rapidly rising stars." She seemed not to realize how rarely that happpens even with a pair of good friends of the same sex who are alike in a wide variety of other ways. One inevitably gets a few, or even many, steps ahead of the other as the years pass. If there had to be a difference, Lois's behavior made it clear that she very much wanted her fortunes to increase faster than Jack's. As typically happens when one partner strongly feels that way, the other soon pulls decisively ahead.

It upset Lois to feel that she had fallen behind Jack, and that the gap was widening. Since she still clung to the belief that he had selected her because she too was destined to be a winner, there was no way for her to escape the feeling that she was disappointing him. That would have been too naked an admission, one that left her vulnerable, at least in her own view. She therefore did what most others in this position do, and switched from defense to offense. It became "Keep your goddam lawnmower" time. As she put it angrily, "I'll bet the bastard thinks he's *outgrowing* me, just because his career is doing better than mine."

We searched hard for even a smidgen of evidence in Jack's comments and behavior that that represented his view. There was none to be found. He loved Lois and spoke about her year in and year out in a consistently admiring and affectionate manner. Apparently none of his words or actions registered with her. She had already made up her mind that *he* thought he was too good for her, though what she really meant, and couldn't bring herself to say, was that *she* no longer felt good enough for him. Not only was she being rejected, the rejection was taking place in plain view of everyone who knew either one of them. There was no time to waste. The sense of urgency that was palpable in her voice reflected her desire to contain any damage already done to her reputation and prevent more from being inflicted. Lois had managed to create her own private hell.

It didn't stay private for long. With her personal life starting to crumble, she began to concentrate even more single-mindedly on her career. This was a typical reaction during the 1970s and 1980s for women in their twenties, thirties, and forties whose personal lives had begun to fall apart, and for those who couldn't find an acceptable personal life to begin with. But Lois needed more—instant success, enough to at least equal what Jack had attained. That was going to be difficult to find. She had moved so far up the corporate ladder, there weren't many slots left. Actually, only two seemed realistically within her reach: executive vice president and president. Both were filled by people who, even in Lois's view, were better qualified to hold these positions than she, and who, in addition, weren't about to leave any time soon.

Finally, she hit upon an ingenious solution. It wasn't one that she sat down and figured out. Rather, it occurred to her while she was talking to a friend she hadn't seen for over a year. But once Lois made the remark, she recognized immediately how powerful and full of potential it was. When Lois's friend said to her, "Gee, I see Jack is really doing well," Lois replied, "Yeah, but *his* success is coming at the expense of *my* emotions."

Having struck gold, Lois continued on in this vein for the rest of the lunch. For the first time in months, she felt relieved. After that, every chance she got to tell people what had "really" gone into Jack's success, she repeated the thought. The first time he heard this speech, as it was being delivered in their living room to a couple Lois knew from work, Jack was stunned. Usually quiet while Lois did most of the talking, this time he openly retorted, "That's not how it was." Lois just turned to him and said, "How would you know? You're always so lost in your work." Lois then turned to the couple and stated flatly, "The husband's success always comes at the expense of the wife."

In an era that was milking the "woman as victim" theme for all it was worth (since it served as a justification for still more outrage), the statement had a contemporary ring of rightness to it. However, Lois was more aware than most that *unsuccessful* men are the real drain on the women with whom they pair up. A few months before Lois met Jack, she dated—and then dropped—a man who seemed attractive and interesting, at least to some of her friends. "Why did you stop seeing him?" we asked Lois. "Because he's not going anywhere," she replied without a moment's hesitation. Unlike the many women who gravitate to them, like moths to a flame, Lois didn't want to be romantically involved with losers. In her words, "I've got enough headaches of my own. I don't need his." Over the years, when discussing women friends who had married men who, as Lois described them, "couldn't get out of their own way" and "kept making trouble for themselves," she made it clear that life with a man who was doing well was easier.

Unless, that is, he started to do *very* well. As long as her partner's achievements were moderate, Lois had no trouble handling them, and she could devote herself fully to realizing her own ambitions. It was only when renown came to him but not to her that this strategy collapsed. Scrambling now to save face, she hit upon the theme that his accomplishments had come at her expense. The proof that this was blatantly false could be found in the record of her previous comments. Prior to Jack's success, she never once stated that his work was taking a toll on her emotions. She didn't say it because she didn't feel it; in fact, she repeatedly mentioned to him, and to us, that she was amazed at how much he had accomplished and still had plenty of time for her and Stacey. "He's so *organized*," she said, with more envy than admiration, fourteen months before the cover story appeared. "He really has his act together."

More to the point, Lois allowed her own career to interfere with her personal life far more frequently and severely than Jack did. She compounded the problem by talking endlessly about work-related subjects with him (primarily petty office squabbles) during evenings and weekends. It was clear that, with Jack at last a success, she was projecting onto him a label that better described her own practices. In the Afterword we'll discuss the guilt feelings of working mothers with children under the age of six. However, when Lois and other equally ambitious women spoke about this guilt, and they did so frequently, we found that it also had another meaning.

Lois regularly said, "I'm always working late, and I feel bad about neglecting my daughter and my husband." She meant it, but the words were being voiced because she also wanted everyone to know how much *she* was suffering, not her family. There was no question in her mind that she would one day be a huge success. There was equally little question in her mind that attaining success required many sacrifices. The biggest sacrifice was—in fact, had to be—her personal life. As far as she was concerned, she had to make a choice: have one or the other, a satisfying love life or a successful career, but not both.

Since she was determined to achieve fame and fortune through her work, she deliberately broadcast the message that she was sacrificing her personal life. "The gods don't let you have both," she might as well have been saying, "so I want them to know that I have offered up my husband and child."

The gods were supposed to be appeased by these offerings and grant her in return what she was really after—success, which she wanted much more than the things she was giving up. This is one of the best examples we've encountered of magical thinking in modern life. However, the event was taking place in the United States in the 1980s, not classical Greece in the eighth century B.C., so she had to make her plea to the public, not to the gods. Lois therefore repeatedly told her tale of suffering to coworkers and friends. She never understood why she felt compelled to do this, but the real reason was simple: there is no sense in making a sacrifice unless someone else hears about it.

Lois was thinking like a martyr looking for a future payoff, not one atoning for a past sin. When all was said and done, Lois's strategy was immensely self-congratulatory. As she went up to the podium and re-

ceived her award before the imaginary cheering thousands (not to mention the imaginary millions more watching on television), she wanted to
be in a position to *have to* apologize for achieving success at the expense
of her loved ones. She knew that the speech would be well received, and
she wouldn't have to add, "But you, my beloved fans, know that such
sacrifices are always necessary, aren't they?" Every moment of suffering
was just one more moment of triumph that she would be able to share
with her audience of admirers when acclaim finally came her way.

"WHAT I GAVE UP TO MARRY YOU"

Lois must not have appeased her public very well, for they never granted
her what she wanted in return for her offerings. The magical thinking
produced only hardship, for herself and for those close to her. But since
it shaped so much of her thought and behavior, it is hardly surprising that
when Jack achieved success she quickly began to accuse him of having
neglected his wife and child in order to attain it. He had done no such
thing. And if he had, the success that she so resented would probably
never have become his in the first place.

After eleven stormy months of nonstop conflict, Jack and Lois got a
divorce. When people ask her about Jack now, Lois almost automatically
replies that his success "is no longer coming at the expense of my emotions *and* my career. Let it be someone else's." Although she remarked
more than once after the divorce that "It's time for me to really come into
my own," she was recently fired. The officials who made the decision
concluded that "she had become too abrasive and difficult to work with.
We were getting a lot of complaints." They had a few of their own, too.
Two of Lois's assistants, now both at other firms, commented that "She's
impossible—scattered, frantic, and insulting. I'm glad they got rid of
her." After being out of work for almost a year, and doing some free-lance
consulting for $2,500 a month, she just landed a full-time position for
$65,000 per annum. "It's the best thing I could find," she said, making
the most of it, and then added, "I'm thinking of filing an age discrimination lawsuit—I made more than this ten years ago when I was thirty-
four."

Despite the traumatic events that finally occurred, Lois had it easy relative to the large number of women who marry men who become successful slowly, instead of overnight. For it allowed her to have a number of
years of comparative tranquility before her house of cards collapsed. The
wives of doctors, dentists, lawyers, accountants, and small-business owners, on the other hand, have to start saving face much earlier in their

marriages if, like Lois, they are concerned above all about impressing the world with their solo achievements. It is difficult but worthwhile to compare the two kinds of self-inflicted pain: Lois's is similar to hitting one's thumb with a hammer, while that of women in the latter category is similar to that which results from wearing a pair of shoes that look good but are too small.

Their husbands' credentials, income, or assets present such women with a challenge almost from the day the honeymoon is over. Less than 1% of the women in this position were as candid as a nurse who said to us outright, two weeks after marrying a physician, "So much for the romance—now the living room brawls begin," with their friends having ringside seats. And that is exactly what happened, as she argued with him fiercely whenever company was present about which of the two was more sophisticated where various aspects of medicine and health care were concerned. ("I start an I.V. [intravenous hook-up] much better than you do," said she.)

There is something sad about seeing women with so much going for them who manage to throw away what they may not be able to find again. Yet that is what the majority of members of our sample did. They became so caught up in the intense competition with a spouse that they undermined their own marriages. In the heat of battle, they don't even consider that possibility. They want to win, and they feel that their husbands are preventing them from doing so. Yet if they hadn't married in the first place they would have no way of deciding whether they were ahead or behind, winning or losing—or so we thought. It was revealing to find that before their marriages and after their divorces they got into competitive conflicts with someone in their immediate vicinity, at home or work. It merely became more localized and chronic once each had wed a man who, she felt, threatened to outclass her with his achievements.

Anyone who has watched a wide variety of educated couples get into these unending quarrels (not even divorce really puts them to rest) usually comes to the conclusion that the best solution is for the woman to pay greater attention to her professional interests. "If she has pride in her own work," one psychiatrist told us, "she won't care how well *he* is doing because of his." Said a psychologist, "She should put her work first, and her love life will take care of itself." Similar advice is currently offered by thousands of other therapists, and our surveys show these two are representative.

The advice is not only worthless, it compounds the problem, leading in many cases to the collapse of the marriage. Our studies show that the emphasis many women now place on their careers is already so extreme, they are unlikely to have either successful professional or satisfying personal lives. The therapists they turn to for help are unwittingly suggesting that the women throw yet another can of gasoline on this fire raging out of control.

MARRIED TO A SUPERSTAR

Before we see *why* so many successful women are competing with their husbands, and destroying relationships in the process, let us see precisely *how well* they are competing. We want to look at strategy first, then psychology.

The vast majority of women we studied were of the opinion that someone in Lois's position had no choice but to come up with an accomplishment of her own to keep pace with her husband in the eyes of the public. Each achievement of his only adds to the pressure already on her to produce. Her failure to do so is humiliating. She is obviously no match for her partner.

That may indeed be what ambitious women see when they project themselves into the picture. But it isn't even close to the view of the onlookers these women are trying so hard to impress. Instead, the public does something that Lois and the millions of women like her would find astonishing. Summarizing the responses on this subject of the more than 26,000 American business and professional men and women we have surveyed since 1980, we can safely say that *when a white-collar audience sees a woman who is married to an undeniably successful man, they always assume that she too must be someone special, otherwise he would not be with her.*

What is noteworthy is that the members of the audience are so inclined to react this way that they grant her a share of the acclaim even if she is a latecomer, having met and married him after he had produced the work which brought him renown. Of course, if she wants all the applause for herself—and Lois, unfortunately, did—then the portion of his acclaim that the audience automatically gives her will never be enough, no matter how large it is. Even when it is combined with the recognition that her own success has already brought her, she will still feel shortchanged.

Some people are plagued by profound feelings of inferiority. For them, sharing the stage with anyone else is simply out of the question, since they are convinced they will end up looking second best. Subconsciously they say to themselves, "The only way for me to prevent the audience from comparing me to the others present on the stage—and realizing that I don't really belong there—is for me to have the entire stage to myself." Hidden feelings of inadequacy are responsible here for what appears at first glance to be egomania and narcissism.

These are not the people we have been discussing in this or any other chapter of the book. Lois certainly isn't such a person. Her problems are more cultural than psychological; they spring more from a prevailing misconception among working women (about the best ways to attain success) than from individual psychopathology. Lois has long been laboring under the impression that unless *all* the credit for an accomplishment is hers, none of it will be. She must be a solo achiever, or she has not achieved in the first place.

The very idea of basking in her husband's glory would have struck her as ridiculous. Any discussion of the audience's tendency to give the wife part of the husband's credit would have seemed to her beside the point. In that sense, the 1980s represent a complete reversal in attitude from that which prevailed during the 1950s, when women wanted to marry a successful man, or one who soon would be, because they looked forward to enjoying with him the fruits of his success. When we asked them, "And what will your friends think of this pairing?" they immediately replied, "They'll all be green with envy." As a quick check showed, they were right.

By the late 1970s and (even more so) the 1980s a husband who was successful, or who soon would be, had become a menace to his wife's public aspirations. For he provided a standard of reference against which her own accomplishments could finally be measured—or so she feared. Never has there been a more unfounded fear. The audience does nothing of the kind and, in fact, is strongly inclined to give her a generous measure of the credit, even in cases where she couldn't possibly have earned it.

What is bizarre is that, on some subterranean level, Lois understood this. For when a coworker of hers named Pam told Lois about her plan to open a boutique in the central business district, Lois immediately raised the issue of who would get the credit if the store became a success. As she put it, "I'll bet people will say it was because of your husband, and your husband's money, even though he doesn't have all that much." Pam was offended at the thought of that happening, and said so, but she let the matter drop.

The store did even better than Pam expected. As Lois had correctly guessed, the issue of who was responsible for the success began to be raised by friends of Pam and her husband. This time, Pam was more than just mildly offended. "What should I do, Lois?" Pam asked her. Instead of explaining to Pam that this was a normal audience tendency, a knee-jerk reaction not worth agonizing about, Lois did the reverse. Remembering how upset she herself had been only a few weeks earlier when a friend had said to her, "You must be such an asset to Jack," Lois decided to do everything possible to make certain that Pam's husband didn't receive *any* of the praise that resulted from his wife's success. "If I were you," Lois stated firmly, "I'd divorce him. That is the only way you'll ever have your day in the sun."

Lois was always persuasive, so much so that she had made persuasion her profession. But the argument had a compelling logic of its own, especially to Pam, who was no less intent upon having a solo achievement to present to the world than was Lois. That was the reason Pam had quit in the first place and started her own business. Lois repeated her argument about a dozen times in the next few months and, by Pam's own admission, "helped me do what I wanted to anyway." She filed for divorce.

Let's forget for the moment the evidence we've collected from thousands of businesswomen like Pam that shows how her decision to terminate her marriage, particularly for the reasons she used, significantly reduced the chances of her remaining a success. There is another important point here. If Lois had any doubts about what audiences are inclined to do, they should have evaporated when she saw what happened next to Pam. Less than two years after Pam divorced her first husband, she was remarried—this time to Marty, an accountant, to whom she was introduced by a neighbor. Pam had barely been remarried for a month when she and Lois were met on the street one Sunday by Delia, a mutual acquaintance. Much to Pam's surprise, the first question Delia asked once she heard that Pam was married and her store was doing well was, "Is Marty one of your backers?" When the reply she received was "No," Delia persisted, commenting offhandedly, "His accounting smarts sure must come in handy."

As Lois and Pam walked away, both were miffed. Pam spoke first: "Doesn't that stupid ass know I've been in business for three years and only married to Marty for three weeks?" Lois chimed in, "People don't give women in business enough credit—for anything. She wouldn't have said those things to you if you'd been a man."

Lois, above all, should have realized how false her own words were. For she had already witnessed a graphic example of how quickly and easily the audience takes credit away from a successful man and hands a portion of it to his wife. The reason Lois had learned so little from that painful episode was that she misinterpreted what was taking place. She viewed the comment, "You must be such an asset to Jack," as meaning that he was the star, while she was merely a marginal member of the supporting cast. If anything, she wanted the reverse to be the case. Her burning desire to come up with an achievement that was hers—and hers alone—made her destructively hypersensitive to ordinary audience reactions. In fact, it made her destructive to her friends as well.

As the two women continued walking, Lois, trapped in the logic of her own worst fears, finally said angrily to Pam, "There's really only one way to put a stop to this. You're going to have to get rid of Marty too." Pam agreed.

PLAYING TO THE CROWD

To fully understand why Lois, Pam, and the millions of ambitious women like them behave the way they do in such situations, we need two categories—"their partners" and "the public." The two categories are supposed to work harmoniously together, instead of being polar opposites, tearing at the woman in the middle until she feels forced to choose one or the other. Although it would come as a shock to Lois and Pam to hear it, a stable and satisfying personal life significantly enhances the odds that each will be successful in her professional life.

However, it would be a major mistake for us to believe that just because the two categories are useful in our analysis, they are equally real in the world. Their partners are certainly real and, in high school at least, so is their audience. Their peers do indeed scrutinize one another mercilessly at that age. But after high school, the crowd disperses—except in the minds of the disturbed and the ambitious. The disturbed spend the rest of their lives trying to gain admiration from a crowd that they once felt despised them. The ambitious, on the other hand, see themselves as talented and special but want to be absolutely certain to present each achievement to the audience in a way that maximizes the amount of applause it elicits.

Needless to say, the amount of overlap between these two groups of individuals is large, and there are indeed many neurotically ambitious people—those for whom achievement is nothing more than an attempt to find a Band-Aid to cover past hurts. It is important for us to focus on the latter group, however: those whose misperceptions about the best way to achieve and to present those achievements to the public are making them act crazy or mean.

Lois's and Pam's problem was that *they had become so used to coming up with glowing explanations of their own behavior to present to their peers that they continued doing this long after high school ended and their peers no longer cared.* Looking at it from their point of view for a moment will help us understand why this is one change Lois and Pam couldn't accept, even though their failure to do so is ruining their lives.

People who want their achievements to be noticed typically have a difficult task on their hands. An applauding throng may not emerge. The crowd may be more interested at the time in the work of someone else in the field. The most widely used substitute for a real audience is an imaginary one, especially among those who are convinced that "the real thing will soon be mine, in any event." In that case they aren't fantasizing, they are merely borrowing—from themselves. It is a temporary loan from their own future renown. And as long as they truly believe that it will one day be theirs, they can easily allow themselves to spend their whole lives waiting for it, one day at a time.

The key point is that Lois believed her audience to be real. From her point of view, it was almost as physical a fact as her dining room table. She could allow herself to hear this cheering mob in her mind, and not consider herself deranged, because she was convinced that it was destined to be hers eventually if she didn't make any silly mistakes. Had someone told her that her audience was imaginary, she would have viewed that person, not herself, as insane. Having literally devoted her entire adolescence and adulthood to winning acclaim from this invisible throng, she would have been horrified to realize that only a small handful of people cared whether she succeeded or failed, or even whether she lived or died.

Like the vast majority of other ambitious women we studied, Lois overestimated drastically the *size* of her audience and the *degree* to which its members thought about her. She was certain that, in her words, "the number of people who regularly follow the ups and downs of my career is in the hundreds." We next asked, "Since they are located in a variety of places, how are they all kept informed?" Her reply was, "Word gets around." However, we found that to be true for most working people only when they got fired. This is the type of news that turns out to travel fastest—faster even than news of one's death.

While the person who was fired may view the matter egocentrically and say, "See, they are indeed talking about me because they're interested in me," we found that most people spreading the word were far more interested in saving their own skins. Pointing to someone else who got sacked gave them a sense of relief, since *they* weren't the ones who were let go. In essence, they were saying what the survivors of calamities have said for millennia: "Thank goodness it wasn't me. I'm still okay." In short, based upon our interviews with the people involved, we would estimate that four individuals were sincerely interested in the ups and downs of Lois's career, not the three hundred she assumed. Another forty who knew that she had been fired mentioned it at least once, but only as part of an office gossip session. When Lois called to tell her, even Pam greeted the news with, "Gee, that's awful. What are you going to do now?" Then, with the conversation finished, she promptly forgot about it and went back to dwelling upon plans for her store.

Which brings us to the question of how much of each day people spent thinking about Lois and her life. She was convinced that the three hundred spent an average of "twenty to thirty minutes a day," adding that "for some it's more—maybe an hour—and others, only a few minutes."

This is an extraordinary remark. To see why, consider Pam's reply when we asked her how many minutes a day she spent thinking about Lois. (The question was deliberately buried among five other inquiries whose purpose was to serve as a smoke screen.) Pam casually responded, "I don't think about her at all. Why would I? She's not in pain or anything, is she? We talk about twice a week, and I guess I think about her while we're talking, but not otherwise." Other people on Lois's list candidly said the same.

Lois's picture of hundreds of people sitting around pondering her fate, envying her abilities, cheering her on, and vicariously participating in what she labeled "my many victories, large and small," was flatly contradicted by the facts. Virtually all the people she believed were thinking about her were thinking about themselves instead. Amusingly, more than 30% told us that they thought she spent twenty to thirty minutes a day thinking about *them*. We found that the only person besides themselves whom they were likely to have thought about for any length of time each day—and even then, it was only for a few minutes once or twice a week—was a boss they disliked.

It is important for the reader not to have the wrong impression of Lois's remarks. Most people react to her estimates as though the words had been produced by someone pathologically self-involved. But, if instead of telling others her audience estimates we get theirs first, we find that most women in her position produce comparable figures. In fact, the more devoted to seeking acclaim people are, the more likely their estimates are to be this high or even higher. It's just that no one has pinned them down before and made them quantify their feeling of being the center of attention. They have no reason to do this on their own, since it is ego-deflating, and they are reluctant to engage in such a conversation with someone else. Avoiding the numbers allows them to escape an accusation of grandiosity. Nevertheless, like Lois, they are certain that their quest will ultimately be successful, so they quietly borrow what they are sure will one day be theirs. The point is that they believe in the reality of their imaginary audience.

"KEEP YOUR EYE ON THE BALL"

A devil's advocate might argue, "Perhaps the audience Lois and Pam envision daily isn't so imaginary after all. Since 1970, there has been a new audience, one that is interested first and foremost in any woman who achieves, especially in the business world. The audience is receptive and huge, and once she becomes outstanding in her field she might well become the recipient of its thunderous applause."

That is true, and we are especially aware of its existence because we have been carefully monitoring its likes and dislikes. However, someone needs to tell its members that as long as they keep trying to lay claim to that audience, they will never produce the achievements necessary to do so.

The situation is analogous to an experience Lois had in Manhattan's Central Park. When she was still an executive at the cosmetics company, a baseball team from a major TV station challenged her firm's team to a game. Many companies have employees who band together voluntarily as members of the firm's official jogging or baseball team (large firms may have more than one such team). Lois's long working hours and lack of interest in the sport prevented her from joining. "I work out at the health club near my apartment," she commented, shrugging off the topic. This time, eager to meet some of the famous people on the other team, she decided to participate. As a senior officer, she was able to do this, though the regular members weren't exactly thrilled about her decision.

She was given third base as her position. Lois had her new team uniform on and was excited. It had just come back from the tailor to whom she had taken it, as she remarked, "to make me look more athletic and sexy." She had also invited Pam and a few other friends to the game, in order to have a cheering section of her own. The game was in the second inning, with no score yet. Lois turned to her friends and the spectators on the sidelines to give them still another eyes-wide nod and ask wordlessly, "How'm I doing?"

Just then the batter, one of the popular evening newscasters whom she had wanted so much to meet, hit a line drive that, as Lois put it, "nearly took my head off." The smile on her face turned to horror as she pivoted just in time to have the ball graze her forehead, sending her baseball cap and sunglasses flying. Fortunately she was unhurt, except for a small scratch on the side of her nose. She remained in the game. But when the other team was finally out, and she came off the field to sit down, a well-known producer from the TV team said to her gently, "Why don't *you* keep your eye on the ball and let your fans take care of themselves."

For Lois and the millions like her this is a priceless piece of advice, one that has even more crucial implications off the playing field than on. During the game she merely sustained a glancing blow; the problems she suffered at work and at home as a result of ignoring the advice were direct hits that have repeatedly sent her reeling. Nevertheless, she believed in the reality of her imaginary audience, and could see it in her mind every bit as clearly as the people watching her from the sidelines at the baseball diamond. The spectators in her mind are even more real in some ways than the ones at the field, since they never leave. They aren't there for a game; they are there just for her.

Since they focus exclusively on Lois and her daily activities, it is understandable that she thinks of them as a captive audience. But since they never go away, she constantly has to come up with something new to entertain and appease them. Collectively, they are like a ravenous pet that must continually be fed. As she well knows, her audience doesn't care what she achieved in previous months or years, or what she will attain in the future. It wants to know what she has done *today* to merit acclaim. Do these imaginary spectators constitute her captive audience— or would it be more accurate to say that she is their captive?

Their reality in her mind makes it easy for her to resolve inner conflicts about which to please, her partner or her public. Given that her partner—any partner—is external and is an obstacle to the solo bow she wants to take, while her admiring throng is internal and not about to go away, it is hardly surprising that she keeps deciding in favor of the many instead of the one. After 1970 it became even easier for her to favor her public, rather than her private, life.

Now the payoff was bigger, and visible at last. Dozens of new women's magazines soon glutted the newsstands, proving that none of the thoughts about her own future fame were fictional. She knew she was a woman who, for starters, should readily be able to elicit applause from her female peers throughout the nation. Then she would move on to bigger and better things. As Lois put it, "I'd like to have my name known *worldwide*." In short, the celebrity status given successful businesswomen after 1970 helped erase the doubts any ambitious woman might have had about the reality of the audience she was carrying in her mind. But it also radically reduced the chances that she would have either a satisfying personal or a successful professional life.

For that to happen, she would have to forget the audience and "keep her eye on the ball." Why is that so crucial a guideline, one that we now know separates winners from losers right from the start? There are two reasons. To begin with, it is distracting for people to try to work and, simultaneously, to worry about what any spectators happen to think. Most people can't do their work at all under these circumstances. However, we found that even the actions of workers who claim not to mind being watched are influenced. To be specific, if the work is manual—especially if it is assembly-line and routine—it is likely to be improved by the presence of interested spectators. But if it is mental—especially if it requires thought and originality—it is affected adversely by their presence.

Many of the women we studied told us that they "don't mind having someone looking over my shoulder from time to time while I work." As one put it, "You get used to it after a while." That isn't what the evidence shows, but there is a more serious problem in any event. Remember, we aren't talking about real spectators. The audience watching the women we are discussing is in their minds. Since the mob is internal, it would seem an easy one for any woman to manage. The problem is that while the mob isn't unruly, it is very demanding. In fact, it is so exacting, it ends up harming rather than helping her efforts to excel. It wants a glittering accomplishment every day—and on some days, every hour—no matter how flawed and superficial she knows it really is. Yet the accomplishments most likely to make her wealthy and well-known take decades, not days. Giving the inner mob what *it* wants prevents her in the long run from having what *she* wants. The unrelenting audience pressure causes her to underachieve significantly, which only makes the pressure still more intense.

FROZEN IN AN ACTION POSE

Some of the women we studied sensed how destructive their ravenous internal audience had become in their lives. They tried to turn a deaf ear to it and concentrate on the tasks at hand. In essence, they were giving themselves the advice that Lois had gotten from someone else. They decided simply to do their jobs and, for better or worse, let the results be judged by others, be they real or imaginary.

It didn't work. In spite of a diligent search, we couldn't find even one woman who was able to tell her inner audience to "get lost" and have that happen. Many did tell friends, coworkers and, more typically, their husbands to leave, but that didn't improve matters. In fact, it usually made them worse. The enemy was within, and in ridding themselves of their partners the women were unwittingly making certain that their inner enemy no longer had any external competition. Now its message was the only one to be heard.

Just as we became convinced that women held captive by their inner audience would remain that way for life, we realized that some were indeed breaking free. The reason we didn't notice it sooner is that they were making their escape so quietly. How? By falling in love. They didn't think of this as a way of silencing the mob, yet it did the trick. Here is still another—and in many ways, the most important—reason why women yearning for success need a fulfilling personal life, and need it first. *Most of the talented, energetic, and highly motivated women in our sample who failed did so because instead of being consumed by love (a fate they feared), they were consumed by their invisible audience and rendered frantic, unable either to love or achieve.*

Unfortunately, a woman on her own cannot break the grip of her imaginary audience (nor can a man; there is no gender difference where this problem is concerned). But having a real partner accomplishes the goal without effort. Not because he is big and strong and has a will of iron. Rather, it happens because of something magical that springs up between the two, a feeling for which she is every bit as responsible as he. In the previous chapter we saw that having a partner gives her the distance she needs from coworkers and superiors to do well, not to fight with them excessively and exhaust herself—or get fired—in the process. Here we see that being part of an enduring intimacy gives her something equally essential: the distance she needs to stop thinking about her imaginary fans and just let herself live, instead of constantly fretting.

Why doesn't it happen more often? When people want something this much they usually manage to find it. We've discussed the most important reasons why they don't, but a final one remains: a seemingly simple word—career. Working women who realistically hope to have a personal life should be especially wary of this word. More than 94% of the women we studied talked easily and at length about, as they put it, "my career in retailing [advertising, broadcasting, finance, fashion, etc.]." Every era has its buzz words and slang, most of them silly and harmless. The most pivotal one for women in the 1970s and, especially, 1980s is "career," a term that is drenched with hidden meanings that cause its users serious trouble.

For one thing, the word always connotes "successful" as an unspoken adjective. Would people call their work a career if it had been a string of mediocre performances that led to repeated dismissals? Career never implies failure, even when a bank robber uses it. Every mention of the word when people are describing themselves is a bit of public self-congratulation. Having declared themselves successful in their chosen professions, they have no choice but to defend that stance. It makes no difference whether they *intended* to give this impression; they gave it. They must maintain their public image or the audience, even more alert to signs of failure than of success, will know that something is wrong.

However, the most damaging consequence of using the word "career" has to do with the imaginary, not the real, audience. As researchers, we can talk about Lois's and Pam's careers. We are outside them—interviewing them, their coworkers, families, and friends, piecing together a picture of their lives, seeking patterns and contradictions in their thoughts and behavior. Lois, on the other hand, is supposed to be living her life, not trying to view it nonstop from outside herself. She can't anyway, since people watching her rarely see what she wants them to (though it would upset her terribly to hear it). Basically, she wants all her alleged fans, interesting passersby, and important strangers to always be pleased with what they are seeing. Her frequent use of the term "career" does indeed pull her outside herself—just enough, she hopes, to allow her to anticipate what her audience will see and to cheerlead them into thinking it's wonderful.

When working women use "career" to describe themselves, the word reeks of packaging, promotion, and public relations. They have already condensed their tale for the listener's convenience, leaving out anything that might refute the upbeat impression they are trying so hard to convey. Each wants this to be "the official version" of the story of her professional activities. In providing such a neat package she earnestly hopes that it will be printed exactly as she has delivered it.

The word "career" is a study in persuasion, an attempt by the speaker to convince us that her work is the very core of her being. Describing her involvement with it therefore summarizes her entire existence, her raison d'etre. The personal data that is offered (about boyfriends, husbands, children, etc.) is mere decoration, props for a literary photographer, proof that she is able to manage both home and work successfully.

Experiences have an intangible quality to them that the word "career" is intended to offset. It makes solid and concrete what is usually fleeting and soon forgotten. A working woman who uses the word to describe herself is giving us a summary of her accomplishments, one that she hopes will make us both like her better and think of her life as having real substance. She seriously doubts that it does have substance, and the doubt is well founded. Her use of the term tells us that she is outside herself, looking in. It is hardly surprising that she ends up wondering whether anyone is home. But she has pumped so much emotion into her work life, fought so hard to make it hers and hers alone, she is almost ready to scream, "You can't take this away from me!" even though no one is trying to. The word "career" is a verbal tranquilizer that prevents her from having to scream.

In short, the word "career" poisons both the professional and personal lives of working women. It dooms each to go everywhere pulling a statue of herself, frozen in an action pose. It complicates her introductions to new friends, since she feels forced to say to each, "Hi, I'm Lois, and this person standing beside me is My Career." When greeting old friends, she is in essence compelled to say, "Hi, I'm fine, thank you. Now let me tell you what my career has been up to lately." Anyone who becomes romantically involved with her will be a participant in a public *menage a trois* right from the start.

What is worse is that even when no one is around she has to do her work *and* narrate it, as a performance, at the same time. Otherwise it isn't part of her career. Only that which can be discussed and, best of all, exhibited fills the bill. What she is really trying to do is to write her auto-biography in her mind while she is still in the midst of the experiences about which she is attempting to write. That guarantees that she will be far too self-conscious to do either job well.

Afterword

Ideally, our lives should have a sense of progression. Each stage should have experiences that the ones before didn't contain. The same sense of progress should be apparent in our attainments. Each achievement should surpass the previous ones.

That is not how it is now. The cruelest thing that the social environment in the United States does to young adults is to pressure them to peak too soon. In earlier decades of this century ambitious people would goad one another with coy questions such as, "You realize, don't you, that by the time Mozart was your age he was dead?" The clear implication was, "You haven't made any significant contributions yet to the world of literature, music or art." Now the focus has changed from culture to commerce, and the standard by which achievements are gauged has shifted. The contemporary version of the question is, "You realize, don't you, that by the time Steven Jobs [of Apple Computer] was your age he was worth $250 million?" The implication this time is, "Forget about composing a sonata or sonnet, how come you haven't started your own business yet, and become rich and famous as a result of its success?"

People are trying hard to meet the new demands—harder than they'll ever know. If they have to scrap their personal lives in order to excel, they are willing. It is a valiant and admirable stand, one that requires more courage and determination than most aspirants even think they possess. They are aware of the price they are paying in chronically elevated levels of anxiety, prolonged periods of frustration and conflict, and repeated bouts of depression. The main reason they aren't also painfully lonely much of the time is that they are so frequently annoyed. The anger eases their sense of isolation because they have someone they can grapple with, in their minds at least, hour after hour. It gives them a semblance of company.

Quite apart from the troubling emotional consequences of their quest for success, there are professional problems that are even more disturbing. The key point is that *if we are all supposed to be whiz kids—multimillionaires with our faces on the covers of national magazines by the time we're thirty—what is left for us to do at forty? And heaven help us by the time we reach fifty.*

In the current environment people lose either way. If they do indeed make it big by the time they are thirty, then, much to their surprise, they subsequently fail. They are no match for their own past. The business press, in particular, will keep measuring their present achievements against their previous ones. They feel perfectly justified in doing this, for they are concerned above all about professional managers, those devoting their lives to running successful businesses—not about men and women who are mere "flashes in the pan," who create companies that do well for a few years and then wither or go bankrupt.

The enormously larger number of people who haven't been conspicuously successful by the time they are thirty are in a bind that is equally awful. What they haven't been told—and are startled to learn—is that they have quietly been removed from the running. Once they pass the age of thirty the public doesn't care about their achievements. The American infatuation with youth and money means that the excitement is missing when a man or woman doesn't attain success until he or she is thirty-seven or forty-seven. The person achieving the goal may be thrilled, but the audience is likely to greet the news with a yawn. Worse still, since the person is no longer young and, presumably, innocent, the public is likely to attribute the profits to deceit. Instead of the national applause about which they had dreamed, people attaining success in their forties and fifties (the most typical time it arrives) are viewed by the public with suspicion and even hostility. No fan clubs are to be seen.

When all is said and done, success in business, whether it arrives before or after thirty, soon leads to failure in the eyes of the public. But if the public has a preference—and it does—it is for tales of youthful achievement. Thirty to fifty years ago the public clamored to see prodigies. Little nine-year-old violinists and pianists were trotted out on stage to display their musical gifts before wealthy audiences dressed in tuxedos and evening gowns. Pre-teen instrumental performers are probably every bit as talented now as were those of yore, but the public is no longer interested. Although a self-righteous explanation is usually offered for the shift ("We don't exploit our young anymore"), any researcher who has studied how the hundreds of thousands of parents at Little League baseball and Pee Wee football games behave know this is rubbish. As we said earlier, the public now wants to see financial prodigies. Any mature adult who attains fame or fortune is viewed as lucky, sneaky, or quaint.

That hasn't prevented highly motivated women from doing anything and everything possible to gain widespread approval in accordance with the new guidelines. Since each is supposed to become a success in business or a profession—and become renowned at it by the time she is thirty—a variety of tricks has come into play. In the previous chapter we discussed the hidden meanings of the word "career." But there is another meaning, a bit of sleight-of-hand that is very useful for any woman seeking public acclaim. Especially as she reaches her late twenties, we found that she is likely to pretend that she has already accomplished an enormous amount. When she was younger, people were awed by her abilities; there were clear signs of great things to come. She was indeed a prodigy.

Americans, we have long been told, don't really value their past. Only their future, into which they gaze ever-hopefully, counts. The behavior of the women we studied contradicts this statement. Everything major that might happen to them in the future is essentially meaningless, since they will be over thirty—or worse, they already are. It must therefore be made to seem as if it happened previously, before the women were thirty. Without realizing it, they are trying to give the public what it wants by making use of a time trick. They must appear sufficiently precocious so that by their early thirties, at the latest, they can look back at a long history of outstanding achievements. They aren't still preparing for success; they have already experienced it. "My career" is a premature autobiography each feels compelled to deliver.

Given the intense pressure in the United States to peak too soon, it is small wonder that more than half the women we studied liked their careers but didn't like their work. Unfortunately, that made their chances of attaining real success nearly zero. And in some corner of her mind, each knew it. For after her listeners left, she wasn't all that surprised that her excited reminiscences—which turned out to be largely exaggerations and distortions—were soon followed by yet another slide into self-pity. Like Lois, she was likely to discover too late (after discarding her personal life) that her use of the word "career" was little more than an apology for her failure to achieve in the only way that the public finds appealing.

However, the really tragic cases are those who manage, by hook or by crook, to attain a high level of pay and position by their early thirties. For the vast majority will spend the next two decades constantly looking over their shoulders, trying to match what they once achieved. In the past, women were pitted in a destructive competition with themselves, trying not to be outclassed by the beauty they possessed during their younger years. The current version of this competition hits early achievers even harder. Bombarded by stories of youthful success, they are unable to escape the feeling that their own lives have become static—heading downhill, if anywhere—old before their time in a youth-obsessed culture.

Before concluding, let us note that virtually every member of our sample stated at the start that she wanted all three things—a career, a husband, and a family. More than three-fourths subsequently found a job, got married and had children. But one question that was always foremost in our minds was which women would find satisfaction in each of these areas, much less in all of them simultaneously.

What we hadn't foreseen more than a quarter of a century ago when we began our study was that the economic world would play a dirty little trick on men and women in their twenties, thirties, and forties. During the last two decades it has become impossible for the large majority to support themselves and their spouses, not to mention raise a family, on just one paycheck. While the upwardly mobile women we studied had no difficulty describing what they would do with the ample incomes they were certain would one day be theirs, the hard fact remains that they did not start to live well until they began to pool their earnings with someone else. Whether the pairs got married or merely lived together was irrelevant, an issue that masks a more important underlying reality: it takes two incomes now to live in large cities at all—the only setting which the majority of driven women in our sample feel is suitable, given the goals for which they are striving.

That makes the cutesy tone in which the vast majority of books and articles on the subject have been written in the last ten years not only irritating but misleading. To make matters worse, many of them deliberately emphasize the competitive aspects of the situation. Harping repeatedly on the question of "Who earns more?" may help sell books, because it plays upon the insecurities of women who are hungry for something to brag about. But it harms the women deeply, for it overlooks the fact that the earnings of men and women aren't nearly as stable as most people have been led to believe. (Each thinks he or she is the only one whose income went down following a job change.) The person earning more than her partner one year may end up earning less than he does the next. Moreover, as we saw in Part Three, if she doesn't yet have a husband and boasts about her high income she is likely to attract a parasite, not a real partner. In short, the cooperative aspects have become even more important than the competitive ones for people who want to live decently. Romance is no longer just a psychological necessity, it is now also a financial one.

That is especially the case for women who want to have children, or who already do. Over and over again we heard working mothers with youngsters under the age of six say that they wish they could spend more time with them. "I feel guilty," they would comment. "This is the time when they need me most." Many added, "There is a selfish reason too: this is the time in their lives when they are the most adorable." This group, more than any other, needs to cut through the battle rhetoric and ideology and understand the forces buffeting them at work and at home.

In all likelihood, the 1970s and 1980s will be viewed in retrospect as a period when women made work—which had become a necessity—into a virtue. Sadly, many made it their only one. To a remarkable degree they resembled soldiers who had been drafted but were making the best of it, singing as they marched proudly off to war, perhaps to die. The women went one by one, perhaps to be divorced and spend their lives alone.

That their quest served themselves instead of their country made them mistakenly conclude that it was voluntary.

It was nothing of the kind. Had they understood this simple but powerful fact, they would not have had to distort their attitudes and emotions so dangerously to avoid the stigma of doing something wholly self-serving. They didn't want to be labeled selfish. "The women's movement" was the smokescreen behind which most of those who were afraid of being labeled egomaniacally grasping and ambitious hid. "Every step forward for me is a step forward for women," many claimed. Yet their biting remarks about the women over whose bodies they gladly walked to take that step clearly revealed that they had a far more personal goal in mind.

Be that as it may, let us accept their lofty rationalizations at face value for the moment. Even had they truly believed that success for themselves was nothing more than a contribution to the general advancement of women, they could not have chosen a worse way of attempting to achieve that success. To keep reminding themselves and others that they were women trying to get ahead was no more useful than it would have been for blacks, Italians, Jews, or Hispanics to do the same. Americans deeply resent lobbies and special-interest groups (unless it is one to which they themselves belong), and eventually respond to them with an effective defense by finding a way to promote their own special interests.

More to the point, groups don't get ahead in the United States. Talented individuals do—by forgetting about their race, religion, gender, or ethnicity long enough to concentrate on the task at hand, and by doing that task as well as they possibly can. Any other approach is simply too distracting to be productive in the long run. And what of the group whose interests we are assuming they sincerely want to advance along with their own? Once the individuals become wealthy or well-known, the group can and will make full use of the success, even if they don't want it to. It will co-opt their achievement in a dozen different ways and make it a symbol of the merits of the entire group.

As we saw in the previous chapter, the women in our study who did best were those who concentrated on their work and let their career story take care of itself. (Truly successful people never have to concoct such a tale, since the public is only too happy to do it for them: "Hey, I used to know her when she was at . . . ") Similarly, the women who did best forgot about their gender while they worked—even if, just as with aspiring blacks, Italians, Jews, or Hispanics, their audience perhaps never did so.

Most women firmly believe that the attainment of success requires sacrifices, and nothing stated anywhere in this book is intended to contradict that belief. However, our study indicates that it is essential for them to make the *right* sacrifices. The large majority are convinced subconsciously that scrapping their personal lives is the best way to move ahead professionally. Even though they complain openly about the lack of love in their lives, the decision to go it alone makes them feel quite virtuous. Despite their complaints they actually wear their loneliness proudly, as a badge, since it appears to be proof of their single-minded devotion to their work. In the preceding chapter we saw that they have an ulterior motive in choosing this particular form of self-denial: when acclaim finally comes their way, they want to be in a position to stand up and take a solo bow.

It is imperative for them to realize that, however saintly they feel for giving up something they want, the world will not reward them for making the wrong sacrifices. They might as well be told by a physician, "You have a serious infection; take one of these pills every four hours," and then, thinking it makes no difference, take instead any pill they happen to have handy. What is so destructive about the way in which most highly motivated women handle their aspirations is that they suffer the pain of not having a fulfilling and enduring intimacy, which they feel they must deny themselves in order to get ahead; and they suffer again when they don't achieve the success for which they made the sacrifice in the first place.

The resulting emotional turmoil has blinded them to a key fact about themselves and their peers: the emergence among the ranks of working women of a major split between the "haves" and the "have-nots." The "haves" consist of happily married women who enjoy both their personal and professional lives; who have partners with whom they pool their incomes and who matter to them as much as, if not more than, their own careers. These are the women moving ahead quietly but steadily in the business world. The "have-nots" are single, divorced, or unhappily married (and hence not far from divorce) women who are devoting all their attention to their work—and enjoying neither their personal nor their professional lives. They have no real intimacy and affection at home, and the pace of their career progress strikes them as frustratingly and even infuriatingly slow.

Magazines, books, newspapers, movies, and television then rub salt in their wounds by reminding them of the large number of women who are currently achieving success. "What? You mean you're thirty-three and aren't earning more than $100,000 a year yet? There is obviously something wrong with you. Here are profiles of six women who are doing so— and their average age is only twenty-nine." Yet another reflection of America's endless appetite for youthful achievement, such stories appear every year in the media, especially now that they have a new group of achievers to highlight. Any woman without a satisfying personal life is hit hard by these goads, because she has no partner to act as buffer between her and them. In most of the cases we've studied she overreacts; too ambitious and impatient to begin with, she becomes even more so, and winds up her own worst enemy both on the job and off.

The irony is that if she copied the right women (quietly competent winners who love their work), instead of the wrong men (loud, blue-collar losers who love to show off); made the right sacrifices (some of her leisure and social time, a trade-off that the attainment of success seems to require), instead of discarding her personal life (which she needs in order to feel glad she is alive); and got rid of her outrage-addicted tough-guy stance, rather than seeking a reason each day to be indignant and resentful, she would maximize her chances of ultimately achieving a $100,000 income. However, with luck she won't attain it by the age of twenty-nine, and then become an object of public pity for the next two decades while people wonder why her career is a mere shadow of its former self.

It is now clear that unless a working woman has *both* a satisfying personal and professional life, she is likely to end up with neither. Fortunately, it takes surprisingly little effort for her to improve the situation substantially. Changes in the right direction build on themselves, making additional progress easier. Repeatedly during our study we were struck by a simple finding: Any woman who wants more love in her life can have it merely by letting the subject once again matter. For more than two decades now, it really hasn't. Maybe that is about to change, and there is at least one critically important reason it should: nothing is more liberating than love.

Appendix
on Methodology

Appendix
on Methodology

The simplifying assumption of a neat distinction between cohort and period effects, as exemplified in such worthwhile works as G. H. Elder Jr., *Children of the Great Depression: Social Change in Life Experience* (Chicago: University of Chicago Press, 1974), and R. A. Easterlin, *Birth and Fortune: the Impact of Numbers on Personal Welfare* (New York: Basic Books, 1980), quickly loses its relevance in an ongoing long-term study using data collected contemporaneously instead of retrospectively. For example, many attitudes and behaviors that first emerged in upwardly mobile college-educated urban groups tended to spread to white-collar and then blue-collar suburban residents, with a mean lag time of 2.7 and 4.1 years respectively for the period 1959 through 1984, a process that is revealingly modeled by a multifocal diffusion equation with an appropriately chosen Green's function. Moreover, as R. C. Kessler and D. F. Greenberg in *Linear Panel Analysis: Models of Quantitative Change* (New York: Academic Press, 1981) and H. Carter and P. C. Glick in *Marriage and Divorce: A Social and Economic Study* (Cambridge: Harvard University Press, 1976) have emphasized, historical factors often exert their most important effects indirectly via changes in the structure of many hundreds of local economic landscapes, not an assumed homogeneous national one (except in anomalous circumstances such as the Depression), and that makes the migratory patterns of sample members a dimension of utmost importance.

Since our focus from the start was on which women would succeed (and why) both professionally and maritally, not so much where they did so, changes in residential and occupational setting were anticipated and monitored carefully throughout. The nature of the personal and business relationships terminated or attenuated by a move, as well as the quality and durability of the new ones established elsewhere, constituted an essential part of our analysis, particularly as they acted to express the differing aspirations of sample members during the various stages of their lives, aspirations that were clearly influenced by an ever-shifting mix of cohort and historical pressures and opportunities.

Random selection of a sample of sufficient size was accomplished in part using RAND Corporation's computer-generated table, *A Million Random Digits* (Glencoe: Free Press, 1955), and the five-digit account numbers of customers at nine stockbrokerage firms; five national and four regional. Each individual was told that interviews at regular intervals would be necessary in addition to follow-up questionnaires. Another 1,500 members were selected from sixteen colleges and graduate schools that represented a cross-section of United States institutions of higher education in 1958–1959. A third sample consisted of 1,518 school-age children of the sample of investor families. The cost savings associated with cluster sampling were not the main reason for making our selections from a total of approximately two dozen brokerage firms and universities. Although we were aware that almost all varieties of clustering in sample design decrease the precision of sample estimates since less new data about the population is obtained by selecting additional people from the same cluster than by choosing people at random, background similarity was viewed as not necessarily a disadvantage in a long-term study emphasizing differential rates of promotion, pay increases, and marital stability. Initial differences among sample members, although smaller in some cases than we would have liked, soon widened and, in fact, facilitated the study of developmental changes by decade.

Attention was paid throughout to inter-, as well as intra-group differences, both professionally and maritally. Repeated comparisons, at least on an annual basis, were made between sample means and population means by utilizing, among other sources, College Placement Council, *Salary Surveys*; Endicott, *Trends in Employment of College and University Graduates in Business and Industry*; United States Bureau of Labor Statistics, *Employment of Recent Graduates*; National Science Foundation, *Two Years after the College Degree*; data on "Consumer Income" and "Educational Attainment" from United States Bureau of the Census, *Current Population Reports* on mean earnings of four-year college graduates; United States Bureau of the Census, 1960, 1970, and 1980 Census of Population, *Occupational Characteristics, Earnings by Occupation and Education* and *Occupations of Persons with High Earnings*; United States Department of Labor, *Employment and Earnings*; American Council on Education/UCLA, *National Norms for Entering College Freshmen* (various years); United States Bureau of the Census, *Current Population Reports*, "Number, Timing and Duration of Marriages and Divorces in the United States," "Marital Status and Living Arrangements," "Families Maintained by Female Householders," "Fertility of American Women"; United States National Center for Health Statistics, *Monthly Vital Statistics Reports*, "Divorces by Marriage Cohort," "National Estimates of Marital Dissolution and Survivorship," "Trends and Differentials in Birth to Unmarried Women," "Births, Marriages, Divorces and Deaths."

While the initial series of questions were intended to elicit information about annual earnings (from employment, inter-family transfers and/ or investment) and growth in company size (among the self-employed and small business owners) or promotions (among employees), as well as dating patterns and marital satisfaction, the respondents themselves were the first to volunteer this information in career contexts. For example, respondents were seeking to justify what, in certain instances, were substantial pay decreases, on the grounds that such a decrease heightened the chances of later advancement at another firm or their own. The number of respondent references to occupation was so much higher than anticipated in these early interviews, even among women who were unemployed at the time, it was clear that this factor could not be omitted from any serious investigation of financial success or failure that resulted from employment or investment and its connection to their personal lives. The careers of these individuals provided the backgrounds against which financially related and interpersonal activities of every sort were interpreted.

To ensure consistent data coverage in the occupational area, each sample member was asked to provide a list of the half-dozen coworkers with whom the frequency of her on-the-job interaction was highest and/ or of greatest importance. The explanation offered for the request was that, as part of the dimension of job satisfaction, brief reviews emphasizing positive and negative features of each coworker would be useful. Highly critical comments across the board, with no coworkers excepted, did indeed serve to indicate an elevated level of job dissatisfaction as measured by differential rates of subsequent job change. Nevertheless, the lists turned out to be of great utility in maintaining continuous contact with each member. In fact, the sample size would have suffered significantly more attrition (8.9%; 307 out of 3,466 as of January 1985) had it not been for the lists, which were updated annually if the same employment position obtained, or within four months after each employment shift. In hundreds of instances, when the post office, phone company records, or residential neighbors were unable to specify the new address, phone number, or institutional affiliation, if any, of a sample member who had moved to an unknown location and thus threatened to become lost to follow-up inquiries, the inner circle of coworkers in each case was able to help us restore contact by offering the name and/or location of the new employer and/or place of residence.

Close coworkers, in addition to being what were often the only knowledgeable link between past and present varieties of employment of sample members, also provided valuable information about factors involved in the move, a subject they were more willing to discuss freely now that the person in question was no longer with the firm. Considerable care was exercised to make certain that the inquiries appeared to be off-the-record probes about the firm rather than about any specific individual who was no longer there. This was necessary since it was not uncommon for sample members to once again find positions at previous employers at future dates. Moreover, the information gathered from coworkers of sample members assisted us in determining what the overall rate of turnover was at the firm during the period under examination, a critical reference level against which to measure the frequency of job changes by sample members in that particular industry or company.

Similar considerations applied to changing levels of demand within each occupation, as monitored on a current basis using monthly indices such as *Engineer/Scientist Demand Index* by Deutsch, Shea, and Evans, Inc., calculated from want-ad placements. The expansion and contraction of employment demand within any given occupation had a calculable effect on the women discussed in this work, but we have given prominence to psychological and psychosocial factors in career development, as opposed to hasty reactions necessitated by external factors, particularly by rapidly shrinking demand, such as that which teachers at all levels faced in the early 1970s. The statistical basis for the decision was that the proportion of career shifts undertaken by members of our sample three or more years after graduation from college or graduate school which were not responses to changing job-market conditions far exceeded those that were.

A concerted effort was made throughout the study to obtain reliable data on consumption expenditures by sample members, among other things to assess their impact on career development. Again, sample and stratum means, on the one hand, and population means, on the other, were compared annually; for instance, during the 1970s as a national average, 2.6% and 8.2% (versus our 1.7% and 12.8%) of consumption outlays were devoted to alcohol and tobacco and recreation, respectively, with consistent decreases in the case of the former commodities as income rose above $7,000 (3% of $7,000–7,999; 2.7% of $12,000–14,999; 2% of $25,000), and consistent increases in outlays for recreation (6%, 7.8% and 11.3% in the three income categories cited above). For further details, see United States Department of Labor, Bureau of Labor Statistics, *Average Annual Expenditures for Commodity and Service Groups Classified by Nine Family Characteristics, 1972 and 1973*, Consumer Expenditure Series: Interview Survey, 1972 and 1973, Report 455–3, 1976. One of the many conclusions to emerge from our data was that, using constant-dollar three-year income averaging as a standard, more than 71% of the women in the sample slipped to a lower income level briefly (eight months, on average) at least once during the period under study, and were significantly more likely to maintain the consumption pattern established in the previous three-year income span than to decrease expenditures to bring them more into line with reduced earnings. This imbalance had the effect of compelling the individual to shelve temporarily career plans in exchange for an income more closely matched to current consumption outlays. Nonetheless, as was clear from repeated comparisons of the results obtained from comprehensive questionnaires administered to the entire sample at three-year intervals—in which information about psychological, economic, and social attitudes, group affiliation and identification, as well as more standard data on income, education, and marital status, was collected and assessed with respect to background and biographical factors—a prolonged period of reduced earnings (on the order of forty-three months) was usually required for a significant modification by working women of previously stated career objectives.

One effective way to get beyond some of the limitations associated with the combination of stratified and cluster sampling we employed was to regularly test tentative conclusions by using interested self-employed, employee, managerial, and homemaking volunteers. Although here too self-selection introduces distortions on its own—which are then frequently compounded by researcher bias—we believe that much invaluable information of a practical nature was obtained (and which was needed for the italicized conclusions and recommendations in the current work to be presented correctly) by proceeding carefully and remaining mindful of the results discussed in R. Rosenthal, *Experimenter Effects in Behavior Research* (New York: Irvington Publishers, 1976); R. A. Jones, *Self-Fulfilling Prophecies: Social, Psychological and Physiological Effects of Expectancies* (Hillsdale, New Jersey: L. Erlbaum Associates, Publishers, 1977); J. Cohen, *Statistical Power Analysis for the Behavioral Sciences* (New York: Academic Press, 1977) on effect size; and J. W. Pennebaker, *The Psychology of Physical Symptoms* (New York: Springer-Verlag, 1982).

INDEX

INDEX